Moments of Engagement

INTIMATE PSYCHOTHERAPY IN A TECHNOLOGICAL AGE

PETER D. KRAMER, M.D.

PENGUIN BOOKS

PENGUIN BOOKS
Published by the Penguin Group
Penguin Books USA Inc., 375 Hudson Street,
New York, New York 10014, U.S.A.
Penguin Books Ltd, 27 Wrights Lane,
London W8 5TZ, England
Penguin Books Australia Ltd, Ringwood,
Victoria, Australia
Penguin Books Canada Ltd, 10 Alcorn Avenue,
Toronto, Ontario, Canada M4V 3B2
Penguin Books (N.Z.) Ltd, 182–190 Wairau Road,
Auckland 10, New Zealand

Penguin Books Ltd, Registered Offices:
Harmondsworth, Middlesex, England

First published in the United States of America
by W. W. Norton & Company, 1989
Reprinted by arrangement with W. W. Norton & Company, Inc.
Published in Penguin Books 1994

1 3 5 7 9 10 8 6 4 2

Portions of the material in the "When It Works" chapter are reprinted
by permission of the publisher from "Integrated Psychiatric Treatment
of a Dying Patient," by Peter D. Kramer, *General Hospital Psychiatry*,
5: 291–299. Copyright 1983 by Elsevier Science Publishing Co., Inc.

THE LIBRARY OF CONGRESS HAS CATALOGUED THE HARDCOVER AS FOLLOWS:
Kramer, Peter D.
Moments of engagement: intimate psychotherapy in a
technological age/Peter D. Kramer.
p. cm.
Includes index.
ISBN 0-393-70075-5 (hc.)
ISBN 0 14 02.3790 9 (pbk.)
1. Psychotherapy. I. Title.
RC480.K69   1989
616.89′14—dc19   88-33271

Printed in the United States of America
Set in Janson

For Rachel

Contents

Preface

Since the fall of 1985, I have written a monthly column for psychiatrists about what it is like to practice in the profession today. I wondered at first whether the possibilities of this topic would not be soon exhausted. Instead I found that the core of our experience—how it is to sit with patients in an era in which the study of the mind, from both biological and psychological viewpoints, is in such flux—was difficult to define directly and interesting enough to warrant repeated approaches from different vantages.

This book constitutes one more attempt to say how it is today to try to meet patients with immediacy. It is directed to those within the healing professions, but, although some of the language is technical, I hope it will also serve as a chance for others interested in psychotherapy and psychiatry to listen in on a private dialogue or to "look over the shoulder" of a psychiatrist, in order to make sense of the ways in which those who deal with problems of mind daily think about the mind now.

The material of these essays is straightforward. This is a book of stories, and the stories are mainly about my work with patients. Most of these stories are from my residency, although I reach back to medical school and even to the psychoanalysis where I was a patient, as well as forward to recent years. I have chosen to concentrate on the training period, when the diverse conceptual strands from which the profession is woven are still apparent, in order to illustrate the clash of emotions and ideas which forms our identity.

The book opens with a sequence of four brief chapters about moments in which patient and therapist first make contact. In the second section, each chapter begins with a vignette from residency which sets into motion the discussion of an important psychiatric tool—medication, stratagem, interpretation, support, empathy, eclecticism. The final section contains two quite different attempts to step back and see psychotherapy from a changed perspective. But whether by case vignette, technical example, consideration of definitions and paradoxes, or autobiography, my intent is through interconnected stories and thoughts to say how it is to work with the mind and the self today and how it is to be the person who does that work.

I mean also for this book to be an homage, or a way of saying thank you, to the teachers who over many years helped me understand what a profession is and what a physician should aspire to. With many seminar leaders, supervisors, therapists, and administrators I have had the sort of special relationship that makes learning a joy. With others, as the reader will see, I have wrestled; but in wrestling, too, one can find valuable mentorship.

It is these teachers—their acts and their character—whom I think of when I reach a difficult juncture with a patient. For me it is my teachers and colleagues who define the profession. Their work, not what is contained in any textbook, is what we do; their knowledge is what we know; their beliefs are what we believe.

I should also thank John Schwartz, publisher of *The Psychiatric Times*, where my column "Practicing" appears. John provides me what every writer needs, and here I am by ellipsis slightly distorting something John Cheever wrote: "the inestimable gifts of a large, discerning, and responsive group of readers and enough money to . . . buy a new suit every other year."[1] Most of the material in this book is new, but certain chapters contain bits and pieces of some of the columns.

It is customary in these introductions to thank one's patients, and I wish there were a more than perfunctory way to do so. I have tried to alter their stories enough to ensure privacy, but I hope I have remained true to the spirit of our work together. A colleague once commented that my essays were less about practicing psychiatry than about the privilege of being a psychiatrist, and this assessment feels right to me. I think the reader will see that my patients were and are extraordinary people and fine teachers, too.

Moments of Engagement

Close Reaching

Some time ago, I supervised a social worker who, though otherwise skilled at what she did, showed a discomfort with conflict or aggression so persistent — and she was really unbudgeable — that I began to become annoyed with her. It seemed she could not confront any patient, however gently, and whenever patients began to deal with angry feelings, she tried to divert the discussion. If despite her efforts a patient remained focused on anger, the social worker was unable to make use of the material or to contain it.

One day she described an encounter with a schizoid and borderline psychotic woman. The social worker said she had at first been reluctant to bring this episode to my attention, but she believed I should hear about it.

Toward the middle of a session, the patient had begun to describe some disturbing happenings at her job and in social settings, and as the telling proceeded she became more and more aware of her anger at those who had disappointed her. Her account became mildly paranoid and her voice rose until it was clear she was in danger of losing control — something which had happened more than once outside the office.

As was her habit, the social worker was trying quietly to tone down the encounter, but somehow she had fallen behind the patient, and it was clear now that she was in danger of being included in a paranoid fantasy.

As the rage heightened, the patient's features took on an ugly look. She leaped out of her chair at the therapist. And instead of backing off to protect herself, the therapist moved up toward the patient to embrace her.

The patient cried and then sat back down and began telling her story, how she felt unlovable, how she longed for contact. Therapy began.

In recounting this incident in supervision, the social worker again extended her arms and rose up out of her chair. I had gone skiing the weekend before, and her motion reminded me of the instruction to rise up and into the turn. Rising into the turn is counterintuitive for the novice; it seems to thrust the body down the mountain just as momentum is increasing. But it is the only way to maintain control.

This image of rising toward the enraged patient has stuck in my mind.

I think I like it because it defies theoretical comprehension. On the surface, this intervention — and it is a therapeutic intervention — draws nothing from considerations of unconscious constellations or cognitive schemata or family structure. Though we may imagine that it affected the patient's inner world in any of these spheres, we have no reason to believe the intervention was planned with any theory in mind, or even planned at all.

It is not even a professionally sanctioned act, transgressing as it does the taboo against therapists' touching their patients and every rule about protecting oneself with the potentially violent patient. She should never have put herself in such a situation, we can say of my supervisee. We can recommend her act to no one — it should come with one of those disclaimers attached to certain demonstrations on television, not to attempt it yourself.

The story made me appreciate the special strengths that accompanied the social worker's failing. Because she had experienced her patient's need and yearning throughout the session, she was able to respond to the hopeless woman inside the angry one instantly, without falsity or hesitation.

In addition to the empathy between the social worker and the patient, there must have been some between the social worker and me, because as I listened to her account I anticipated the ending.

While she was talking, my mind had wandered to medical school days. It had been my good fortune to be one of the last students from my school to do the surgical emergency room practicum at the old Boston City Hospital emergency room. Because of the changeover in staff, the E.R. was partly manned by non-academic physicians, and I came under the tutelage of a remarkable doctor from India.

I clerked under him on one of those days (the government soon began staggering payments to avoid just these problems) when all the welfare checks were issued and the E.R. was swamped with gunshot and knife wounds and the many injuries associated with alcoholism. That night the police wheeled in an enormous drunken brute with deep gashes around the eye, all bleeding profusely. It took four cops to hold the man on the stretcher. He was screaming and threatening and foaming at the mouth, and of course the police threatened back.

My mentor asked the police to leave the room—this was one of those boxcar first-aid rooms, with barely enough space for us to maneuver around the pallet and nowhere to hide—and he and I were left alone with the dangerous patient. The Indian doctor talked calmly to the man, asking whether he had lost consciousness, addressing him with the directness and deference usually accorded a corporate executive worried over his blood pressure.

For my part, I was left in a heightened and embarrassing inner state. I found I was filled with fear and rage, but these emotions were suddenly without an object. I was an outsider to the calm intercourse between the surgeon and his patient.

The surgeon placed a small blue sterile sheet with a square hole in it over the drunkard's face and begun stitching the cuts. To lie in a state of near-blindness while someone wields a needle around the eye creates apprehension in normal and sober people, but the work went on without incident.

Afterwards, I said to my teacher, "I didn't even see you inject the Novocain."

"Oh," he said. "I work without anesthesia in these cases."

There is extraordinary power in being able to disarm aggression by failing to meet threat with threat. I am aware that I have little of that power.

As my colleague rose from her chair, an ending so consonant with my daydreamed recollection, I understood that she had a talent that would serve her well despite her flaw.

At the same time, the flaw was already fading. For in telling me the story, which she had considered not recounting, the social worker was expressing awareness of my annoyance and in effect confronting me. I might have dressed her down: How could you let the session get so out of hand? Why can you never anticipate aggression? You managed to escape, but at what cost to the treatment relationship? You have aroused expectations you can never meet. And so forth.

The conflict she had ignored with the patient she risked with me.

To put it differently, the moment of engagement in therapy served as a moment of engagement in supervision. The moment occurred well into the therapy and well into the course of my collaboration with the social worker, but I think its timing need not trouble us. Like an element of a short story—the climax, for example, or the denouement—the moment of engagement may occur early or late or only by implication or not at all. But if not at all, as in the experimental story without a climax, we may ask how the trick has been pulled off or wonder whether we have not been cheated a bit.

When they do occur, it seems to me a common characteristic of such moments that they have reverberations outside the work. They tend to find echoes in different areas of the life of the patient and, on occasion, of the therapist and even the therapist's supervisor.

Nor is it unusual, as happened when the social worker rose toward her paranoid patient, for the process of engagement to contain and illustrate tensions among the formal demands of psychotherapy, the rules of the professions, and our instincts as healers. So that we may hope, by thinking about these moments, to learn something about our treatments, our calling, and ourselves.

Myth

They say the biggest influence on the therapy you practice—and the therapy you aspire to, your *imago* of therapy—is the therapy you experience as a patient. And this truth holds for me, if you add the admission that I remember few details of the treatment.

I do recall distinctly the setting: an antique, high-ceilinged flat fronting on Regents Park near Baker Street in London. The waiting room was paneled in mahogany, the walls lined with glass-doored wooden bookcases filled with old volumes in several languages. The carpets were worn orientals and the furniture so heavy and ornate it could only have come from pre-war Germany. The ensemble was familiar to me. It reproduced exactly the taste of the German Jewish grandmother in whose more modest Manhattan apartment I had spent some months in early childhood when my father was hospitalized for tuberculosis.

Although my analysis took place in *tabula rasa*-style anonymity, I gathered that the Regents Park flat belonged to an older analyst—the woman I occasionally saw addressing the maid in the pantry, which I passed on my way to the bathroom—from whom my analyst rented his consulting room. In decor the consulting room resembled the rest of the house, so I could assume nothing about my analyst's taste, other than that since he chose to rent these rooms he may have shared a certain comfortable and fusty continental sensibility.

He appeared to be in his middle fifties and he had a marked South African accent. (I still cannot read the words ego or superego without imagining the long 'e' to be pronounced the way an American would pronounce a long 'a'.) He was modestly overweight and given to wearing muddy-colored, shapeless suits, as if the physical, and ornamentation in particular, had little significance for him.

I treated him as if he were older and more frail than his appearance indicated, and after I discovered that he was a nonstop cigarette smoker between sessions—often I saw him sneak off to the tobacconist to pick up a pack of filterless cigarettes and a tabloid paper—I began to imagine that he would soon die of a heart attack. He ascribed this fantasy to transference; I feared he would die as I had feared my father would when I was three years old.

My first meeting with my analyst was inauspicious. He interviewed me from behind a desk—something which I believe is little done any more in the States—and I had trouble settling in to tell my story. When I complained that I had been able to say more to the referring psychiatrist, a Dr. Couch (yes) who was visiting London from my undergraduate college in the States, my analyst replied quietly, "Perhaps you felt more pressure," and I imagined I detected irritation at my implied criticism. I wonder if this trace of emotion did not emerge precisely because we were still sitting facing one another and he was not entirely in role. Once the analysis proper began he took on a perfectly selfless posture; I had to magnify this hint of pride to ascribe to him anything other than a neutral focus on my psyche.

His initial history-taking was perfunctory. He made no attempt to elicit or characterize particular symptoms. Certainly there was no formal mental status testing. By contemporary standards my analyst cannot be said to have made any attempt at diagnosis. I laid out my case as well as I could, and before the end of the hour he suggested that we begin an analysis. I was to lie on the couch and say whatever came into my mind.

We would meet twice one week and three times the next, as much time as he could give me and all I could afford, even at the modest fee he proposed. Later we increased to three and four. The schedule alternated because he traveled to Holland every other weekend to teach child psychoanalysis there—the only substantial detail he told me about his life outside the office.

I did not warm to my analyst immediately and, though I threw myself into free association with vigor because I wanted to appear cooperative and bright, my faith in the method grew only slowly.

[8]

One day I managed toward the end of an hour to remember a fragment from the past night's dream involving the word "Penthesilea."

Penthesilea? he asked.

Don't you know? I chided him — Penelope's cat in the *Odyssey*. My kindly maiden-aunt Latin teacher in high school had named her own cat Penthesilea. I went on to associate to the warmth of the Latin teacher, the domesticity of cats, and the admirable fidelity of Penelope.

No, the analyst ventured. This train of thought sounded false. And though he did not recognize the name Penthesilea, he doubted I had the reference right.

I left the session angry at him for his ignorance. Once home I went straight for a classical handbook, awarded me as a prize for my studies by this same Latin teacher.[1]

To my bewilderment, the entry under Penthesilea had nothing to do with Penelope. I read the passage repeatedly, overcome with wonder.

Penthesilea was a queen of the Amazons, a race of warrior women who slew their male offspring at birth and cut off the right breast of girl children "so as not to interfere with the bow arm."

Her involvement was with Achilles, not Odysseus. She killed many Greeks, but her lance shattered on Achilles' magic armor. "He wounded her in the breast with his sword, and as she debated whether to ask for mercy he impaled her and her horse with his spear. When she fell he gloated over her but when he removed her helmet and saw the wonder of her beauty, 'like a child of Zeus sleeping,' he fell wildly in love with her and was filled with remorse."

This material suggested I harbored a different unconscious image of women than that implied by the cat, the Latin teacher, and the faithful wife. Also implicit was a different picture of my intentions toward women.

But, but . . . I wanted to protest. I could swear I had never read this passage, indeed never known anything about Queen Penthesilea nor the habits of the filicidal, one-breasted Amazons — and yet, and yet. The word had arisen in my dream. I had reported it in therapy and insisted that it represented my attitude toward women. And I had known right where to go to find the reference.

In the sessions preceding the dream we had been talking about my relations with women. Max — in my thoughts I always referred to my

[9]

analyst by his first name—had implied that I was drawn to women who were bitchier than I gave them credit for being.

Also, I was just at that time settling on a thesis topic—I was in England on an honorific two-year graduate scholarship in modern litera-ture—and had chosen one which would put me in competition with a woman named Penman.

Penelope, Penthesilea, Penman. P-e-n words were multiplying. I could hardly argue that the dream, the reference, and my mistake were coincidence. With embarrassment and some other emotion, a combina-tion of excitement and the pleasant resignation of one giving himself over to the inevitable, I went to the next session and confessed to the revised interpretation of the dream.

Further association led to issues about putting pen to paper—I had wanted on finishing college to write a novel but had somehow gotten myself bogged down in the graduate studies the scholarship demanded—and then to more general questions about achievement and whether my lack of satisfaction with my accomplishments did not relate to inhibi-tions regarding that other p-e-n-word analysts look for and even, confess-ing the most banal, to castration anxiety.

I was in for a nickel all right, and a less skilled therapist might have enjoyed the bravura performance and left well enough alone. But it was hard to snow Max even with cooperation.

He suggested we examine what my insistence that Penthesilea meant the same as Penelope had to do with my opinion of him. Why had I imagined he would swallow the false story, and why had I felt such contempt when he did not? It was true, I realized, that I considered Max my intellectual inferior and treated him with disdain. Just as I in fantasy overstated the power of women, I underestimated the power of men. Although I feared men, too. For wasn't the way I broached this subject—the way I tried to pick a fight with Max—a bit prissy? Why did I hide my challenge behind an obscure classical referent?

In the unconscious, it seemed, I lived in a violent world of threaten-ing women and alternately incompetent and frightening men. And how, by the way, did this unacknowledged schema relate to those days before age five when my father became sickly and my mother and her mother assumed control?

Und so weiter. The therapy had begun.

From that moment, and with increasing certainty as similar moments recurred in therapy, I was convinced of the basic tenets of psychoanalysis: that conscious life is governed by mental fantasy; that this fantasy resides in a part of the mind not readily accessible to consciousness; that the unconscious is not a filing cabinet but an active, dynamic component of the mind; that the subject of this dynamism is inner conflict; that the conflict regards difficult-to-acknowledge emotions, especially those related to sexuality and violence; that these conflicts have roots in early development; and that the full scope of the unconscious and its fantasy is expressed through dream materials and associations in conjunction with the transference and the transference resistance. And that the results of unexamined neurotic conflict are expressed both in acute symptoms—lack of pleasure in accomplishment, failure to write, unsatisfying relations with girlfriends—and in character style—a subtle priggishness only imperfectly disguised by my American blue jeans and flannel shirts.

These beliefs became central to my life in London and formed the foundation of my thought about psychotherapy and the functioning of the mind for years thereafter.

For the therapist there are many pleasures in therapy: parental pride in a cautious patient's venturing a new risk; the illicit enjoyment of voyeurism; feelings of competence in diagnosis or power in strategic interventions. But in one way or another each of these is tainted, ambiguous, ordinary. I wonder if there is any moment so specific to therapy as this one, or so satisfying: the making of a perfect tripartite interpretation which crystallizes these three selves, the selves of the present, the past, and the transference. The commotion stops. For an instant, before the thousand lies reassert themselves, the patient knows his hopes and fears, and he understands his contribution through fantasy to the world which troubles him.[2]

There are, we as a field and I as a student have with time discovered, many ways to join with patients. To the extent that they all lead to productive therapy, these ways ought all to be equal. And yet there is something about interpretation—about Penthesilea—which makes it dearest to my heart.

I say "dearest to my heart" in the way one speaks of a first love, one which in retrospect seems unworldly, a love which one has betrayed once and then twice and then daily. An unlikely love in the profession I know today—but does one ever find a better?

Nor is this weakness mine alone. The other day I received from a local health maintenance organization a mailing extolling brief, low-cost therapy focused on patients' strengths. In it, a founding leader of the HMO mental health movement began his essay by quoting from Freud's 1918 address to the Fifth International Psychoanalytic Congress. In order to reach a greater mass of the population, including the poor, Freud wrote, we may need—and this is the phrase the HMO psychiatrist cited—"to alloy the pure gold of analysis freely with the copper of direct suggestion."

The pure gold of analysis. Penthesilea as the golden moment. How can anyone write, or even quote or think, such phrases today without irony? Irony stands at the door, along with the neurobiologist and many others, but let us keep it outside a moment longer and ask whether it is sentiment only or something else that makes us talk of gold.

Many things make the analytic relationship attractive. For me one has always stood out: it rests on the belief that the truth sets men free.

Freud is often accused of pessimism, but by current standards we must call him a Pollyanna. That the truth should rid us of disease—the idea is visionary. Freud's pessimism lies in his beliefs about the nature of this liberating truth: we harbor violent and incestuous fantasies. But what seemed grim to a different generation is, and this change itself owes much to Freud, now a commonplace. Today, acknowledging our perversity is a price we will gladly pay if we can thereby rid ourselves of our malaise. Taking our animal origin as a given, what remains is pure optimism.

Much else is imperfect about psychoanalysis and Freud's views of mental illness and normal development, but for me this one quality, the reliance on expression of inner truth as a curative agent, makes the method irresistibly attractive.

The source of cure, we discover, is not in the analyst, adept though he may be. Symptoms or maladaptive personality traits develop through the cleverness of the patient, through the complexity of the contortions he puts himself through to avoid disorganizing pain. The same mind that created the problem can solve it; the Gordian knot unties itself. Perhaps other therapies, quick ones which avoid dependency, can cut the knot in one stroke; but at what cost to the patient's belief about locus of control?

Penthesilea appeals to me as an example because it shows off this aspect of the method so clearly. There is nothing fancy about Max's interpretation. He says only, "I think not." His genius is in his patience and his forbearance and his faith in the method. And it is a genius. Max created an environment in which I was free and bound to make errors and to recognize them. The therapy can be seen as a series of moments of engagement separated by less important periods in which the work of therapy seemed to be going well.

The other aspect of Max's genius was his unwavering faith in the method. He betrayed no doubts, and on the contrary great firmness, in his application of the different principles of psychoanalysis—neutrality, abstinence, and reliance on interpretation for cure.

This consistency avoided the conflict among psychiatric roles so evident in the social worker's rising toward the patient. In the quiet of the psychoanalyst's consulting room, an interaction occurs which is beyond reproach (how odd to be able to say this now, in light of Freud's need to defend his methods against moral attack) and yet of enormous power. The distracting voices beyond the walls are not heard.

As for the content of Penthesilea, my belief in its uniqueness diminishes with time.

The story of the paranoid patient is, after all, not so different from Penthesilea. Both incidents center on a confusion of love and violence. We can say of the social worker's intervention that when the patient began to see her as an Amazon, hostile and threatening, she countered this projection by showing herself to be Penelope, patient and accepting. This wordless transference interpretation—"Your image of me, and of the world, is more threatening than it need be"—allowed the patient to experience her violence and her neediness as her own.

We can even say that my struggle, as a supervisor, with the social worker had to do with where she stood on the Pen-woman spectrum and where I imagined she should stand. And we may wonder whether hidden concern over this spectrum, and an accompanying exaggerated emphasis on the importance of intellectual acknowledgment of conflict, was not my own persistent flaw.

[13]

*   *   *   *   *

Finding myself at the end of medical school with a few weeks free before the start of internship, I decided to team up with a classmate and take a cheap flight to Europe to celebrate our last days of liberty.

We were headed for Paris via Brussels, but the flight was canceled, and after various delays we found ourselves on a stopover in London, where I had finished my analysis with Max four years earlier. I thought he would like to know I was on my way to becoming a psychiatrist, and in any case the landing in London seemed like kismet, so I called his old number.

A worried voice referred me to the Hampstead Clinic, where Max was on the faculty. At the Hampstead there was more hesitation on the other end.

Who was calling?

Thinking on my feet, I said simply, "Dr. Kramer."

"Oh, Dr. Kramer," the secretary acknowledged, mistaking me for someone else. Evidently I hadn't heard. The doctor had died the weekend before.

I felt that old sense of dislocation. It was not just that I was standing exhausted in an airport phone booth learning that my analyst had died. It seemed I was still in the analysis. I had graduated, and he had died; there was some lesson here, if only I could grasp it, about the Oedipus complex, about competition, maturation, and independence.

And what of this trip to London? I could have fought harder for a seat on that plane to Luxembourg. All happenings must be treated as meaningful. How badly I had wanted to see him, how worried I had been I would find him dead.

I must still have been in my doctor persona, for I asked the secretary how, how had he died?

"Of a heart attack," she said.

"Ah, yes. I had once suspected. . . . Had he a history of heart disease?"

"No," she said. It had taken everyone by surprise. In fact, when he was admitted to hospital, the surgeons treated him for a bleeding ulcer.

The rankest beginner's mistake, to leave heart disease out of the differential when the patient complains of abdominal pain. God, it made me angry.

I had known, of course. The doctors had not suspected, but I had. In all the world only I had known that Max had heart disease. I had told him.

Coincidence, it is easy enough to argue. I still believe, even at this remove from the treatment and from his death, that I knew. I had sensed his frailty.

It is characteristic, it seems to me, of good dynamic therapy that, despite all concealment, the patient comes to know the therapist with great immediacy. Is the therapist trustworthy or secretly cruel, confident or anxious, loving or withholding, generous or self-absorbed, sick or well? The analysis is very much with one specific person.

I wonder whether Max's death—the precise death I had during the therapy imagined and insisted on, and the belief in which he had, correctly enough from one point of view, ascribed to my own supersensitivity—did not open a chink of doubt in the armor of my faith in interpretation. I loved the method, but I loved the man more. My naïve empathy had been as accurate as Max's studied explanation of it. Certainly his death made a contribution, for better or worse, to my own style as a therapist. I trust my instinct—I sit with my unjustifiable feelings about my patients longer than I otherwise might. And when patients reveal their fantasies about me, I listen.

Silence

No carpets here. Gray linoleum tile covered the floor. No windows either. The reflective side of a one-way mirror took up most of one wall, and a naked microphone hung from the ceiling, as in an interrogation cell. To sit on, there were battered plastic Eames chairs.

The patient was a stubborn-looking young black man recently released from the inpatient research unit where he had unsuccessfully completed an innovative medication and behavior modification protocol for schizophrenia. He remained, as he had been for months, virtually mute.

I had been his psychiatrist before he was transferred to the research unit, when he was first admitted to the general hospital inpatient ward. His parents told me his story then. He was a normal boy, they said, interested in sports, contented, the kind of boy who does well in school without having to be pushed. He had friends, never many, and his closest companions were cousins, but that's how boys were in the family. He was their only child.

Toward the end of high school things began to change. (Our most terrible question: when did things begin to change?) He stayed in his room more. He slept less, and at odd hours. His face took on a hostile look, and he muttered things about the man next door. One day he took to the car windows with a two-by-four.

In the bleak consulting room in the basement of the community mental health center, his parents sat beside him.

The father was enormous, a physical presence. He had begun as a manual laborer and then risen through a stint in the Marines to skilled machine work. Now he had his own small company. Effort, he always demanded of his boy, more discipline and effort. When I was in the Marines, the father once told me, we played tackle football on gravel. He was a proud man, a modestly successful member of a family which included well-to-do farmers and a lawyer in this generation. But as I read the situation he was the softer parent. The boy—I, too, thought of him as a boy—had brought him to his knees.

The wife was still something of a mystery, camouflaged more completely in the black community. When we spoke she never moved to meet me half way. Her face remained fixed in a certain expression—sadness, perhaps, or else it was a scowl. She wore outdated hats which to my eye gave her a crazy-lady quality, although she was sane as could be. Too passive for my taste, maybe, too stoically reconciled to her son's fate. But I could as easily have said she was more realistic than the father or I. We still had hope.

No one had been able to break the patient's silence, so he was referred back to me. There was a challenge in the referral. I was the guy in the group who imagined therapy worked for everything, the one who liked tough cases.

I did, and I liked Gary. It must have been the unanalyzed oedipal conflict in me. I half enjoyed his stubbornness. I thought it was directed against his father.

But even I had no interest in sitting alone in a room with an impassive young man, searching for hints in his expression, guessing out loud at his emotions. I can say I had too much respect for dynamic therapy to use it in that way. The dialogue of dynamic therapy is a subtle one; it depends on the patient's cooperative search for signs to make meaning out of chaos. And besides, I had already made a fool of myself that way on the inpatient unit.

So this time I was trying family therapy.

It was our third session. I had gotten a sentence out of Gary last time. The parents disagreed about something, coming one step short of an argument, and I saw a smile steal across the son's immobile face. What makes you smile? I had insisted. He'd had this image, he said, of something he did when he played with toys: a picture of blowing up G. I. Joe.

[18]

That's what he does, the father said. If he talks at all, he talks about games.

That's right, the mother nodded.

Here was my hypothesis: the boy's muteness—even his psychosis, if we think we can explain psychosis in terms of the intelligent mind—had its roots in family conflict. On the parental level, the conflict concerned the different values mother and father brought to the marriage. The parents met in a southern rural community where members of the father's family were prominent landowners. He began life with less parochial values than hers, and he was now an assimilated northerner. Father wanted to see the boy go to college, choose a profession, succeed.

Mother remained attached to the world of the black farm family, the Baptist Church, and maternal power over children. She was already angry at her husband for wrenching her away from her home, although to complain about his success would have been unthinkable. And she did not want to lose her son to the father's family.

This explained why she was so little perturbed at her son's condition. At least he was at home. At least he was hers. She was nonverbal anyway; she spoke in two-word sentences. She had named the boy after Gary Cooper, strong and silent. As a rebuke to her husband? Let him talk his way into the white man's world, let him display his physical power and brag of his days in the Marines. She sat quietly with her arms crossed, a sufficient counterweight.

The boy, of course, played his own role. No mother can assign a part so completely. He must have had his needs: thirst for the love his mother doled out sparingly, hope for refuge from the fears she taught, a drive to find weapons against a dominating father. Blow up G. I. Joe. And now, his explicit dreams and his father's ruined, he sat in silent opposition to him and to me and the world we stood for.

I was working during these same weeks with a deaf-mute psychotic woman, so I was focused on the question of therapy in silence. I was looking for a simple first step. If only the mother could trust the father and release the son, if only the son could express his fear and anger directly, if only the son could move toward the father, forcing the mother to move with him.

For some reason I remembered something I had once seen done by

Carl Whitaker, the crazy spiritual father of a generation of family therapists. I was in my medical internship year in Wisconsin, and I snuck off
regularly to Whitaker's family psychiatry seminar for residents. He was
working with a psychotic child, two angry siblings, and feuding parents.
The mother was the outsider, a histrionic woman with a hard-to-diag-
nose wasting physical illness. While the co-therapist talked with the
crazy child, Whitaker—wouldn't he just—got up from his chair and
walked behind the mother and began giving her a backrub. As his meaty
hands played over her delicate shoulders and neck, the family seemed to
fall away from its anger. They must have seen the mother as she saw
herself at her best, a beautiful woman of sorrow.

I remember how liberating the moment was for me. To touch a
patient, to comfort her directly—how stunning and refreshing it was to
watch a senior therapist break the rules. (It was this moment as much as
any which prepared me years later to admire my intuitive social worker.)
No *tabula rasa*, no amplifying of small signals, no fantasized image of the
caring parent. Here was lantern-jawed Carl Whitaker, bigger than life,
kneading the base of a patient's neck with his large thumbs.

In the windowless room I turned to the boy and said, I want you to
do something now. I want you to stand behind your father and give him
a backrub.

I thought he might. I thought I knew the rules of the game. The boy
must not speak, he must not show emotion nor take initiative, but he
will obey commands. This was his rebellion, to be acquiescent but
unreachable.

He stood now with his hands on his father's shoulders. The hands
were small, and the neck was thick and strong. The boy stared blankly
but the hands moved. At first they were slow and tentative. I said
nothing. He warmed to the task. The fingers moved to the front of the
neck, and the G. I. Joe smile crept across the boy's face. He was thinking
of strangling the father. I did nothing.

And then the boy began to dig his hands into his father's shoulders
and to roll the thumbs into the muscle of the neck. There was a fluidity
to the motion that had been absent from all the boy's movements from
the day I met him. Tears began to roll down the father's cheeks. Out of
the strong came forth sweetness. The mother moved to touch her
husband's hand. And I saw tears on the boy's stony face.

I wish I could say that from that moment he spoke. When I was frustrated in my work with the deaf woman, my supervisor used to say, what is your goal in the therapy? Do you want her to hear? The question was just; my expectations were too high in exactly this way.

The boy remained impassive and isolated. But he did move toward me. One day we went for a walk around the mental health center, and for a few minutes we joined a pickup basketball game. He was not much of an athlete, I was sad to discover, and he mixed awkwardly with the other kids. But he seemed to warm to my interest. He began to talk of his fantasies. He wanted to be a Marine like his father. A good compromise, I thought. A military career would allow him to identify with his father and grow to manhood without challenging the mother's fears that she would lose her son as he changed social class.

The backrub had one unexpected result. I fell in love with the mother. "Fall in love" may be too strong; I mean for it to express the immediacy of a certain sort of event. There are breakthroughs in therapy, moments when we begin to see beneath surface signs to essential and endearing human qualities. To be concrete, the next time the mother visited I found myself thinking, "What a lovely hat."

The parents seemed more at ease with one another. From somewhere came permission for the boy to leave home.

The boy did join the military. To me he still looked obviously disturbed, but the treating psychiatrist is often a poor judge of progress in the seriously troubled patient; time and again studies have shown clinicians to underestimate the progress of patients who are improved but ill. Not only did the Army accept Gary at the recruiting station, they observed him for two weeks in a preliminary boot camp and gave the OK to send him on for basic training far from home.

How sweet it is to stretch our legs after the cramped and finicking work of dynamic therapy. How liberating to make bold strokes.

There is a distinctive satisfaction in pulling off a successful strategic intervention. People use the analogy of judo; a small change in balance causes the opponent's force to work against himself. Not that the relationship is adversarial; the similarity has to do with the overwhelming strength of families and the astonishing way in which a measured intervention can alter its direction.

[21]

This pleasure is the pleasure of applying technology with skill. The backrub was social engineering. Reestablish the conventional generational boundaries within the family, and all will be well.

And there was a doctorly aspect to the backrub. Although the particular intervention may stand out as unusual, even bizarre, the sequence of diagnosis and action is recognizable. Do this, we are used to saying. Take this pill, stay away from salty foods, elevate your foot, stop smoking, put yourself in my hands.

To be more precise, the backrub was a halfway therapy, in this sense: if, as a therapist, I already had one foot in the world of doctorly technology, I still stood with the other planted firmly in the world of meaning. Whatever else I believed about schizophrenia, I continued to act as if specific symptoms had specific meanings—that the pathoplasticity of the illness arose out of temperament, individual history, and current unconscious conflict. The boy's violence and silence signified something—not "mere" genetic illness. Truth, I imagined, was still important.

But my belief about what to do with truth had changed. Understanding of the family constellation had no need to go beyond my own mind. If my analysis of the structure was accurate, and my intervention well tailored, the truth would be borne out in recovery, without a need for insight on the part of the family.

The patient's job was to obey. The rest would follow.

For the therapist raised on psychoanalysis there is something uncomfortable in this new arrangement. Knowing what we do of the unconscious, how can we be content to leave our patient in the dark? We miss the patient's resistance, and his collaboration. We miss his constant correction of our ideas, his discovering, and taking responsibility for, something similar to but slightly different from what we had imagined.

And yet, we may be able to see ways in which this moment hangs together with the others. For the boy, the backrub contained the familiar confusion of hatred and longing. Like the paranoid woman who moved to attack the social worker, he began with fear and rage, and he ended in experiencing love.

The problem for us is that cognition played a minor role, or none at all, in this experience. Anything coherent that happened in the boy's mind was only an incidental consequence of the family therapy. If the treatment was working as I intended, the mechanism of action was not intellectual but structural.

As the boy moved toward the father, the father rose in value within the family, and the mother was guided to deal directly with her husband. The crucial gesture was not the backrub but her reaching to touch her husband's hand. If she could find her security in her husband instead of her son, and if the son were freed to identify with his outward-facing father, the boy would be able to grow.

We can imagine this treatment occurring in the boy's absence. We would work with the parents, and the son's psychosis would melt away. It was not insight that set him free, but his parents. Insights, like the flowers that bloom in the spring, have nothing to do with the case.

We can perhaps hold on to a sense of commonality by considering the story differently. What if, as in my psychoanalysis with Max, the therapist was not so well hidden here as he imagined?

When in response to the tears in the father's eyes I remembered, "Out of the strong came forth sweetness," I was thinking in the mother's Biblical language. Perhaps it was not the backrub at all but a change in my perception of the mother which constituted the moment of engagement. Perhaps our emblem should be the therapist admiring the hat.

We recognize this moment, too. It is Penthesilea once more. The mother still sits with her arms crossed, but where once I saw defiance I now see warmth and protectiveness; I understand that all her fierceness is in support of her son, her family. Penthesilea into Penelope.

Family therapy depends in part on role-playing. Support the father, a supervisor might suggest. Sit beside him. Mimic his gestures, tailor the pace of your speech to his. Your unspoken respect will force the mother to take him into account.

If it is true that the therapist's subtle gestures of regard guide the family, might therapy not have depended on empathy and insight after all, in this sense: as I came to love and understand the mother, her husband was moved to love her, too, and her son to fear her less? As she found support in her own generation, the mother could let go of her son. So that the metamorphosis in the therapist which took place in the room, in the presence of the family, was the catalyst for change. Far though this therapy was from psychoanalysis, Max's work, imperfectly completed we must note, was not wholly wasted.

[23]

*   *   *   *   *

Gary's departure did not end my contact with the Steadwells, to give the family a name. I knew even then I would want some day to write about them and had asked their permission to do so. The parents responded by inviting me to their home.

The house stood in a quiet, modest part of the black ghetto. Once or twice had I set foot in a sitting room in this neighborhood, as part of an emergency call to evaluate a patient for certification. I wondered how often a white man was invited here as a guest.

The living room was done in fluffy pink and rose, with mass-produced paintings on veneered walls, religious statuary on side tables, and couches covered in clear plastic. What it most resembled from my own world was the kibbutz apartment (in orange tones) of distant relatives in Israel. What tied the two together in my mind, besides visual similarity, was a mixed sense of dignity and tawdriness, of unnecessary formality— something sad about what the two families reached for from the outside culture.

The living room was not meant for use, and after some minutes the Steadwells invited me into the real living area, the kitchen and recreation room. We had no agenda other than to thank each other for some undefined thing. Because our pretext for meeting was my intention to write about them, the Steadwells began to retell their family history.

We drank some beer, and, when the moment was right, the father brought out the albums. First the square black-and-white snapshots. The Steadwells hand-in-hand at Yankee Stadium. Now standing proudly beside a new Oldsmobile. Here was Mrs. Steadwell, youthful in gay dresses, her tight-lipped smile unambiguously lovely. And at last the baby on clouds of white pillows. Can we ever see these images—the photos perhaps more powerful than the moments they depict were at the time—without brimming over with sentiment?

Now the large man stands beside his small son, glove in hand, again at Yankee Stadium. And beside another Oldsmobile. A small boy and a large pumpkin. Fourth and fifth birthdays with Gary in flannel pants with suspenders and starched white shirts. Gary and school friends. Church suppers. Family events.

"You see how bright-eyed he was?"

[24]

His face did look expressive. Or was the smile a little distant?

"He was always a quiet boy."

Many people have tried to say what it is about photographs. For the first time I understood how important they are to families, how badly we need them to document the good times.

The evening was a test of my beliefs about parents and children and mental illness. What influences development? So much is unknown. Subtle neglect, subtle seduction, overly intense hopes and fears, the silent struggle between mother and father over the boy's soul. I had no evidence for any of this, nor did I know what among it would matter if I did.

You raise what you think is a normal boy for 15, 16, 17 years, almost two decades of fights and hugs and secret self-pity and unwarranted pride and suppressed and overeager love—were you too indulgent, too pushy, too punitive? Were you different from other parents? Where did the stiff, blank, hostile, unreachable child, a parody of your worst secret anger and loneliness and confusion, no longer wholly a person, where did he come from?

The evening was also a test of my beliefs about psychotherapy. One aspect of the invitation now had become clear to me. Like a priest, I was meant to absolve. Absolution is a therapeutic function of which I had never before been so aware.

"I can see you have been good parents," I said.

They told me how Gary was doing in the Army. Not well, it sounded to me, but I expressed hope. Theorists debate today about "upward interpretation" or "incomplete interpretation," where a therapist alludes to only the most easily tolerated part of an unconscious conflict; but if we were honest we would admit that the outright lie is also part of psychotherapy. And not only to support fragile egos in patients with primitive personality structures—lying is just a necessity of human discourse, and the therapeutic relationship is not exempt from having to depend on it now and again.

As I left, I glanced into Gary's room. It was a boy's room, with posters of sports heroes on the walls and a full sized baseball glove on the shelf.

"One night he smashed the stereo," the father said, pointing to it. Other than the broken amplifier I saw no hint of anything out of the ordinary.

The parents invited me to come back soon, but we both knew I likely would not.

*   *   *   *   *

In truth, I had done something potentially worse than lying in this case.

Besides the family therapy, Gary came to me every two weeks for medication. Since we were not sure he took pills reliably, we had him on intramuscular depot Prolixin at a dose worked out on the research ward — a very high dose, but he seemed to show some response to it.

On a day off from his introductory military training, he had come to me for a shot. This is my strongest physical memory of him, the feel of his arm and shoulder as I gave him Prolixin. Nurses mostly give the injections nowadays, but for some reason I treated Gary myself, because he was not in the "community support" clinic or because he came in at off hours.

He was a muscular boy and Prolixin is unbelievably viscous. God, how I hated Prolixin. If I gave him a shot straight into the deltoid, the stuff would ooze back out at me, so I had to make a z-track and bury the needle deep. Even so, I always lost some.

I know and believe in all the evidence about antipsychotics. The best predictor of relapse in hospitalized psychotic patients is failure to take medication. The most powerful prophylactic against relapse is depot phenothiazine. We used it more in those days anyway, because the evidence on tardive dyskinesia was weaker. But I hated to give it. What a load of medication it was, and for what slight effect. The worst thing was, Gary seemed not to mind. He seemed immune to the pain.

He had learned at long last that he needed the shots to function. He guessed — I guessed too — that if he asked the Army for an antipsychotic, he would be discharged. When he was sent to a base far from here, he asked, what should he do?

We decided he should find a civilian doctor off the base and get an injection on his leave time. I did not know how this deception accorded with any agreement he had made with the military, and I did not want to know. The military had made the judgment to take him, and I had no intention of interfering with their decision. Perhaps, I told myself, the structured environment would do him good. (This is our eternal hope, that the military will do our patients good, a final myth in cases where there are no answers.) If he stayed with it long enough to move to a sensitive position, to combat duty, say, and I knew about it—I would face that day when it arose. For the moment, I was grateful to be sworn to confidentiality.

Find a doctor, I said. If need be, the doctor could call me and I would speak with him. I reminded Gary of side effects—I remember hyperthermia worried me the most—and sent him on his way.

How entirely bizarre this relationship had become, how far from the hands-off treatment I had imagined my profession to entail. The mental health center, the boy's illness, the family's hopes, issues of money and social class, my position as doctor, the medical and psychotherapeutic technology available to me—so many external factors had shaped my behavior.

As a child, I loved a Mark Twain story about two elderly, morally rigid sisters who take on the care of a child whose quarantined mother is ill with typhoid. When the child herself becomes weak and dies, out of compassion the once puritanical sisters forge letters from her to the mother. At last the mother, too, dies, and an angel of the Lord appears before the sisters, who had always condemned lying absolutely ("All lies are sinful . . . all lies are forbidden.") The sisters confess their weakness to the angel, and he whispers his decree. The final chapter of the story consists of one sentence, which is also the title of the story: "Was it Heaven? Or Hell?"[1] For me, a parallel question hung over my work in residency: was it a fulfillment of the spirit of Max's work, or a betrayal?

For better or for worse, my work with the Steadwells moved me toward a less rigid understanding of psychotherapy. I still saw patients first through the lenses of dynamic theory. But, this early in residency, my sense of what it is appropriate for a psychiatrist to do had already changed utterly.

Gary was released from the military after a number of weeks. He had taken no medicine and had been unable to adapt to day-to-day demands. Getting up on time, following routine orders—simple tasks became too much for him. What surprised me was how long he stayed in, given his condition. I telephoned someone at the base but got few details.

For his troubles Gary earned the right to be treated free at Veterans Administration hospitals. I learned this when a V. A. inpatient psychiatrist called me for information during a subsequent hospitalization. So our relationship bore practical fruit. He was now, as he had wished, forever tied to the military. Good for him, I thought. In the end, the illness had defeated my efforts, but I was glad Gary had taken a chance on his dream and glad he got something for it.

I spoke to Gary and his parents now and then, over a number of months, but the moment had passed. They had adjusted to his chronic illness. I have always wondered whether I could have done better for Gary. We did seem to connect for a short while. Whether these moments are washed away or whether, as the analysts believe, nothing is forgotten, I do not know.

Intrusions

It is a Sunday afternoon. Upstairs the television drones a murmur of sports noise, here in the kitchen the children are demanding food and attention. As in a detective story, the telephone rings.

A patient is about to enter my life, that other quieter and more turbulent life. Time and again there are these half-welcome calls, in the office, on the answering machine, or like today, at home on a weekend afternoon, people proposing a relationship with themselves or with other, unknown, people.

On the line is a senior psychiatrist in our small city, a man who has never before called me at home. I could delay the moment, suggest I call back later. But because I hear urgency in his voice, or because of his position and my fear of alienating him, or perhaps merely because I am irritated by any referral, by the work it will entail, by the obscene intimacy of it, I choose to take it now, when I can give only partial attention. I may know, too, that I risk creating, here in this kitchen, an objective situation which will serve as a simpler, less conflicted outlet for irritation.

I shove peanut buttered bread at the children and shake my head into the phone, "No, no, not an unreasonable time. I understand. Go ahead."

He is calling on behalf of his wife's cousin's family. The cousin is a widower, and his eldest daughter is in trouble.

A relative. Already my mind is racing, wondering why me, why at this hour. I pull the cord into the dining room and half shut the door.

A lovely girl, he is saying, he has known her all her life. She had just graduated from college and headed off to Guatemala to do volunteer work with a relief agency, but within days of arrival she fell ill with a fever, and when she recovered—or did her altered behavior precede the illness?—she began to relate to others strangely. She thought the villagers were after her. She accused the head of the agency of staring at her provocatively. Today she threw herself in front of a bus, not in a suicide attempt but to escape imagined pursuers. Fortunately the driver saw her in time.

I find I am thinking the defensive thoughts of the modern doctor. Cynical thoughts. The lovely girl will sue me over the delusion I have attacked her. And more personal defensive thoughts: she will run in front of a car, and I will have to live with her forever, in guilty memory. She will attack my sense of nurturance, damage my confidence as a father.

The side door opens. My wife has returned from her errands. Covering the phone for an instant, I stick my head back into the kitchen. Bread and juice are everywhere. "Sorry. Couldn't help it. Important call. Fill you in later." I know she would prefer a breathing space before taking over.

To be fair to myself, I am also thinking all the nosologic doctorly thoughts. Schizophrenia? A young adult with new-onset psychosis—demographically schizophrenia is the most likely. I set this diagnosis aside, only partly on professional grounds. As a father I cannot stand the idea that I might raise children—these very children who at this very moment are paying for my minor neglect—who 16 years from now will wake up to see the world as an unremittingly terrifying place, and then deteriorate further.

Manic-depressive illness then. Likely in a bright girl who turns paranoid. Or a post-encephalitic syndrome? What do I know about the viruses of Latin America?

And then why would anyone choose me for such a case? I see mainly outpatients. Surely others are better prepared than I to coordinate the care of a first-break psychotic.

Unless his hypothesis is homesickness, an exaggeration of the usual late adolescent separation-individuation issues. But then why not choose someone from the analytic crowd he usually refers to? Are there, I wonder, ugly family secrets which the referring doctor would just as soon see addressed by a more distant colleague?

Or else it is the ambiguity of the case that made him think of me. Is this how he sees me? The man to handle a troubling family case which may, on the other hand, turn out to be physical and very sad. Psychotherapy or drugs. I'm a utility infielder, fair glove, fair bat, flexible.

I hear him saying, you are young. You have the resilience to take on sticky cases.

"I'm fairly busy," I say, "but . . ."

My practice is full (luxurious state!), as full as my wife and I have agreed it should be. But there is always room for a special case.

In a small community, there are many special cases. Friends of friends and their children or parents, referrals from the doctors I work with most often, members of the university community, people in the local government, famous people, people treated by someone I trained with in a distant city and who since moving here have held on to my name in case they got into trouble again, people whose dilemmas make them appealing for one reason or another.

And then the sorts of clinical puzzles that interest me.

This case is special already, by more than one criterion, so I know I will take it. But I raise a small barrier, to elicit information, to let the colleague know I know I am taking on trouble.

He says, "I think you'd be good with her. She's never had any real difficulties. She might have had a touch of anorexia in high school — I remember hearing something of the sort from my daughter. But nothing that required treatment."

Anorexia clusters with affective disorder or identity problems. He wants to let me know the case is benign.

He answers other questions without my having to ask. No borderline traits he knows of. A bright girl, a pleasant girl. "It's a lovely family. Observant Catholics. The mother died eight years ago, of cancer. She may have had a period of depression after one of the children's births."

More good news in the guise of bad. Affective loading. Unless the mother had a touch of alcoholism or schizophrenia and raised the daughter in some aberrant way. Would my informant tell me if he were aware of frank child abuse? I wish I had a better sense of the family I am entering; it feels dangerous to approach them naked.

"The father is a top executive at _____." He names a national firm with a local office. Good insurance and the ability to make the copayment. I dislike this aspect of private practice. But I attend to it.

Our negotiating is mostly done.

"If she needs immediate hospitalization, I'm not sure I'd be the right person." I name the inpatient psychiatrist I'd send her on to.

More boundary-setting.

"The father wants her at home. He'll cooperate in any way he can."

We have laid down the ground rules.

The girl's plane is arriving midday tomorrow.

Fine, I say. I'll see her at eight-thirty tomorrow night, if the father doesn't take her right to the hospital.

My schedule is full tomorrow afternoon. And I want to leave time for the patient to show whether she can live at home. If she can control herself for a few hours, we'll start work together. After my kids' bedtime.

"I told the father if it were my daughter you are the person I would most want her to see."

The coup de grace. Because the other reason we take cases, the joy of private practice where patients come to you because they want to see you, you in particular, is narcissism. Is there a subtle insult in the flattery my colleague has just proffered? Has he heard my reluctance and interpreted it as self-absorption? No matter. The covert accusation is overwhelmed by the pleasure of the surface compliment.

But even taken straightforwardly, what does it mean? When I was in training, these accolades were reserved for men (mostly) over 50 — more likely in their sixties. This is an era, or a case, where things other than wisdom are valued.

"Well, thank you for thinking of me. I look forward to meeting her."

I reopen the kitchen door, to hang up the phone and confront the mess I have created.

I hope the young woman comes. I want to see who my colleague thinks I am.

*   *   *   *   *

There is, I am aware, a sour or disturbing note in this telephone conversation, something not quite what we should wish or expect. Surely we can attribute this minor falsity of tone to the Sunday afternoon and the distraction my own family presents, or rather to the sketchiness of the case and to the natural anxiety we all feel before meeting a patient and having a myriad of possibilities collapse into one simple and familiar problem. Once we see the patient, everything will be clear.

Or perhaps not. Because what is disturbing about the conversation is, at base, the different intruders who stand between doctor and patient: the referring physician, the insurance company, malpractice lawyers, the complexity of my own life. These were largely absent, or present in quite different and more acceptable ways, in my own therapy and the therapies I conducted in residency.

And in truth the intruders are unlikely to fade away in the impending encounter.

Given my image of the referring doctor and his relationship to the patient's family, I am unlikely to prescribe (much less to perform) a backrub. Or if, contrary to my self-protecting impulse, I do engage in an unconventional therapy, I will have to ask myself whether I have done it just to shock or offend him. He might as well be in the room with me.

And the others. The insurance company, certainly. If outpatient coverage extends only to 20 visits, the young woman will be in the hospital tonight, I can tell you that. This is no 20-visit outpatient case.

And, yes, the malpractice lawyers, hers and mine. I don't worry about them much, but they will be there. They look askance at backrubs and extended arms, I imagine. They want a diagnosis, and formal mental status testing, and documentation of suicide risk. They want me to make explicit things I might prefer to do by feel. Perhaps I should call in a consultant early on, to guarantee my own safety. It is true, what all the newspaper articles say, the lawyers make us — patient and doctor — adversaries in advance.

My own wife and children are onlookers, too. I am most aware of their role when I consider whether to agree to treat an intrusive patient with a personality disorder. I used to pride myself on taking on all comers. But today, can I afford the phone calls at midnight, the emergency sessions? If I do take on patients with poor self-control, I will without question choose a therapy which "establishes firm boundaries" and "discourages acting-out." My own social situation will help determine the treatment I choose.

I suppose I am aware of these last onlookers because of my memories of wilder cowboy days in residency, and also because I imagined my own psychoanalyst to have been unmarried. No woman would let a man out of the house in the awful suits Max wore. Perhaps he was widower. (Now, years later, I can just barely imagine him married—as Rumpole of the Bailey is married; he was very much a Rumpole figure in dress and deportment.)

These are different *imagos* of the therapist: the young idealist and the solitary priest, each fixed singlemindedly on the pain of others. A third image is the happily married, overly stable figure—à la Will and Ariel Durant.[1] The inevitable compromises of real marriage, pleasant and necessary though they may be, give rise to a quite different sense of the healer.

Except for essays on defined conditions such as pregnancy or illness, little has been written about the effect of the therapist's life circumstances on therapy. But I think therapies rely almost as much on the therapist's perception of his place in life as on the patient's fantasies; or, more precisely, the two interact. My identity as father is already evident in my overoptimistic rejection of the obvious diagnosis of schizophrenia. For the therapist to feel himself a parent—what worse betrayal can we imagine for a patient struggling, if she is, with identity and autonomy?

We are here no longer talking about onlookers but multiple roles for the doctor in the room with the patient. Already I anticipate being father, insurance company proxy, community stalwart, legal opponent, and small businessman.

Having once alluded to these roles and intruders, I will be silent about them. They are the givens of the social circumstances in which we practice; their importance can hardly be overemphasized, but they stand beyond the subject matter of these essays. I do not want to give the impression of being unaware of the effect of external circumstances on our work, but at the same time there is more than enough to say about the inner workings of psychiatry.

The other element which makes the telephone conversation uncomfortable—it is a somewhat ungenerous dialogue in a profession I think of as above all generous—is a painfully evident excess of clinical distance. Distance is a necessary part of today's psychiatry, in which diagnosis and formulation are central and the choice of interventions is great. Constraints internal to the profession make us approach patients with caution. Putting aside our functions as bearers of different societal values, we find within ourselves a confusion of psychiatric roles: neurologist, diagnostician, psychopharmacologist, and psychotherapist. This is before we consider whether the psychotherapist must be a blank screen, play actor, prescriptive behaviorist, paradoxical coaxer, or supportive friend. We will not be surprised if it takes some time before the patient and I meet one another.

*   *   *   *   *

The trouble with these cases is that they take so damn long to come into focus. Schizophrenia, bipolar illness, hysteria, epilepsy, difficulty separating, trauma. The more we wonder about, the more we hear. And even if we imagine we know what the answer is, there is the sticky problem of coming to an agreement with this person, the patient.

In the first meeting with the paranoid young woman and her father, even simple information is hard to come by. She is frightened, clinging, and empty. Her problems seem to be on an animal level. Like a beaten dog. With every statement she looks to her father or to me for confirmation.

The father is decisive and clear. Maybe he and I can step aside and get a handle on this thing. But the price will be the daughter's trust. So I try to work with her directly.

I adopt a vague style, in order to ally with the patient. But I see the father is beginning to consider me a milksop. I will lose the case entirely if I don't show some backbone. I make my voice loud and sharp to assuage his doubts; then I catch myself and return to the daughter for more history.

She understands it may seem crazy, but she knows CIA operatives are after her. She has kept vigil for days, avoiding sleep or finding, when she drops off despite herself, that she is pursued in nightmares more awful even than waking life: men and women force themselves on her. Maybe this all began with a college boyfriend; he may have worked for the Agency.

In my office, the depth of her terror is evident. She starts at the sound of a passing fire truck. A car horn blares, and her features take on a look of desperation.

Mixed with the paranoia are ordinary concerns of a college graduate. Should she resume her volunteer work in Guatemala or apply to graduate school in international studies? What should she tell her boyfriend? Living at home will be a humiliating setback. Should she look for a job and an apartment?

[35]

The organization of her denial, or her willingness to turn to her father, or his evident concern—something reassures me. I will agree to try to treat her out of hospital.

Why not start with some Mellaril tonight, to take the edge off things, to allow sleep?

Yes, she agrees, she would be grateful for some relief. Although she is wary about putting anything artificial into her body.

I discuss side effects in a vague and incomprehensible way, relieved when she asks no questions. Standard practice. We do not dwell on drug risks with an acutely psychotic patient we are hoping to keep out of hospital. There will be time later for honesty; to be explicit now would be immoral on more subtle grounds. But I expect to pay a price for this delay in full disclosure.

I do, in fact, take a moment with the father alone, to mention extrapyramidal side effects and tardive dyskinesia. And I give him a small prescription for an antiparkinsonian for his daughter, to be initiated if needed.

This choice, too, is ordinary, an option recommended in standard writings about management of the psychotic patient.[2] But unbeknownst, for now, to the patient, I have already acted on fantasies she is sure to have, treating her as an invalid and allying with her father. Well, we will sort it all out in time.

First we have the diagnostic phase, and if we take it seriously it is never as straightforward as we wish. The patient will see an internist and, because of the possible history of febrile illness, a neurologist.

The question is, which neurologist? The one who finds clinically important dysrhythmias in every electroencephalogram or the one who never finds any? The father and the internist choose a middle-of-the-road man, and the reading comes back positive, but in a nonspecific way: indicative of a static process, centrencephalic epilepsy, probably familial, an incidental finding unrelated to the patient's symptoms. The neurologist recommends against treatment with an antiepileptic.

I know that there are neurologists who almost never diagnose centrencephalic epilepsy or who if they do consider it an indicator of underlying temporal lobe dysfunction. And if, as I suspect despite the consultation, the dysrhythmia is significant, does it result from a recent mild encephalitis (and will it resolve), or is it genetic? We may be in the diagnostic phase for some time.

The family member with the epilepsy was the mother. When the mother was the age her daughter is now, and just when she set out to leave her own family, she began to experience grand mal convulsions. These persisted while she was single and then disappeared the day she married.

So the mystery is pushed back a generation. A mother who functioned best within the structure of a family. Epilepsy? Separation anxiety? Did she or didn't she? Likewise for the daughter.

I arrange to inspect the mother's medical records, but I have no belief they will clarify matters.

There is nothing for it but to push on. We do repeat EEGs and CT and NMR scans and neuropsychiatric testing. Amidst all the poking and probing, I come to know the patient.

She is, as promised, a lovely girl. A many-sided young woman like other young women just out of college. Idealistic, angry, romantic, bright, funny, perceptive, undirected, unsure of herself—although she may have a bit more of each of these traits than her peers, which is either fine or ominous. And she has this particular problem, the paranoia.

She stares at the rug, stealing an occasional glance at me. She is recovering from the worst sort of terror and, residual paranoia aside, she must wonder whether she can trust me to save her from another episode.

Aware of inevitable issues of control, I try to avoid intruding in any easily stereotyped way. Not too forceful, not too kindly, I rely on time, along with the medicine about which I have been so disingenuous, to do its work. Like the patient, I am looking away. We postpone getting to know one another and hope that this delay is therapeutic.

The important issues—fear, sex, parents—are still too overwhelming to handle. But as the psychosis recedes, she begins to talk about the safe subjects, things any young woman might discuss. So far I have mostly let her go her own way in comfort. But now, when she mentions the theme of her senior thesis, something about hypocrisy in international political dealings, I repeat the word hypocrisy once or twice, staring meaningfully.

[37]

She begins to talk about an episode in her childhood when her mother, whom she until now has characterized as loving, was out of control. They fought over food, as children and parents will. Finally the mother grabbed the girl's hair, pulled the head back over the chair, forced meat into the girl's mouth, and held the jaw shut until the girl swallowed. The mother force-fed the girl this way many times, off and on for weeks. The girl told her father, but he said she was exaggerating.

As she might be here in the office. The story smacks a bit of newspaper accounts of abuse. Still, our tendency these days is mostly to believe these stories, and when not paranoid this young woman has seemed straightforward enough. I can ask the father and the girl's sisters—but if they do not confirm the patient's story, whom shall I believe? If the account is fabricated or embellished, it shows the patient knows me well. I can identify with all the actors. Who cannot imagine the terror of a child resisting her mother's wild intrusions? The young woman's pain and terror strike me with new force.

But I also feel relief, and not only in empathy with the young woman's relief at broaching the forbidden subject. Mine is relief that the case is taking shape at last.

Here is a young woman who with effort and at a cost—under real provocation or imagined—maintained boundaries between herself and a needy and loving mother, only to have that mother die of a terrible illness, perhaps as the daughter had often wished. And now when it is time to act as a mature woman herself, and to leave the father who protected and failed her, she finds herself unable to separate. This is a story we know, one we can work with.

I have a good sense of how it continues, how it repeats itself. For instance, I expect to learn that the young man, the one she imagines works for the CIA, rekindled her sense of being invaded, probably through a sexual act she considered a violation but which she enjoyed as well. Beyond its oedipal overtones, this pleasurable violation may have aroused in her a terrible realization: that she loves and needs, as well as fears and hates, intrusions she experiences as abusive.

And of course she is asking whether she can trust me. My diagnostic doggedness may make her feel I will dismiss as meaningless her understanding of her individual history.

Meanwhile, the session is not over. As she prepares to leave, the

[38]

young women adds "one more thing." About the medication – she has not taken it. She wonders: since she is feeling a bit better, will I insist she take it?

I do not yet quite realize that the material of the session has been crystallized into this one question, do not yet see that it is I who am at once invasive and titillating. Having made me privy to the first secret, she is testing me to see where I stand.

Without thought or theory, for better and for worse, I hear myself say: "I won't force it down your throat."

The young woman has two feelings about me. On the one hand, I have created a safe environment to which she can return and where she feels understood. On the other, I hold her at a distance and examine her, I order tests, have blood drawn, push pills, and devise strategies to manipulate her. I make her feel safe and I terrify her.

Like her mother, I am Penelope and Penthesilea both.[3]

We can treat what our teachers could not. We mourn the loss of the delicate skills needed to manage psychosis without medication, but not so much that we fail to medicate. There is no turning back, and thank God there isn't. We are here to make patients better. But having insisted, appropriately, on EEGs and neuroleptics, and having argued out loud among ourselves about anticonvulsants, we should not be surprised to find it has become hard to reach the patient.

Perhaps we do not mind the barriers. Faced naked, patients are threatening. They exhaust us. We say we enjoy sailing close-hauled, but in truth we are ready to let the motor do the work and to see the sail luff.

Or perhaps therapy is hardy. We have brought the doubt, the haste, the partial honesty, the interruptions and variety of the outside world into the consulting room, but in truth there is something exhilarating in still being able to make therapy work amidst the turmoil. We are mountain goats leaping from one point of balance to another, we are scrappers and street fighters, we are compromisers who teach our patients the art of the possible.

The young woman home from Guatemala and I do in the end make contact.[4] And if I have now become the figures I once longed for and feared, Penelope and Penthesilea—well, isn't that just the price of growing up?

We ought not to overemphasize the hindrances of multiple roles and intruders. I do wonder whether it was not once possible to meet patients with more immediacy. But even before pills and tests and consultants, the issues were the same. Terror and longing tend to become intertwined, if only because from childhood the sense of our own weakness and our own strength, and the weakness and strength of those around us, is so exaggerated. We are not surprised to find our old friends Penelope and Penthesilea at hand.

Tools of the Trade

The
Mind-Mind-Body-Problem
Problem

Some years ago, a group of researchers at the University of Minnesota looked into the careers of residents who had been considered either mentally disturbed or just disturbing to the teaching program. The disturbed residents had done a bit more poorly than their peers, although most of them ended up pursuing "satisfactory" careers in psychiatry. But from among the disturbing residents were drawn some of the program's most successful graduates: department chairmen, honored clinicians, influential scientists, leaders of the field.[1]

I ran across the study early in residency and, giving myself the benefit of the doubt, took heart from it.

My problem, from a certain point of view, was that I knew too much. I had entered medical school certain I would become a psychiatrist, so I spent extensive elective time caring for psychiatric patients, there and in internship. As a result, I came to residency with five years of clinical experience—all of it psychodynamic.

I had also picked up a slight doctor's swagger in internship, having gotten used to ordering nurses around at all hours, and I considered myself a fair medical diagnostician. I had done my neurology under a nationally renowned epileptologist and thought I had a sense of what was a seizure and what wasn't.

In this puffed up condition, like a lamb to the slaughter, I entered my first psychiatry residency placement, an inpatient ward headed by a hardened convert to neuropsychiatry.

The unit was one of the great centers for its time of a certain sort of psychiatry. The milieu structure was tight and effective. Patients were placed on a buddy system and, though the group names were somewhat different, in effect were moved like summer campers from chipmunk to beaver status depending on their ability to assume responsibility. It was assumed that if someone did not get better quickly with first line medications and the pressures of the milieu, there was something really wrong with him.

What was said to be wrong with nonresponders was often a disorder at the cutting edge of science—adult "minimal brain dysfunction" masquerading as schizophrenia, subtle temporal lobe variants, neuroendocrine syndromes manifesting as anorexia—entities which had barely been proven to exist at all but which in their own way neatly explained patients' symptoms and lab results.

The ward chief's favorite idiosyncratically used medicine was Dilantin, which he employed in the treatment of certain patients who appeared to be personality disordered but who could be shown to have neurological "soft signs."

For a young doctor trained in dynamic therapy and conventional neurology and accustomed to a leadership role, entering this ward was like commitment to the looney bin.

I was seen as a troublemaker almost immediately. The nurses told me that the ward chief had decided a personality disordered patient of mine should be placed on Dilantin, and I refused to write the order. I said I was a licensed doctor, and I had to believe in what I was doing. The ward chief wrote the order. When the patient continued to progress slowly, my divisive spirit was to blame.[2]

I will spare the reader my many bitter and bittersweet stories of conflict with social workers and nurses (and of my growing, if grudging, respect for them and for the ward chief) and move right ahead to the case that broke me.

My collapse came during the hospital stay of an affable, unflinchingly suicidal young man—let us call him Alex—who had decided on the basis of reading Kurt Vonnegut and Albert Camus that "pain in the world" made living illogical. (Forever after my neurological-disorder sensors have twitched on hearing college students mention these two; Rainer Maria Rilke is a third. They are not to be confused with Anne Sexton, Sylvia Plath, and Stevie Smith, who accompany depression in apparent borderline syndromes.)

Our patient had come close to killing himself: he came to us from intensive care. He was in no way psychotic, nor even agitated; indeed, he had a charming, self-abnegating quality which presented a real danger on the ward, since it gave him the power to pull impressionable young women to suicide with him. In his calm and pleasant voice he would tell me, "You can do what you want here, but when I leave the hospital I'm going to kill myself."

How a resident views suicide is to some degree a measure of his acculturation into the profession. I was not yet so entirely a psychiatrist as to consider philosophical suicide in the young and healthy an impossibility, but I had worked enough with suicidal patients to view this young man as ill, not spiritually troubled. The question was: with what illness, and on the basis of what pathology? But for his recent attempt and current threat, Alex looked like an ordinary college kid. To some of the nurses he seemed like an amiable, if misguided, younger brother. In others he induced rage. One nurse yelled that if he wanted to kill himself, he should lie about his intentions, earn a discharge, and get down to business. Alex said he was too honest to lie, and why should he bother? He would achieve his goal in time.

As the ward dynamics unfolded, I labeled the young man border-line—but this is just the sort of arbitrary diagnosis George Vaillant has in mind when he compares "borderlines" to the tar baby in Uncle Remus and says the diagnosis is iatrogenic.[3] From the patient's perspective, it was only our unreasonable insistence that he live that made him a "splitter."

Alex had some schizoid traits, to be sure, and there was an abruptness to the changes in direction in his late adolescent development that seemed not quite right: he had been a biology major and had one day realized that dissection was unjust, and at about the same time he had given up horseback riding on similar grounds. But all in all he seemed different only in degree from the run-of-the-mill student who intellectualizes his struggle with identity and separation.

I presented Alex to my off-ward supervisor, an eminent phenomenologist. The encounter heightened my belief in the borderline diagnosis. The supervisor became irritated with me, as if I must be missing the obvious, and demanded to come to the ward to interview the patient himself.

Of course, it was just as I had said. Beyond the insistence on suicide there was nothing particular he could get out of Alex. "Schizophrenic," the supervisor said, despite the lack of evidence of hallucinations or delusions—despite the phenomena. "Schizophrenic"—as if the boy's cool stubbornness had the power to make the supervisor revert to the years of his own training when anything unexplainable was schizophrenia.

"The most difficult patient I've ever seen," the supervisor pronounced as he left the ward. He was prone to hyperbole, but this verdict served to make Alex all the more important.

To the ward chief, the case was a *forme fruste* of epilepsy. The pain he saw as the young man's inadequate account of derealization, the schizoid traits resulted from depersonalization, and the access of existential *angst* was a form of hyperreligiosity. I think the way the boy abandoned biology for literature was the clincher for the chief. As a scientist, he was quick (and in this case I think correct) to see this incomprehensible change in preference as the equivalent of a religious conversion, a marker for temporal lobe seizure disorder.

After two normal EEGs, the chief had me order a third, and when that showed a single temporal lobe spike, read by the neurologists as nondiagnostic, he walked me over to the order sheet and had me write for Dilantin.

By then, I was willing to do it. I had resisted as long as I could, longer than was seemly, and here after all was a case with *something* to point to on the tracing.

The boy got better instantly—two days after the drug hit a therapeutic blood level. He stopped fomenting suicides and began to charm histrionic young women patients into health. Weeks later—and I am not exaggerating here, in my memory it was more like a matter of days—this most dangerous patient was back at college happily studying biology with no follow-up care beyond the drug.

And I got better instantly as well. The nurses no longer squabbled with me nor I with them; the chief stood back and let me manage my cases as I wanted, which is to say as he wanted; even my fellow residents noticed a change for the better. I felt myself again. Life outside the ward seemed less complicated. I was in from the cold.

And ruined. No matter that some might see the patient's recovery as a flight (from our ward's craziness) to health. No matter either that subsequent attempts by a group at NIMH to substantiate my mentor's belief in Dilantin-responsive borderline states led nowhere.

I was ruined forever. To this day I cannot hear a college-aged young man complain of social distance and a diffusion of identity without wondering whether to get an EEG.

It is not just this one symptom that begins to sound medical. The clutching at the heart which may be panic anxiety, the lassitude which hints at depression or hypothyroidism, periodic phenomena of any sort—in how many interviews does a patient seem not at all organic?

Someone might protest that this episode in my training was idiosyncratic and overdetermined. The boy's rebellion, which turned out to be a biological disturbance, mirrored my own too closely; no doubt I was overly influenced by his conversion.

I don't dispute this interpretation: I tell this story on myself precisely because the parallels between patient and therapist are so evident. But I would argue that what was impressive to me about the disappearance of Alex's symptoms was not only that I shared them but also that, for the most part, they were common altogether. And not just common but central to adolescence.

It is the absorption of the ordinary into the organic which is most impressive. It no longer disturbs us that that florid mania responds to lithium. Almost everyone now considers bipolar affective disorder an illness, easy to segregate mentally from common human experience (although in truth there is a spectrum of manifestations here as well—we all know manicky individuals who flourish, including leaders in the field of psychiatry). But for rebelliousness and anomie to be disorders of the brain—here our very world view is at issue.

Were the sorrows of young Werther electrophysiological aberrations? And that other suicidal youth, Chateaubriand's René, what do we make of his wanderings? Is identity formation a legitimate intellectual task, or is the adolescent urge for separation and individuation merely endocrine and neurophysiological instability? Would Dilantin (or, nowadays, Tegretol) in the drinking water answer the questions of young adulthood?

What is stunning about this formative experience—and anyone who begins as a psychotherapist and goes on to medicate patients will have a number of such epiphanies—is the power it has to influence the way we see the world.[4]

But why not look at the episode from a different perspective? I was cured by the patient's taking Dilantin. I was no longer disturbed nor disturbing, no longer narcissistic nor passive-aggressive nor depressed. What Dilantin had to do with the young man's recovery can be disputed; what happened to me is clear. Why is the whole episode not merely further proof that psychological troubles respond to psychosocial treatment? I mean, in forming my identity as a psychiatrist, why didn't I put the episode to that use?

I don't think there is a simple answer to this question. We might just say that the physical has primacy in our society; but then that is an anthropologist's observation, not an explanation at all.[5]

This episode, and others that followed it, resulted in a particular change in my own abilities as a psychotherapist. To me, having known how it was before the fall, when all I heard was the patient's unconscious speaking straight to mine, it is as if I were left with an acquired hearing deficit, minor at times, impossible to ignore at others. I had lost that most desirable attitude in psychotherapists, the unfocused and yet persistent concentration which a medical school mentor called "close reaching" or "sailing close to the wind."

*   *   *   *   *

Who today can sit with a "hysteroid dysphoric" patient without having his mind wander to MAO inhibitors? Is there anxiety without a mental lapse in the direction of Xanax? A mood swing without Tegretol? Rage without lithium? I don't mean necessarily that we prescribe these drugs, though of course sometimes we do and should; but even in those cases when we do not and should not, we are weakened by having one more excuse to avoid that most painful of tasks, feeling what the patient feels.

When psychotherapeutic drugs were being developed, early opponents claimed they would interfere with patients' ability to focus on the difficult task of self-examination. It has turned out that what drugs do for patients in psychotherapy is complicated. For some depressed or psychotic patients, therapy is barely possible without drugs, immensely helpful with them; drugs allow certain patients the mental relief necessary for concentration on hard problems. Other patients, once the issue of medication arises, focus on physical diagnoses and drug effects rather than heartbreak, and some feel well enough on medication to opt out of therapies we think they need.

And yet mostly, in my experience, drugs are much like time and money; they can intrude on therapy as the resistance or serve it as identifiable objects of projection and speculation. We are comfortable with this sort of intrusion and can work with it. Where drugs do interfere (and not least for those ever-rebellious residents) is in the minds of therapists.

For us, I would say, the possibility of purely physical diagnosis and cure is a special distraction, different from the urge to write oneself a note to pick up milk on the way home and different also from the conflict over whether to raise the issue of an unpaid bill now or later in the hour.

I do not have in mind only our own failings in empathy. Of course, a stray thought about medication (or ECT *can* arise from a sadistic impulse or discomfort with intimacy, but it can also arise, and this is what makes it so especially confusing, from what is most central to our profession, the quest for cure. And it can legitimately arise at any stage in treatment, when a certain symptom worsens or when the nature of a symptom becomes clear.

The necessary incursion into psychotherapy of thought about the role of the physical is on the increase. After many failures because of overambitious research goals, investigators are at last succeeding in delineating biological markers associated with personality styles. The work of the Harvard psychologist Jerome Kagan and others on toddler and child temperament appears to demonstrate that what Kagan calls "inhibition," which has to do with shyness and introversion, is congenital or at least set early in life and is correlated with certain physiological characteristics, such as high and invariant heart rate, increased sleeping muscle tone, and other markers of differing neuroendocrine control evident even in infancy.

Personality, the last bastion of the pure psychotherapist, may soon be perceived to have major biological determinants and to respond to pharmacologic intervention. In an imaginable future, we may not so much ask how a patient's childhood experiences determined his avoidant personality disorder as—the much weaker question—what shaped the particular manifestations of his biologically inhibited temperament.

This future is already here. I recently had occasion to do marriage counseling with a couple in which the husband labeled the wife overly aggressive and controlling, while the wife complained that her husband was insufficiently sexually motivated. This is a typical family therapy case involving a fixed maladaptive interaction between people of differing personality styles. But a few weeks into our work, I saw an incidental report from a gynecologist indicating that the wife had high testosterone levels. Do we take this datum into account in deciding how much change in aggressiveness or sexual demand we will expect in her? (Or, before that decision, do the hormone levels influence our belief about the accuracy of the two spouses' reports of the causes of their conflict?) For a psychotherapist in this case, might there be an ethical difficulty—a question of good or bad faith—in ignoring the research on "high-T" women?

So far, speculation about physiology and temperament remains ahead of the evidence. And we know that environment influences character formation, so it is not likely that we will ever look back on the psychotherapy of obsessional or hysterical personality traits with the skepticism, wonder, and even horror with which we now view certain excesses in the dynamic treatment of parents of autistic children. But the example of the psychotherapy of autism is a telling one, a touchstone for the issue of bad faith.[6] From the time of its description, there was good evidence that autism was a medical, neurodevelopmental disorder; at first there was room for other theories as well, but the neurological evidence grew until it became overwhelming. At what point did it become bad faith to treat autism as if it had a large psychodynamic component?

I believe it is already bad faith for psychiatrists not to consider biological therapies for many acute conditions and even some common chronic disorders. But this state of things may present a paradox for the field.

If it is true that psychotherapy is as delicate as I imagine it to be, it may happen that those psychiatrists (or medically well-trained psychologists or social workers) who have the hearing deficit I have alluded to—

the need to consider biology frequently when their mind should be on dynamic issues—will be less good therapists for certain patients, including, by the way, some who have biological disorders, than those psychiatrists who practice in bad faith by consistently ignoring the biological and attending only to the psychosocial.

*   *   *   *   *

I want to illustrate the hearing disorder as I experience it by considering a single moment of a clumsy therapy containing nothing so exotic as derealization, temporal lobe spikes, or philosophical suicide.

A young man came to my office on the advice of a gastroenterologist whom he had seen for refractory diarrhea. The diarrhea was so severe and so sudden in onset that it prevented the patient from traveling on business, and of course it utterly debilitated him. He had pursued cures in the realm of internal medicine for over a year, without satisfaction.

I found the young man to be obsessional and rigid, traits he masked with a superficial affability which struck me more as a mechanically learned skill than a true reflection of an inner state. He was likable and successful enough socially, but I felt there to be emanating from him rage which was controlled only by the imposition of his stiff character style. By history, it seemed the anger originated in a struggle with an overbearing father who died before the young man had a chance to reconcile with or confront him. And I knew the patient had panic anxiety.

Something within him seemed hard to reach, and I believed that his stifled emotional self should be the focus of our work. But I sensed also that he might not engage if I did not best his internists, and fast. So we talked about the bowels and about modern theories of panic anxiety, and I started him on Xanax, eventually raising the dose to eight milligrams daily, twice the maximum daily dose in the PDR, but a common regimen in these parts.

I gave the agoraphobia a name, and like a good behaviorist I sent the patient on ever longer journeys. He did well.

The diarrhea disappeared, as did a number of other discomforts which had at first seemed unrelated, but the patient never felt quite himself. Partly it was that the drug slowed his thought and action, but mostly it was what was wrong between him and the world.

I remember hearing a story about a certain way of treating obsessional patients. The patient goes on and on about circumstantial issues, avoiding all expression of emotion. For his part, the therapist stares at the ceiling, twiddles his thumbs, fidgets in his chair, perhaps even hums a tune rudely. At last the patient yells at the therapist, "I can't stand it. Here I am spilling my guts to you, and all you do is look at the ceiling and say nothing. Can't you see I'm suffering? I'm furious at you."

"Good," the therapist says. "Let's talk about that."

Mostly I dislike this story. The teller is showing off, ill disguising his pride in imagined emotional superiority. The approach may work, but treating patients cruelly and discourteously, even if these attitudes are only feigned, is too close to the reality of our sadistic impulses to have a place in our armamentarium. What I do like is the emphasis on the need with patients of this sort to capitalize on the moments of emotion, whatever the ostensible focus. These moments are precious.

My anxious patient and I fiddled with medicines. I tried lowering the dose and adding antidepressants, then raising the dose again. Nothing worked, and we decided to taper the Xanax and then institute antidepressants afresh if symptoms recurred.

Now tapering Xanax is not a task for the weak of heart. The drug is more addictive than anyone suspected when it first came on the market. We dropped the dose slowly while maintaining the frequency of dosing. I encouraged my patient to begin the session by updating me on his symptoms and then to go on and talk about his family and work and his troubling memories.

One day, in the middle of a session, he let out a cry from the heart. "I can't go on like this. It seems it will last forever. When will I find peace?" There was for the first time pain in his voice. His eyes filled with tears of frustration, and he sighed—almost moaned—with disappointment.

I was focused on distinguishing among benzodiazepine withdrawal, rebound anxiety, and return of the underlying condition. (This consideration always reminds me of the political argument in the sixties over whether popular negative response to civil rights or anti-war demonstrations was "backlash," a true reaction to the provocative political maneuver, or "out-from-behind-the-rocks," merely a manifestation of existing beliefs.) I probed further for symptoms, turned the possibilities over in my mind, discussed them with my patient. Perhaps he could only come off Xanax under cover of clonazepam, if this was withdrawal, or after the addition of trazodone (since imipramine had failed), if we were seeing a recrudescence of the presenting complaint.

In short, I missed the moment. It was hours later, after the end of the work day, before I considered the possibility that his outcry had to do not with panic anxiety—and after all he was not suffering true panic anxiety now, my thinking was all based on "sounds-like" diagnosis—but with his conflicted self.

Even if he had been referring to his anxiety disease, how had I overlooked the opportunity to amplify his expression of heartfelt emotion? We were in the room together at last, and I had acted obsessionally. Like his father, I had ignored his need and demanded false maturity. And where were my ordinary psychotherapeutic instincts? A mere grunt of empathy for his pain would have been better than my dispassionate analysis of alternatives.

Perhaps the moment would recur, or perhaps I could in some way retrieve it—with time most lost opportunities can be recaptured. But there is no substitute for being available the first time, nothing quite so powerful as acknowledging pain just when the patient is able to express it. And I had waited so long for this very chance.

I was listening wrong.

But, someone might argue, it seems most likely he was in a state of continuous mini-withdrawal from the Xanax. Those are just the circumstances in which patients say that sort of thing.

Yes, but that is just the problem. It may be withdrawal. You can't avoid considering the physical, but when you do the mental slips from your grasp.

And aren't we all in mini-withdrawal—I mean, premenstrual or postmenstrual, or pre- or postictal, or phobic, or cyclothymic, or addictive, or rejection-sensitive, or chronically dysphoric, or developmentally immature, or a bit sociopathic, or minimally brain dysfunctional, or paranoid, or subject to rage attacks, or sleep disordered, or truly physically ill and treated with one or another potentially psychotropic medication? To whom can one listen right?

$$*\quad*\quad*\quad*\quad*$$

But can't we just split the prescribing doctor off from the therapist?

This suggestion misunderstands the problem. The problem is inherent in the patient and our understanding of him. It colors every moment

[53]

of therapy; it is a condition of therapy, a danger and an opportunity. What should the therapist do when the patient begins to associate meaningfully to symptoms the therapist believes to be autonomous and physical, and what does the medicating doctor do when he finds the patient's important moments of emotional expression are occurring in the office with him, over somatic issues? Separating functions only creates two puzzled people, three if we count the patient.[7]

If I am treating an asthmatic patient for mood swings and a pulmonary specialist is titrating his steroids, I am no less confused over whether to ascribe meaning to a new bout of discouragement. It doesn't matter where the physical influence on mood originates, with another doctor, with me as the prescribing doctor, or within the patient; we still have to know to what degree we can consider mental phenomena to be based on dynamic conflict. The goal is not for the therapist to know less; the goal is always to know more. Ignorance of physical causation is not a boon; in today's world it is a form of bad faith.

And who can long for the good old days? The obsessional, somatizing patient—and this is how my panic patient would have been dismissively characterized—was never a pleasure to treat. Without the right diagnosis and without psychotherapeutic medication, it is unlikely this patient could have been induced into treatment at all, and uncertain that he would have benefited.

Again, this is just the issue. Psychiatric medication is truly one of the "miracles of modern science." Not to consider physical disease and treatment is malpractice, not just legally but morally. If attention to the physical didn't work, the dilemma would disappear. The point is, it does work. If we are good at what we do, we will consider the physical again and again.

* * * * *

I am a great afficionado of antidepressants. Neuroleptics scare me for the obvious reasons, and mostly I have little use for the benzodiazepines, but it is hard not to admire imipramine. It does so many things so well. Imipramine is to psychiatry what broad-spectrum antibiotics are to general practice medicine.

Depression, anxiety, panic, bulimia, anorexia, insomnia, diarrhea, migraine, pseudodementia, memory loss, cocaine addiction, obsessionality, hyperactivity, enuresis, nightmares, globus hystericus, derealization and depersonalization—I have seen imipramine work for a myriad of symptoms, and so have all general psychiatrists. We struggle to differentiate demoralization from depression, but the truth is we have seen antidepressants work for both. If you ask a general psychiatrist for an informal consultation about a case—the sort of thing you might do on lunch break during a conference, or in passing on the beach if your families summer together—likely as not he will say, I can't comment on the psychotherapy side, but I have to tell you I had a patient like that once, and I tried him on imipramine. . . .

Psychiatrists like to trade stories about subtle effect of drugs. I remember from years back a preliminary result reported at a conference at McLean about anxiolytics. The study compared Librium and Valium, two drugs whose gross effects are indistinguishable. The hypothesis was that Valium had a slight euphoriant effect, made patients feel better in a subtle way, not just less anxious. There was no measurable difference in outcome between the two in a clinical trial, except for this one—the patients on Valium reported liking their doctors better. Nice feedback loop.

I think antidepressants make doctors feel better. They allow us, like the colleagues we envy (ophthalmologists come to mind), to isolate a problem and eradicate it. If you run a mixed practice, it is a wonderful thing to have a percentage of patients walk in, get better fast, and respond with gratitude. And if you are, like many psychotherapists, someone who was raised to think of him- or herself as bright but not handy, there is also a seductive satisfaction in mastering a mildly "technological" treatment.

Even in the majority of cases where medication is best supplemented by psychotherapy, the antidepressant pill is a wonderful colleague. The relief that the patient feels, particularly if sleep or concentration is restored, is a powerful placebo for the healing alliance.

I became aware of how much this collaboration meant to me when a plastic surgeon referred me a young woman for depression following partly successful reconstructive surgery. What sort of depression? I asked. Sleep, appetite, tearfulness. Fine, I said, and scheduled her.

But in my office, the story was different. She had been self-conscious for years because of her deformity, depressed for as long as she could remember. No endogenous symptoms, no psychomotor retardation.

Just a sad young woman at odds with her image of herself. Damn. More slogging. And then I caught myself—it was late on a Friday but I caught myself nonetheless—what had come over me? I teach psychotherapy, I tell myself I enjoy it, but here I was feeling burdened by the prospect of having to treat depression empty-handed.

I remember it used to be said that one of the impediments to high achievement in women was a tempting and socially acceptable alternative to hard work; you didn't have to be Wagner, you could marry him. (Speak about hard work!) I don't know why Wagner was chosen; I don't think it was because he was the most loathsome man one could imagine marrying. At the moment when I caught myself, I realized that in some sense I had found it easier to marry the curative agent than to be it.

*   *   *   *   *

Although perhaps I am being, as we are wont to say to patients, too hard on myself. Psychotherapeutic medications are not an alternative to psychotherapy; they are a part of it. Marriage to medication, or at least cotherapy with it, is an unavoidable part of honest psychiatric work. (Perhaps what I should say is, since we're already cohabiting, it would be honest to marry.)

When we are lucky, medications can function as, or provide, interpretations. What I mean by this statement is not arcane, but I want to spend a moment first saying what I do *not* mean. I do not have in mind here merely the way that patients see the act of being recommended a medication.

Certainly, to be prescribed for has meaning. A patient may feel his fear that he is crazy or unlikable has just been confirmed, or he may come to believe he is well loved because he has been given something. The act may be seen as nurturant or sadistic or both.

Consider, to take an extreme case, the prescribing of a monoamine oxidase inhibitor. It is a rich act, an act replete with overtones. If you were given an MAOI, might you not wonder if the prescribing doctor didn't find you overly dramatic and out of control? Isn't there a slight insult in the choice? Or would you find the prescriber sophisticated and capable of subtlety? Or kindly, to see past mere vegetative signs to the pure pain beneath?

The act of prescribing affects how the patient sees us and how he imagines we see him; indirectly, through his revised sense of our opinion, it affects his self-image.

We are used to dealing with complications of this sort. They may be unfortunate if they raise issues which the patient is not prepared to handle, or fortunate if they confront the patient with a reality he has avoided but is ready to address. We dislike the intrusion of such consequential acts into the therapy because they are unplanned, but they occur often enough, and we can accommodate to interpreting them or living with them as we see fit.

When I say medications can function as interpretations, I have in mind something which is more startling and less subject to our control: direct drug effects. The medication acts on the patient, and in so doing it serves as a cotherapist. Perhaps this idea is best made clear through an example.

An internist referred me a chronically somatizing patient. I saw her twice and realized she had a serious medical problem and referred her back for further care. My impression after two meetings was that she would be difficult to work with in therapy. She was not psychologically minded, and she had a long history of vague maladies. Worse, to the extent that she possessed nonmedical explanations for her misfortunes, she attributed them to stresses caused by unsympathetic family members—she was a blamer. I believed she had a longstanding "anaclitic depression" related to numerous losses early in life, but I doubted she would be willing to focus on what I saw as a major impediment to her recovery, namely her sense of the fragility of human relations and its effect on the way she approached others.

In time the woman returned to my care. She had been treated for her illness, but now her undiagnosable physical symptoms were much worse—the illness had heightened her sense of the unreliability of the world, and the resultant anxiety had increased her focus on her physical symptoms and the failings of her family. She had suicidal thoughts without suffering any vegetative signs of depression except sleep disturbance.

Anaclitic or characterologic depressions are not supposed to respond to antidepressants, but I tried them anyway, and the physical symptoms disappeared. This in itself is not noteworthy; anyone who has used

[57]

antidepressants with somatizing patients has had this result now and then, and of course these symptoms on occasion respond to placebo.

The woman felt much better globally. She had energy and enthusiasm which had been lost to her for years. Projects she had postponed were now completed with ease. She evidently had suffered a treatable "biological" depression after all. This, too, we half expect. All depressions are both biological and psychological; our emerging understanding of the nature of depression is just the sort of development that makes us anticipate an end to the mind-body dichotomy.

But what meant most to me was what the patient began to say. "It was me after all," she told me. She saw that she had created her own trouble within the family. She patched up old quarrels and began to create a new family life. "It wasn't just my husband, it was me," she said, and not in the guilt-inducing tone of the false confession which is meant to be contradicted. She understood that she had created her own environment, and we could go on to try to understand why.

Anyone who has worked with the sort of patient I am trying to depict will understand how remarkable this transformation was. The medication substituted for months of therapy in a patient who would likely not have stayed in treatment beyond a few weeks. Often we wish we could just get patients to see things a certain way, if only for a moment – and this wish results in much bad therapy: "Can't you imagine how your husband must see it?" said in an insistent tone of voice.

But the difference between the depressed and the euthymic, the relief the patient felt when the antidepressants kicked in, was so great that she understood – experienced – the possibility that the world was altogether a different place from what she had imagined it to be. I didn't have to say, "Can't you see what you're doing?" The medication allowed her to see.

This is what I mean when I say that medications can act as interpretations, and part of what I mean when I say they are cotherapists. To let a person experience the world differently is an extraordinary intervention, quite independent of the meaning of taking a drug. And it seems to me that any good therapist must accept such powerful help, although to do so entails a cost in terms of our confidence in and mastery of older ways of speaking to patients.

*   *   *   *   *

If we do accept medicines on the terms I have just discussed, and it seems to me we must, then there are other consequences, one of which I will just touch on: thoughts about medication are bound to turn up as telltale components of countertransference.

I have hinted at this topic in asking about the transference meaning of being offered an MAO inhibitor. Let us say you believe as a psychiatrist that MAOIs are useful in treating "hysteroid dysphoria" or, to use a nicer term, "rejection-sensitive dysphoria" (or, to be nasty, "emotionally unstable character disorder"). You are listening to the pain of a young woman, and you think, my goodness, we ought to consider an MAOI for her.

What has just happened? One possibility is that you are experiencing what I call true countertransference, the feelings in the therapist elicited by the transference. The patient is communicating vulnerability to rejection, and the way you come to understand that communication is by discovering that your mind has wandered to MAOIs.

Another possibility is that you are in the grip of what I prefer to call reverse transference (some people also call this experience countertransference, but I think the distinction is worth trying to maintain), feelings which arise from the therapist's distortions with much more minor input from the patient. You are, I am trying to say, angry at the patient for reasons of your own, and this anger leads you to name-calling. But instead of maligning her as a damned frustrating, provocative hysteric, you have a more acceptable doctorly thought, that you should help her with a drug which has that very meaning to you and which will subject her to a rigid diet and put her at risk of hypertensive crisis and stroke.

Or there may be some other meaning, for instance that you would like more distance from this young woman, and you know that introducing the idea of a medication which entails such complex instructions will create that distance; if you became aware of this thought, you would want to know whether this desire was therapeutic and then decide how else to create distance or how to overcome this urge in yourself.

I would say there is a new requirement in therapy, namely that we know the meaning of medications for ourselves, because thoughts about medications have inevitably become part of the way we communicate with ourselves. I mean this in the way that one of my teachers might have said to me: perhaps you want to think further about your urge to use a confrontative interpretation. What does confrontation mean to you? Deep down do you consider it to be aggressive or helpful? What sort of patient do you consider confronting in this way?

A thought experiment: consider what it means in the middle of an hour to have the stray thought of prescribing: lithium, neuroleptics, anticonvulsants. Or amphetamine. Or adding thyroid supplementation to antidepressants.

Equally, there are forms of psychological awareness which can help us in prescribing.

Some time after my work with the suicidal young man who loved Vonnegut, I treated a woman for what she called "nothing spells" or "black spells." She had been referred to me for therapy for depression. These spells were only the most easily defined part of her problem. She was dissatisfied with her job and marriage, so much so that she was provocatively inattentive to both. She acted on her boredom in ways which annoyed and alienated her husband and her parents, to whom she had heretofore remained close.

In therapy, the patient showed a bland, sleepy-eyed appreciation for my interpretations, but nothing I said seemed to hit home. Then she began to talk to me about her secret love of poetry and her absolute passion for Rainer Maria Rilke.

I sent her to a local neurologist for an EEG, on which I wrote "Rule out temporal lobe epilepsy." The neurologist took his own history and called me to say he thought there was no indication for the EEG. I asked him to get it anyway.

Shortly thereafter he called back. He hated to admit it—he had the tracing re-read by a colleague to be certain—but the woman had bilateral temporal lobe spikes. How had I made the diagnosis, he wanted to know, and could he examine my office notes? I told him how certain of the woman's perceptions and behaviors could be reconceptualized as déjà vu, hypergraphia, hyperreligiosity, and so forth.

But the truth is: the moment I heard about Rilke, I felt the strong urge to put this woman on Tegretol.

This diagnostic coup had a humbling sequel. I did place the patient on Tegretol. It had no effect, so I kept raising the dose until she was lethargic and dopey. After I discontinued the medication, she seemed markedly less depressed, and she returned to her work and marriage with much greater focus. She thanked me for having poisoned her with

Tegretol: "Being slowed down gave me time to think," she said. Perhaps she was right about how the intervention worked. Or perhaps the brief trial of medicine had a lasting effect. Or we may wonder whether another force was at work. For example, it might be that the patient's sense of having "gotten to me"—put me in the wrong through my overmedicating her—allowed her to move on in other spheres.

I still don't know what to make of this case diagnostically. But in terms of psychotherapy, I now have a better purchase on it—because I see that it is necessary also to look at these interactions from the reverse perspective. In terms of monitoring my countertransference, I should have understood that when I have a stray thought in the direction of Tegretol, I am expressing an unacknowledged awareness that the patient has a problem in identity formation—that was where the problems in job and marriage seemed to originate. Or rather, I am irritated by the patient, whom I consider naughty and overly rebellious; in the countertransference, I was, because of the patient' blandness, identified with her frustrated parents. To think about Tegretol is to signal to myself that the patient has certain intrapsychic and interpersonal traits similar to those of the suicidal "borderline" young man; to consider Tegretol may mean that a seemingly reasonable patient is "getting to me," the way the young man got to my off-ward supervisor.

*   *   *   *   *

But if medications are cotherapists and interpretations, and if our thoughts about medication are aids in diagnosis and in understanding of the countertransference, we pay a price for these benefits. I have so far approached this issue through a focus on the therapist's concentration; but the distraction of the physical also has, it seems to me, a direct effect on the tenets of psychotherapeutic practice.

My psychoanalysis with Max was guided by the principle that "everything which interferes with the course of treatment must be interpreted as the resistance." If I was late for a session because the Tube was behind schedule—well, the Tube was often often behind schedule, and why hadn't I taken that into account? Did I secretly hope there would not be enough time to discuss a certain delicate topic? Or was I expressing contempt? Better wrongly to attribute meaning than to allow circumstance to undermine treatment.

And this principle extended to resistant thoughts as well. To deny that a behavior or feeling or cognition contained significance was to subvert the treatment. Psychoanalysis works best when every aspect of the patient's life can be deemed meaningful.

But what if what interferes with the progress of therapy is the thought that a symptom is biological?

I recently treated a woman who had a sensation of disorientation and lightheadedness in the presence of a bowel disorder whose exact nature was unclear. The identifying details are unimportant—indeed, it is disturbing to consider just how unimportant they are. The patient occasionally had fever accompanying diarrhea, and many diagnoses were entertained, from unusual infectious diseases to endocrine disorders to ulcerative colitis.

On the off chance that her ailment might be mental, she came to see me. All her symptoms responded to Xanax and a mild antidiarrheal, and then to Xanax alone. Finally the symptoms disappeared, and she discontinued all medication.

As in the case of the anaclitic depressed patient whose view of the world was transformed by imipramine, this patient got globally better. Friends remarked on how much happier she looked—and she asked them what they were talking about, because she could scarcely remember how she had felt in the preceding months. It seemed to me that she suffered a difficult-to-define affective disorder; although her symptoms were like those of anxiety, the course of her remission resembled recovery from depression. Later, the sensation of lightheadedness and a queasy feeling in the gut returned, in the intermittent pattern of panic attacks.

Meanwhile we were engaged in psychotherapy. Experiences in childhood had predisposed her to extremes in self-image. She was alternately tough and helpless, desirable and worthless. Years before our meeting, she had been thrown into a depression by a failed love relationship, and in some ways she remained attached to the man who had rejected her.

While in treatment, the patient began an affair with a generally appropriate man. She came in one day to say she had suffered a terrible week. Starting the previous weekend, her physical and mental symptoms had returned, and only recently had they remitted.

"I guess I had a panic attack," she said. She was well read on the subject, and she understood herself to have had a random and spontaneous manifestation of a biological disorder. She felt she might have had a touch of the flu and wondered whether physical debilitation might not in her case lower the threshold for an outpouring of catecholamines.

We talked more about the events of the weekend. The new boy-friend, it seemed, had become insistent on their committing themselves more fully to the relationship. Might she have been more deeply threatened by this development than she let on?

Well, of course she might and then again perhaps not.

The significance of her social life was very much in question, which made it difficult to demand that the patient focus on her reactions to the boyfriend. Indeed, the significance of significance was in question: I could not say with assurance that any of her thoughts or feelings, however seemingly meaningful, had any relationship to her disabling anxiety. How frustrating to have a patient develop symptoms in the face of pressures to "make a commitment"—and as a therapist to be unable to demand cleanly that she look at how these events are connected.

I was uncomfortable at her attempt to ignore the role of her unconscious, but I would also have been uncomfortable if she had taken it for granted that her symptoms were psychogenic. If she had thrown herself into the psychodynamic work with blind devotion, I might have experienced myself as a fraud.

And even if I did have a hunch about this one episode—I suppose the way I have told it, it does sound psychogenic—I had no confidence I would have the same belief about the next one. Patients do seem to have "spontaneous" panic attacks. The illness has some of the feel of a physical disorder with psychogenic exacerbations, like certain forms of asthma, where nonspecific physical or psychic stress can predispose to an increased frequency of symptoms, without each episode necessarily being caused by a particular psychic stimulus.

What does it say about psychoanalysis if the basic motive beneath all symptoms, anxiety, is now just assumed to be nonspecific in this way? Further, what does it say about our choice of treatment?

Dynamic therapy depends on the negotiation of an agreement between therapist and patient regarding the meaning of symptoms.[8] How can we propose such a therapy as the treatment of choice for an ailment the significance of whose manifestations is so ambiguous? (Perhaps it is not by chance that Salvador Minuchin developed his structural family therapy in the course of work with families with children suffering psychosomatic disorders; such cases make difficult any agreement between therapist and parents as to the role of emotions in the child's symptoms. It is easier to use a therapy which bypasses the resistance and requires no negotiation as to the meaningfulness of symptoms.)

This problem persists whether or not we believe that the "anxiety disease" in this woman originated in psychic conflict. I did believe that developmental issues and their consequences in adult life contributed to the onset of the illness, whatever genetic or other biological factors may also have had a role.[9] But such an opinion about the origin of the disorder only slightly mitigates the difficulty, which is that once the disease is present very important events in the patient's affective life may be random occurrences; this uncertainty weakens a therapy which demands that the patient examine the current conflictual underpinnings of her emotions. The fiction that all occurrences in life are meaningful has become difficult to maintain.

*   *   *   *   *

Therapy is best when simplest. Our therapy is no longer simple. We have a choice of frequently seeing our patients through biological lenses or standing in an uncomfortable relationship to the imperatives of our profession and to contemporary reality. In either case, therapy has changed. Old-fashioned psychodynamic psychotherapy is gone. It cannot be done today. What we do today is different.

I suppose this is one meaning of the vignette in the previous chapter about the paranoid young woman who presented a diagnostic challenge. There is no old-fashioned, simple way to face such a patient; too many possible interpretive lenses stand in the way of our seeing her plainly.

This is our sometimes uncomfortable posture in an era before the much-anticipated "integration" of psychiatric perspectives: when we serve our patients in good faith, our minds are partly on the mind-body problem, but then our minds are not fully on matters of mind.

We like to imagine that our situation is unique, that only we have to dance between two worlds. So it is well to remember that Freud struggled with the same dichotomy. From the start, in his studies of hysteria, he weighed evidence for neurosis, in the physical sense, against the new concept of psychical determinants of mental and behavioral symptoms. Only later, and because the biology of his time had little reliable to say about mental phenomena, did he take the posture, adopted and exaggerated by his followers, of giving a perfunctory nod in the direction of *soma* and attending single-mindedly to *psyche*.

The brief period of absolute dominance of psychical theories of illness in psychiatry will almost certainly turn out to be an aberration, our current state the norm. That period had its faults, not least the complacency of psychotherapists. As recently as the days of my medical schooling, psychiatric residencies taught little beyond psychological theories of mind. An iconoclastic journal article about a famous residency program described a first-year experience centered on students' interpreting the loose associations of schizophrenics; the patients didn't get better, but residents did—at fulfilling the expectations of their supervisors. The therapeutic behavior which then was considered most compassionate, and most skillful, a few years later seemed ignorant or cruel.

Some assertive biological phenomenologists take their energy from anger at the excesses of their time in training. But having come in at the end of those days, I remember their pleasant qualities, not least a prejudice for intent consideration of what patients said. The central challenge was the challenge of listening and responding; there was a sense of excitement over the delicate art to be learned, the art of a certain sort of dialogue, with rules about when to speak and what to say.

This art depended on heroic dedication to a focus on the hidden meaning of feelings and acts. It is hard now to find that dedication, and hard even to know whether we ought to want to find it. A frustrated student today is likely to turn away from refining his dynamic therapeutic skills and instead seek out another sort of solution.

In my own training I expected to master one subtle art, and instead I learned parts of the dozen crafts which make up the profession. The excitement lay in finding ways to weave together diverse strands of knowledge. I am, of course, grateful to the demanding neuropsychiatric ward chief. He inducted me into the modern world. But like other births, this one was painful, and the gratitude is alloyed by other less happy emotions, among them wistfulness, nostalgia, and doubt. Complexity has its pleasures. But so does single-mindedness, something we may miss as we struggle to hold mind and neurons in mind.

Pièce de Résistance

I don't know what would have happened to me if the inpatient rotation had lasted a full year, as it used to in most residencies, but at the end of six months I had the good fortune to move on to the outpatient service of a mental health center, where I was a fish in water.

At the core of the rotation was an intake group: five residents under the supervision of a crusty and opinionated diagnostician. We met two or three days a week and, in addition to interviewing new patients privately and discussing them together, we would by turns do intakes in front of a one-way mirror, with the rest of the group looking on.

The residency accepted trainees according to the smorgasbord principle, a protégé or two for each sort of faculty member, and as a result the residents were a heterogeneous lot. I was the Freudian in the fivesome. The other four were a monkey spinal fluid researcher, a neo-Kraepelinian, a doctorly type reared in the medical consultation tradition, and — my one ally — a woman who had studied dance and existential therapy in Mexico at Erich Fromm's retreat.

We must have been a challenging group to teach. At first the hard scientists doubted the need for subtle distinctions on the psychotherapy front, and we soft scientists had little tolerance for the way our physiology-minded colleagues pigeonholed patients. But there are no atheists in the foxholes, and, under the pressure patient care created, in the end we all adopted all the religions.

I in particular adopted strategic approaches to patients. In part this was because I felt I already knew a good deal of the basic analytic material the group was being taught, in part because I had developed a special relationship with a special teacher, of whom more will be said in a later chapter. But I think the main attraction of the strategic approach was that it allowed me to show off in dramatic fashion what I already knew — how to size up the dynamics of a case — while avoiding the bored criticism that comes when a resident looks too sweetly empathic before his skeptical peers.

My public moment of glory came shortly after the group had coalesced, when I had the opportunity to interview an impossible patient in front of the one-way mirror. He was a silent young man, fat and stubborn and effeminate in his appearance. He was, as we say, apparently attending to internal stimuli. Accompanying him was a helpless and loving mother who had that superficially adoring and harmless look we all know thinly covers a propensity for rage and paranoia.

The boy's chart was thick, filled with notations of missed appointments and the other usual indicators of the musical therapists game. Taking my cue from it, I began by addressing the complaisant and hostile mother: "You don't have much luck with doctors." This is one of those Milton Erickson openings, a question to which either reply is positive. I went on in this way, ignoring the boy and asking only questions which would elicit the answer yes.

Saying yes and yes and yes induces a friendly trance, and the mother soon began telling me of her woeful home life with her son. He would not work, talked to no one, and stole money from her bedroom to buy candy and childish toys.

It had been some time since the boy had seen his mother interact cordially with a doctor, and he moved to seduce her back to his world, sidling up and putting his arm around her shoulder. When he found his playing footsie did not stop her or me, he began to talk, at first with loose associations dripping with contempt. Using a reframing move, I complimented him for participating so nicely in the interview, but continued mostly to shower my attentions on his mother, one adult to another. In time, the boy began to join in quite coherently, expressing his ambivalence over jobs and fear of leaving the house and so forth. He wanted help.

But by now the mother had broached a sensitive subject. The boy entered her bedroom each night and frightened her. This was the real reason she had come here, to learn how to keep him out. She was

[68]

worried for her safety. But at the same time, mother and son were billing and cooing right in front of me.

I let the farce continue until he was virtually in her lap—while she asked for help, at last with a discernible tone of sincere need audible above the seduction and the anger. Would I care for her son?

"Look at you two," I roared. "You don't need a psychiatrist, you need a divorce lawyer."

The mother readily agreed. This metaphor was no metaphor to her. She was married to a maniac, and the bedroom was getting too hot.

But couldn't they see me again? she pleaded. No one had understood her situation before. And the boy spoke so well with me.

I asked her if she knew a locksmith in her area. She did. I said I would see them if she managed to get a lock for her bedroom door.

When I entered the intake group conference room, it was to something like applause.

It is always gratifying to impress your peers with your prowess, but in retrospect I think I took particular pride in this moment for an idiosyncratic reason. I had in effect reproduced the astounding interviews of my psychoanalytic medical school mentors, but I had done it on the cheap.

The typical interviewing *tour de force* in my Freudian medical school was an encounter with just such a schizophrenic patient as the one I had worked with here. The patient would enter mute or babbling word salad, and the understanding interviewer would sit close beside him— this would be in front of a group of 20 onlooking students at various stages in training—and rumble empathic sweet nothings.

The therapeutic instrument was the well-analyzed analyst, a man neither frightened nor disgusted by the patient's unconscious urges expressed through the illness. The interviewer in his soul wanted neither domination nor succor, his chest was a neutral pillow on which the troubled patient could rest his head.

And soon the conversation would turn to the patient's childhood, to memories of a grandmother, perhaps, who had shown occasional kindness amidst the continual abuse wreaked on the child by parents and siblings. The audience held its collective breath as the patient, coherently now and with more feeling than anyone on the ward had ever heard him muster, poured forth his sense of longing and of loss.

The effect of these interviews was odd, because often as not no one on the ward could ever again elicit a moment of lucidity from the patient. The master interviewer had proved it could be done, and his success served to convince the staff that the patient's illness fit a psychological model of resistance and symptom formation through compromise in the face of inner conflict. But moving further was usually a chore, with the result that the effective message to young therapists was that they needed more inner greatness—freedom from their own conflict—if they were to do the job. It was to this peace and harmony that I aspired, although I was aware even as a medical student that it had its annoying, sanctimonious side.

The emphasis in the medical school setting was never on technique, always on the inner state of the therapist. Inquiries about technique were generally interpreted as signs of resistance on the part of students or as a sort of stand-in for sexual curiosity, wanting to know how the parents did it. And although sublimation might have been valued as a high-order defense, this comment about sexual curiosity was meant to embarrass the questioner.

At the beginning of residency, too, discussion of analytic technique was considered premature, even though in my case I had been seeing patients in dynamic therapy for some time and found it hard not to seek out the next level of training. (By contrast, our instruction in the rudiments of dynamic *theory*—the unconscious, transference, countertransference, and the like—was generous, kindly, and scholarly; of course, these qualities are largely a function of the personality of the teacher.) But if analytic technique was reserved for advanced students, well, early in residency I could find the methods of other schools and other masters—Minuchin, Whitaker, Montalvo, Haley, Erickson—spelled out in elementary texts, even popular trade paperbacks.

My interview with the mother and son drew heavily on the experience in empathic, dynamic work I brought with me to residency. Early in the interview, I must have sized up the mother's resistance to interventions and her susceptibility to the sort of paternal seduction hysterics cognitively ignore and behaviorally respond to, and I no doubt had a fair sense of the route to the son through the mother's attention. Perhaps I emanated an ability to bear the pair's craziness—after this public interview I developed a modest reputation within our group as someone who could handle paranoia, with the result that I was referred some quite hair-raising cases. So it would not be fair to say that my empathic self was irrelevant to the therapy.

But in my mind then, the interview was all technique. I made it happen through craft. At least I knew damn well it was not any inner spiritual peace on my part that made the crazy boy act sane. I was aware that I was not unconflicted over the destructive intimacy the mother's intrusive behavior exemplified. I could not flatter myself that I was inwardly neutral about the couple's various impulses, valuing their ids as highly as their superegos. I was not accepting and unjudgmental. I wanted them to do something, and they began to do it.

My inner peace was not at issue. What counted was facility at sizing up situations rapidly and at employing certain manipulative interpersonal skills. In this sort of treatment—for first interviews are treatment, as Harry Stack Sullivan emphasized—what matters is not that the therapist be good, but that he be good at what he does, often a quite separate concern.

*   *   *   *   *

As an aside, I want to say—of course, there was also technique in what the analytic masters did. That technique can even be taught.

There is the manner in which one sits before the patient, the tone of voice, the way interventions are phrased. I don't believe in my years of studying therapy I have ever seen these taught in the context of psychodynamic work. Certainly in my residency the analysts shied away from focusing on technique. Even in supervision the precise form of interventions was rarely discussed. A supervisor might ask whether a trainee was uncomfortable with a certain patient, or overeager for cure. But the details of verbal intercourse—whether to use more active verbs or shorter sentences, whether to delay a certain comment until later in the session, whether to smile or frown—these were either taught in an advanced level of training I never achieved or, as I suspect, not taught at all. Even the usual technical advice in analytic training—interpret character before content, avoid premature interpretation of the positive transference, and so on—came rather late in the game.

By contrast, in the teaching of modern family therapy technique is discussed right away. Muscular empathy—the physical imitation of patient's posture—is an early lesson of the Minuchin school, as are adoption of a family member's language rhythm or word choice, use of seating arrangements to create interpersonal closeness or distance, and so forth.

Probably the central technical intervention in analytic interviews during the engagement phase is the communication of empathy. Traditional psychoanalysts are not used to thinking of empathy as a technique, much less instructing students in it. But outside the world of psychodynamic psychiatry—in the training of internists in interviewing courses, for example—the teaching of empathy is commonplace.

Certain followers of Milton Erickson give regular seminars for neophyte hypnotherapists on techniques related to empathy. For someone trained in dynamic therapy by conventional means, the hypnotists' methods are thought-provoking. Empathy is taught in quite concrete ways. Students are instructed to repeat patients' statements, follow with a platitude or truism, and then slip in a suggestive sentence intended to lead the patient slightly in a certain emotional direction. Or students are taught to listen to the patient's tone of voice, ignoring word content, to gain an empathic picture of the patient which does not rely on the ostensible material of the patient's narrative. Later, students may be asked to focus exclusively on the patient's posture, facial expression, word choice, or hand movements. Instructors present a nosology useful for empathy in hypnosis: Are the patient's inner statements made in urban terms or rural? Are they analytic or synthetic? What sort of story or metaphor would be meaningful to the patient?

Such teaching is alien to training in dynamic therapy, although empathy-enhancing skills are no less important in analytic work. These skills probably formed the basis for the interviews I admired in medical school as much as did any purity of heart.

*　　*　　*　　*　　*

And yet the analysts may be right. Students need heart before they need technique. My own insistence on skill bears examining. I entered psychiatry in part to let my intuitive side grow, to decrease my reliance on a cleverness which I understood had roots in aggression and narcissism. So my anger at never being taught enough was a retreat from challenge, a frightened demand.

But this sort of demand is difficult not to make in a psychiatric world in which everyone except the analyst—from biologist to structural family therapist—has access to a plethora of techniques from the first weeks of residency.[1]

Today, I would file the locksmith interview ironically under "*pièces de résistance*," by which I mean *tours de force* which contain a large piece of neurotic resistance. The source of resistance, in this case resistance to concentrating on the task of refining my psychodynamic skills, was my continued competitiveness toward earlier teachers and therapists, a remnant of the contempt for Max expressed via the Penthesilea dream. My unspoken intention was to match them—to achieve the result of turning psychosis into sense—while remaining iconoclastic. (Of course, many individual good things may flow from resistance; residents ought to try to master and enjoy practicing a range of therapies. But we must believe that in the long run it is better for psychotherapists to have less conflicted motivations.)

I remember once, in residency years, returning to medical school and sitting down for a chat with a psychoanalyst whom I had admired as a teacher. He talked about the underappreciated powers of dynamic therapy, and by way of example he cited instances in which he had managed to cure a schizophrenic or borderline personality disordered patient. In response, I aggressively trotted out my Dilantin truimph with the young man who had variously been diagnosed as borderline or schizophrenic. I had cut the Gordian knot—matched his hard-earned achievements with an instant cure in the first months of residency.

The work with the mother and son who needed a locksmith resembles in function this triumph with Dilantin. The result others toil at painstakingly can be achieved with less bother—much less bother if one imagines perfecting the self is a prerequisite for the masterful interview.

Of course one can ask whether cutting the Gordian knot is really the equivalent of untying it—whether there is some extra benefit for the patient in dealing with complexity. But this issue is subtle and contentious.

In the meanwhile, the codification of technology in modern therapies has helped turn the psychiatric profession on its head.

Outside psychiatry, medicine has long been a profession in which young doctors have certain advantages over old—the young enjoy easy familiarity with the most current theories of immunology, and they are adept with the latest antibiotics, diagnostic methods, and surgical approaches. But for many years in psychiatry there was no challenging wisdom and experience. What the young psychotherapist needed he could learn only with time and through apprenticeship. This truth gave the field a certain stability (some would say stultifying stability) and allowed for a slow and predictable sequence of mentorship and growth. Contemporary technique-rich therapies, no less than medications, have upset this pattern and thrown psychiatry into the camp of the rest of medicine.

The result is a change in what we value. When I was a medical student hospital departments were still occasionally built around the wisdom of one or two good men or women. Today, even in those few academic departments where psychotherapy plays a central role, the power is in the hands of subspecialists. One researcher may have made his name in the family treatment of eating disorders, another may be skilled at evaluation strategies, a third may focus on behavioral interventions for obsessive-compulsive symptoms. We are in the age of the specialist and the technician, and if a teacher happens to be wise, generative, patient, and empathic, that is so much "gravy," but hardly the meat of the job.

This shift in authority is also a change in our identity. I entered psychiatry imagining the profession to be a way of being, before all else a training in a certain self-abnegating approach to healing—an exercise in self-discipline. And I held this belief even in the face of evidence that individual psychiatrists, including leaders in the field, were egocentric or power-hungry; these defective exemplars were only imperfect embodiments of a well-understood ideal. Today the ruthless administrator is no longer merely a necessary evil, the sad compromise departments have to make to stay solvent; he is a reasonable member of a business-like community of achievers whose members include wet-lab scientists, pharmacologists, consulting medical specialists, and research-oriented psychotherapists.

There are in truth few concrete results that cannot be achieved through technical interventions in psychotherapy. Anxiety or depression gives way to cognitive restructuring, monosymptomatic phobia to behavioral desensitization in vivo, rebellious acting-out behavior to family restructuring, and so forth. There is no special requirement of inner peace; cognitive, behavioral, and "interpersonal" therapies can be taught via protocols, and certain family therapies were developed from the start to be taught schematically. The movement toward straightforwardly replicable therapies has been inevitable, even Darwinian; those institutions survive best which can pass on their methods most easily. It is clear today to every resident that ordinarily neurotic people can do perfectly competent therapy.

The availability of these discrete powerful tools tends to move the emphasis in residency from wisdom to skill. Now, of course, trainees must have both. Residents need technique because they need a rest from vulnerability. There is nothing like an early sense of mastery to give a young doctor confidence, the awareness of his own adeptness which is a prerequisite for prudent risk-taking. The corresponding danger, however, is that he will locate the source of that confidence in his cleverness and intellect, while remaining uncertain and defensive about his underdeveloped emotional strengths—his patience, empathy, quiet judgment, and stable familiarity with his own fears, disgust, lust, and aggression.

Incidents in my own training like the divorce/locksmith interview made me wonder whether I was not making myself a victim of a sort of premature maturity. Instead of enhancing my ability to rely on my emotional side, I was settling for mere mechanical skill of the sort I might as readily have exercised in, to stretch a point, pathology or radiology. Or, more exactly, the emotional side I was stimulating was that concerned with decisiveness, wit, and wild intuition.

But there was in truth no better way to turn. A doctor does have to take care of his patients, in the most efficient manner possible. And besides, it was not always clear what teachers of insight-oriented psychotherapy, some of whom were quite fixedly tied to one or another dogmatic school in which they had made their mark, had to offer. The world of subspecialists is not conducive to the nourishment of wisdom, nor does it especially reward wisdom in trainees.

And so I went down the path of technique, stratagem, cunning, and straightforwardly transmissible knowledge, aware of an unsatisfied part of myself which I tried to placate through reading, contact with special teachers who were most often from the clinical faculty, attention to an unsteady internal demand to maintain certain compassionate clinical standards, and discussions over racquetball or lunch with my equally troubled peers.

[75]

*   *   *   *   *

As in the case of medication, there is no going back. After all, my callow interview with the disturbed and enmeshed son and mother did succeed where other approaches had failed. We cannot dismiss the strategic engagement of patients as a parlor trick—it is a valuable addition to our armamentarium. Like pharmacotherapy, strategic therapy (and the many other brief, powerful therapies) is not something you can dabble in and then ignore. Its successes are stunning and economical.

At least I know I can't go home again. Awareness of the availability strategic interventions had an intrusive effect on my focus in dynamic therapy similar to my awareness of biological alternatives.

From the vantage point of traditional psychotherapy, strategic use of the self, and of prescriptions and paradoxes, is the enemy within. Some therapists can perhaps compartmentalize psychiatry in such a way as to consider biology external to the world of psychotherapy (in the preceding chapter, I have argued the opposite), but even the therapist who can banish imipramine from his mind may have repeatedly to ask himself whether or not to reach out more aggressively to certain patients—or to all patients in certain moments. It takes tremendous, and perhaps unwarranted, forbearance to sit empathically with a patient when you have the suspicion that an active combination of manipulations will not so much unblock the therapy as catapult the patient past his problems without therapy in the psychodynamic sense having to occur at all.

We live, as our predecessors did not, with a keen sense that, whatever our method, we are only treating part of the patient. Recently a man was referred to me for cognitive therapy of a panic disorder. He and I discussed his maladaptive cognitions—escalating thoughts, while anxious, that he might die of a heart attack or suffocate. And therapy began, only to falter at a certain point. The more complete thought which so troubled him was, he revealed, that he would die and desert his son, whom he felt he had wronged. The guilt over the son caused the father unconsciously to want to retain his symptoms (to punish himself), as did his remaining unconscious hostility toward the son—it would serve the boy right for the father to die and leave him.

Well, we might say, a dynamic therapy was called for. Yes, but if we precede every cognitive therapy with a dynamic therapy, we will weaken the power of the cognitive work which, after all, depends on the inculcation of a certain paradigm of human behavior and relies on a Socratic teacher-student relationship quite at variance with the enhancement of analyzable transference. And worse, we will sit in the dynamic therapy with our free-floating attention disturbed by the frequent urge to cut out a lot of nonsense by teaching the patient to modify self-defeating imagery or to adopt tailored "action strategies."

Of course, these therapies can be successfully combined and are, as a matter of routine practice, in many therapists' daily work. I will discuss eclecticism at length in a later chapter; I want for the moment only to note that the coexistence of powerful tools in itself creates a new therapy, one of doubt and strength for the therapist.

*　　*　　*　　*　　*

After the applause had died down, our crusty supervisor snapped, "OK, Don Quixote, what's next?" The boy was not suitable for therapy, he said; I should have referred him to a support group for chronic patients.

For a while, the five of us disputed this disposition. The supervisor was too pessimistic, he underestimated the power of our therapies.

To hell with the therapies, keep your eye on the diagnosis, the supervisor insisted: bad prognosis schizophrenia with an intrusive mother. I was free to keep the case, but I had to understand I was bucking the odds.

There is something mesmerizing for the audience in hypnotic therapies. My peers held out for me longer than they should have, but in time they came to their senses. The kid needed a medication adjustment. Realistically, nothing would separate the pathological mother and son.

And of course they were right. If the mother found a locksmith, I would be trapped by my own glibness into treating the untreatable. I was in the position the master psychoanalysts who consulted on cases had been able to avoid: I had to go on and work with the patients.

The too-successful interview may reveal a part of a patient or family which is unlikely to be sustained, under any treatment regimen. I had created the illusion of a patient where there was none. By saying I could do nothing if the mother could not locate and employ a locksmith, I had in a superficial way followed Carl Whitaker's dictum to make your impotence your ally. But in reality I had supplied too much of the

[77]

motivation for the characters in the drama. The patient existed only because of my energy.

This is the other illusion of technique: that we can easily create patients. Therapy comes from the patients; a few we can trick into health with our more intrusive interventions, but mostly we fool ourselves if we believe we can cure those who would rather stay ill.

And in the weeks that followed, despite the adjunctive services of a locksmith, I did fail with the mother and son, referring them in the end to the medication group a good triage nurse would have selected the moment they walked in the clinic door. Unless it is just that I was incompetent—you never know whether more skill or more effort might not turn a case.

As for the residents, we got good very fast, each in our own field. Not that we didn't come to respect one another's specialties. By the end of our six months together, we each admired what the others knew. But later years found each of us in a line of work with a clear relationship to his initial skills and interests. The spinal fluid specialist became a world-renowned psychiatric geneticist; the neo-Kraepelinian heads a respected diagnostic ward; the medical man does consultation/liaison work in the Harvard system; the expressive therapist heads an HMO psychiatric unit which emphasizes brief therapies; and after various detours I am practicing as I had imagined I would back when I was working with Max, writing and seeing patients in a private office.

I sometimes wonder what this says, that we each pretty much ended up doing what we set out to do. Perhaps the residency chose well; it selected and groomed us to excel in one area or another, and we ran true to form. After all, we were adults when we started. But I wonder also whether this excess of successes in just those fields we began in does not hint at premature closure, at a triumph in our training of skill over wisdom, of work over play. Our inertia no doubt owed something to our competitiveness and our fear of failing in strange domains. But was it perhaps not also the result of a residency, and a profession, that had trouble transcending its heterogeneous strengths, one which lacked a central theme?

My own mixed feelings about certain dichotomies—between technical facility and self-knowledge, cunning and naïve compassion, science and craft, examined empathy and spontaneous empathy, patience and short-term efficacy, cure and understanding—continued through the outpatient rotation and after. It might be possible, I feared, to become skilled without growing in wisdom. That did not turn out to be true either; there was growth, but it came in areas I had not considered when my aspirations were focused on dealing with inner conflicts of ancient origin.

Limits of Interpretation

In the teaching of individual psychotherapy, a distinction is generally drawn between exploration and support. Bright and psychologically-minded patients are considered candidates for psychotherapy based on insight and interpretation, while those less endowed merit mere restabilization through encouragement of their inherent strengths. This distinction is today perhaps no longer defended with much vigor, but it remains a central concept in the triage of patients, the selection of treatment modalities, and the supervision of residents.

In the opening chapters of this book, I implicitly questioned this dichotomy from one side by likening my psychoanalyst's dynamic interpretation of a dream to a social worker's reassuring gesture toward a paranoid woman. Here were widely different methods of treatment—psychoanalysis and straightforward psychotherapeutic support—for patients with differing levels of ego strength and developmental maturity. And yet both interventions could be seen to depend upon the expression of a single idea about the dangerousness or trustworthiness of certain female figures; there is a way of understanding both as turning on the correction of fantasy through interpretation. Many therapies, even the most primitively supportive, can be conceptualized as interpretive at their core.

It seems to me equally important to approach the dichotomy from the other side and consider the merits (and ubiquity) of support.

In medical school, with the first psychiatric patient I ever faced, I learned something about the power and limitations of interpretation. I knew from the start I wanted to become a psychiatrist, and I knew also I would become anxious if I spent two years doing preclinical work before ever meeting a psychiatric patient, so while taking the basic didactic courses in my first year, I spent my spare time in what turned into an informal four-year elective in the psychiatry department at Beth Israel Hospital in Boston. In the first weeks, after I attended a couple of intake team meetings, the psychiatrists in charge allowed me to evaluate an outpatient.

He was a truck driver who for eight or twelve years had suffered from constant headaches. The ambulatory care unit found no physical cause and referred him upstairs to us.

I felt under pressure to make a formulation, so in our first meeting I got right to the heart of the trucker's problem. Disappointments in his social life had rearoused dependency needs rooted in childhood and made him ambivalent about work. I understood the headaches as symbolizing the pain of his recent and prior losses and at the same time providing secondary gain. I noted that the headaches only became disabling when he was driving his truck; they would force him to stop and eat, and they made him late in his work. I don't know that I laid the whole picture out, but at the end of the hour I interpreted connections between headaches, doughnut stops, feelings of neediness, and work problems.

The second session he was late for the appointment with me, a failing which I promptly interpreted as resistance to the first interpretation. I never saw the patient again — but I did hear from him. He said he was no longer coming in because he had no more headaches. The medical ambulatory care unit confirmed the report of his recovery. I had cured the man in two visits.

The headaches recurred in a few months, but the patient took care to go elsewhere for his second evaluation. I learned about his progess by chance, during an early clinical experience at another hospital. Part of me did not understand how a patient could find relief from such a painful symptom and not stick with the treatment which had wrought the miracle. Part of me understood perfectly well. Pure interpretation is useless.

There is no point in dwelling on the failings of my attack on the hapless teamster. No one contends that mere self-knowledge, dumped artlessly on an unwilling subject, has the power to cure. Even I, at the time, did not believe in what I did. (Beyond frightening the patient into a "flight into health," I think I scared myself with my own power.) Having been treated by a skilled and subtle psychoanalyst, I knew better than to imagine technique consists in beating a patient over the head with insight. I had been overanxious to display competence, and the patient paid the price for a performance aimed, clumsily, at my teachers.

If interpretations are forceful enough, they can elicit dramatic responses: a decade of headaches and then all of a sudden none. But the most striking results often occur in contexts where they cannot be expected to be maintained.

It is hard not to favor the confrontative, even brutal interpretation, especially when dealing with something so hard to influence as a chronic pain syndrome. But it is also hard to imagine a patient such as this one succeeding for long without a sense of being supported. We know better than to take away a man's good custom—however self-injurious—without at the same time giving him something of value.

Generally what we give first, if we are able, is a therapeutic alliance, and then if we are doing psychodynamic work we will likely try to prepare the patient for the moment of insight, enabling understanding to evolve from within. But if we have in mind a certain sort of untrusting man, we may predict that by the time the alliance is formed our work will be about done. Interpretation (except the occasional kindly one meant to indicate understanding and thus nurture trust) will have a very minor role in such a course of therapy—and with good reason. Besides being largely irrelevant to the treatment plan, interpretation coming from such a benign source will lack the disruptive force needed to drive away headaches. By the time we have prepared the patient for self-awareness, the interpretation will have been rendered ineffectual.[1]

My first full psychotherapy case was of this alliance-building sort. After completing a couple of evaluations in the Beth Israel ambulatory clinic, I was assigned what was supposed to be an easy patient, an anxious and sad hysteric. But diagnosis rarely says enough about what therapy will hold.

In our first session, the patient told me she had slept with both her obstetrician and her internist. She was a beautiful young woman, upset over the impending failure of an abusive marriage. She came from a neglectful and abusive family. Father had been a gambler and mother a chorine, so the patient had been raised with a single talent, pleasing men.

There are, I know, many ways to approach such a case. But perhaps there are not so many which a first year medical student seeing his first therapy patient can be expected to carry out. My supervisor gave me a sound piece of advice. He told me to propose a 12-session therapy, along the lines of the brief therapies I had read about in a manuscript by James Mann which was circulating in the hospital.[2] Then he said, if you get through the treatment without having slept with the woman, you will have done her a great favor.

I carried out the plan. Being who I was at that stage in my training, I did make many interpretations, but I was aware that their purpose, if any, was to hold us in the room together while frustrating the patient's impulse to treat her anxiety through seduction and self-humiliation. My most frequent interpretation, if it can be called one, was that she would be tempted to terminate prematurely, because she felt anxious and out of control if she was not pleasing a man and abusing herself. She managed to stick with the treatment and within weeks began to demonstrate a touching degree of depth, revealing a solid non-hysterical aspect of the self, capable of bearing deep hurts and carrying on. I wondered at the time and do now whether this presentation of self did not emerge out of an attempt to please the unseduceable man I appeared to be, but even with this reservation I would call the treatment successful.

It was a therapy of support. If I connected childhood abuse and marital abuse and self-abusive instincts in the treatment, it was only to say that I understood her pain and wanted to bear it with her. I had no illusion that insight would help—except insofar as it helped me keep my vows. I was saying, I can see you without the glitter and still bear to be with you. This sort of statement is the essence of support. I suppose we could list a series of things the patient may have learned, about the source of her own goodness and so on. I think support almost always does function as interpretation. But the essence of the therapy was what the supervisor had said it should be, my sitting there and helping the patient sit there without our acting.

What was odd about medical school, and I think about psychotherapy training in general in that era, was that our discussions focused on psychodynamics and insight even when the cases at hand demanded support. We supported patients without having to say why, and we did so not, so far as I was aware, because of any well-worked-out theories about dynamically based supportive therapy, such as are now appearing in the literature, but rather because of unstated, strongly held assumptions about the doctor-patient relationship, assumptions concerning the importance of courtesy, temperateness, patience, and respect for people's limitations. Beth Israel Hospital was an institution with a psychoanalytic orientation, but, more importantly, it was also the kindest, most humane hospital in town on all of its services.

Of course, to my psychiatric training were added all the doctorly experiences of medical school and internship, so that by the time I reached residency I had an odd constitution. Intellectually I believed in insight and interpretation, and I tended to see patients' dynamic conflicts clearly. But viscerally and through hands-on work I was schooled in support.

*　　*　　*　　*　　*

In residency, this inner dialectic came under stress in my work with my first outpatient. She was a borderline retarded, psychotic girl whom I had treated on the inpatient ward. Since she had no other psychiatrist, when she was discharged I continued to work with her. As luck would have it, my assigned outpatient supervisor was a psychoanalyst of the old school—just the sort of person I would have requested if given a choice—who seemed to believe that all patients could be treated by at worst a slightly modified version of the method of free association, clarification, and interpretation.

The congruence of our beliefs did not help me avoid conflict. Rather, it fostered a difficulty of an unexpected sort. The dispute was over the issue of support versus interpretation.

My patient was in her late teens or early twenties; if I think of her as a girl it is because her most striking quality was a sweet immaturity or bland innocence. She had always been less worldly and more attached to her parents, her father in particular, than were her brothers and sisters, and she was deeply affected by her father's early death from cancer. Some days after he died, the girl entered the kitchen to find her mother and brothers eating minestrone soup. To her, it seemed the vegetables were human body parts, perhaps her father's, and she understood her family to be cannibals.

In time she came to the neuropsychiatric inpatient ward and was put under my care. She revealed little of herself. She moved as if by tropism toward the windows, and, though she denied it, she seemed to the staff to be contemplating hurling herself against the glass and throwing herself down the ten stories to the ground. Otherwise she was pleasant and obedient, and when with medication her fear diminished she was discharged to my care.

She came reliably to my office in the mental health center and was glad to talk, usually about daily activities at home. In certain visits she would discuss her psychosis. She had seen signs in the flight of birds and had imagined she could soar off with them; that explained her affinity for windows. Mostly she had been in a state of undifferentiated terror, something she was loath to recall.

A degree of confusion remained with her, and it was hard to tell how much was attributable to her mental illness and how much to an intellectual deficiency. She had graduated high school, and there her I.Q. had tested in the normal range or just below. But she came from a bright and talented family, and I wondered whether the testing might not have overestimated her capacities. As certain children are disadvantaged, she was advantaged. She had lived in symbiosis with her quite brilliant father, a man who had loved and nurtured this least self-sufficient of his children and had made her appear and feel more normal than she otherwise might have. Without him, she acted borderline retarded, though her test scores had deteriorated only slightly.

For years she had felt a special relationship to birds. She drew birds endlessly and said she wanted a career as a bird illustrator. But her work, though loving and detailed, had a childish and inexact quality. She knew a great deal about birds in the way certain preschoolers do about dinosaurs; the facts were always the same, and she could not manipulate or reason with them.

Birds entered into her fantasy life as well. She had not the practical experience nor ingenious imagination of the protagonist of William Wharton's marvelous fictional war memoir, *Birdy*. Her dreams of flying, pecking, and clawing were simple and unelaborated.

So we sat and talked about family members or looked at her bird sketches together, and she came to trust me and to consider the office a safe haven. Much of the treatment was rehabilitative. She began to attend a sheltered workshop. She negotiated privileges with her mother; she learned to drive and went on dates. I was raising a child, helping her balance her capabilities and her urges and this process was difficult because she was enough aware of age-appropriate activities to resent her limitations.

The patient made good progress, and all would have been well except that my task with her was to do psychotherapy.

My supervisor believed strongly that the patient was in need of dynamic self-understanding. In part this assessment stemmed from his impression of her diagnosis.

The neuropsychiatry ward chief had understood the girl to have a variant of minimal brain dysfunction or pervasive developmental disorder. It did not bother him that her I.Q. had tested nearly normal; for someone in her family to be only in the normal range indicated subtle neurologic impairment. The analyst bought none of this so-so-biology. A girl who can graduate high school is workable; in his opinion the ward chief was so caught up in unsupported theorizing that he had lost sight of the well-known characteristics of simple schizophrenia.

The supervisor also believed that beyond the acute stage schizophrenia is amenable to insight-oriented therapy. This tenet was not, I imagine, a function of specific ideas about psychotherapy efficacy. The supervisor saw the world through the lens of psychoanalysis, and for him any honest and helpful conversation would contain elements of clarification, confrontation, and interpretation.

I agreed with the ward chief that some of the girl's disability was organic, but in formulating the case I did not disagree with the supervisor either. The girl had an Electra complex, or whatever is the proper term for a daughter who wants to lay first claim to her father. At least I posited that she had long been jealous of her mother and resentful of mother's role as rule-setter. After her father's death, the girl could not understand how life could go on as usual for others in the family. To her it seemed barbaric that the family could blithely eat soup and make small talk so soon after her father's death, and this horror was evident in the form of her delusions.

My problem was not in seeing the case in dynamic terms but in acting on that vision. When I sat in the room with the girl, I found myself reluctant — in fact unable — to push her.

Part of this difficulty was a matter of belief. Consider the issue of defenses. I could list the patient's defenses — they were transparent. She reacted to stress by withdrawing from reality, most benignly to the world of birds but in the worst case to frank psychosis. She was also capable of the smaller defenses, such as denial, but the retreat to fantasy predominated.

But I was not confident about the dynamic origin of this defensive structure. Was it a response to a seductive father and overly cool mother? Or was it just the case that the girl was easily overwhelmed and had limited capacities to handle complexity of any sort, so that, with the onset of whatever neuroendocrine changes take place in late adolescence and now the loss of her best support, quite benign family relationships became inadequate to keep her afloat? Although I could make a dynamic formulation, this sort of doubt made it hard to put force behind my implementing it.

My supervisor and I might have come to an agreement over these questions if we had struggled with them openly together. But we were not in the sort of supervision in which we addressed practical issues directly. We did not so much as make a treatment plan. In form the supervision paralleled my psychoanalysis with Max. I talked, and the supervisor was silent except to question individual actions I had taken in therapy. The core of supervision was the interpretation of countertransference, including my countertransference resistance to the supervisor's unexpressed image of progress.

I floundered. Without saying just how I should make it right, the supervisor faulted me for the tone and direction of my interactions with the patient. I understood him to expect the case to go much as any psychoanalysis of a neurotic would go — as my therapy with Max had gone — and I found I could not bring this transformation about.

What he wanted, I believed, was for me to hide my care and concern for the girl (and what is all this about a girl anyway? — she's a young woman with disturbingly hostile fantasies) and to be more vigorous in my interpretation of the patient's dynamic conflict. This advice was not given in so many words, but I understood it from the supervisor's irritation at me whenever I became too supportive. Why had I missed this or that opportunity to draw the strands together? The implication was that I had an inner failing which made me too soft on the patient, too seductive.

In this, the supervisor was right, at least this far: much as I tried, I could not bring myself to confront the girl. She felt fragile to me. She had only recently suffered a frank psychosis, and she was still "fuzzy around the edges." Besides, I found that in challenging her I had only the power to upset or frighten. If I ventured toward saying too much, she would pout like a toddler or develop a hawk-like gleam in the eyes. We could then talk about that reaction, of course, but she would leave the session bitter; it felt to me that her need for my support was too great for her to look with perspective at the moments when it felt to her that I was the enemy.

Or rather, the matter was simpler. I just could not push myself past a certain point.

I did venture simple connections. When you have fantasies of vultures it means you yourself are angry, often at your mother. You resent your mother's ability to resume everyday life. It's like that time in fifth grade when your friend moved away and you had those tantrums no one understood; you were angry that others did not share your sense of loss.

But my aim was less to make the patient aware of her dark urges than to make her driven behavior and overwhelming feelings comprehensible. My obvious fondness and concern for the girl were not conducive to the development of the sort of transference most amenable to examination. And my broad interpretation of the defenses was, to the supervisor, second-best psychotherapy, a mere ego psychology substitute for real Freudian tripartite interpretations of transference, developmental trauma, and current neurosis as manifested in the specific symbolic content of symptoms, parapraxes, dreams, and the like.

The supervisor thought I had the kind of trouble I once attributed to the social worker who could not work with aggression. He could not decide whether I was stupid or weak. More precisely, I think I considered me the annoying sort of student who, despite a superficial ability to "speak the language," will always be a bumbling psychotherapist because he is so thoroughly blinded by his own neurosis.

I still see the bird-loving young woman so clearly through my own lenses that I have in telling the story weighted the pans in my own favor. The supervisor's point of view was reasonable, even if I could not bring myself to act on it. And his angry gaze was difficult for me to bear. Imagine having worked so many years and finding oneself unfit to practice, not in the sense that I would ever be prohibited by the organized profession from doing psychotherapy, but in this deep and invisible regard, that I was temperamentally unsuited for it. I had sufficient confidence not to be crushed by this harsh sentence, but it weighed on me heavily enough to make me think carefully about myself and the therapy, and in the end this dogmatic supervision was invaluable.

Why was I so peculiarly paralyzed with this patient? After all, didn't I hope to become a psychoanalyst? At first I tended to consider myself oedipally resistant, lumping my failure to take instruction here with my contrariness on the inpatient ward. I could not obey authority, whether biological or analytic.

If so, this recent failure was more disturbing, because less accessible to consciousness. On the inpatient ward I explicitly refused to do what I did not believe in; now with every intention to act on my supervisor's advice I found I could not. I melted in the patient's presence.

If not oedipal and directed at the supervisor, and no doubt it was in part, this failure could still be considered a result of distorted feelings toward the patient, and we discussed this possibility in supervision. Perhaps I used reaction formation to defend myself from hostile wishes. Was the bird-loving young woman like a younger sister toward whom one is overly solicitous, even smothering, in order to seal off from consciousness murderous impulses? I was capable of that sort of error, and ever since I have asked whether syrupy tendencies in my therapy mask hostility.

In these ways the supervision led to productive avenues of self-examination.

But throughout, I never more than half-believed that my failure to confront the girl stemmed from hidden blind spots and weaknesses. I could not do what the supervisor wanted, but I wondered whether this inability did not stem from an accurate reading of the girl's needs. In any event, I was learning something about the enormous power of perceived reality in therapy; it is nearly impossible for the therapist to act on a reality he does not experience in the room with the patient, nor, in my opinion, should therapists-in-training be asked to do so.

It seemed this way to me: interpretation was all right for this girl, if presented gently. But it was all right precisely because it failed to work fully as interpretation. (And the way I presented interpretations contributed to this failure.) When I pointed out that her dreams of carnage meant her mother's calm enraged her, the patient felt understood. And this understanding was important because it signaled that I was in the room with her and knew what she must be feeling. She did not "make use" of the new point of view herself, did not elaborate on it or generalize it. She used the interpretation to monitor my attentiveness. In a given session, some much less incisive indicator of my regard—a smile or a laugh—might mean as much to her as an interpretation.

Interpretation had no unique role. Suggesting that she would have a greater sense of purpose if she worked and encouraging her to apply for job training had a similar effect to explicating dreams. My understanding of the importance to her of being able to go shopping alone was on a par with any revelation of unconscious aggression. Nor was it clear in a practical sense that hidden rage was more of a problem for this patient than was social awkwardness.

In this therapy, interpretation functioned as support. It carried the primary message: you are important, you are acceptable, and even when your actions are incomprehensible to you, they can be made sense of by someone else.

There were secondary functions of interpretations which involved their stated content, but in an incomplete way. For instance, my giving meaning to aggressive fantasies made them less strange and disturbing for the patient. (The particular meaning attributed might not have mattered much.) This normalization of fantasy then allowed her to share yet more disturbing fantasies, so that she was better and better able to use her birds to talk to me. But some broader view—that she projected anger onto her mother and then responded to her own projection—might forever elude the patient, not least because she was not well enough individuated to demand self-understanding. Of course, this disinterest may be seen as a failure of the therapy; or perhaps if therapy were to go on long enough we would be able to "turn a certain corner" and move from support to insight.

* * * * *

[91]

At this point, we might want to stop and ask whether in choosing the case of a person of limited intellectual capacities I have not stacked the deck against the use of interpretation to cure through the creation of insight. If we are discussing the usefulness of putting ego in id's place, we will want to talk about instances in which the ego is strong and flexible. (Though this objection is cogent, I might ask in reply: if the centrality of support in this case is self-evident, then why did the supervisor and I struggle?)

The mix of support and insight in a course of psychotherapy obviously ought to vary according to the patient's capacity for integrating different forms of information. But before calling this case atypical, I would like to consider a moment from a treatment I conducted with a more sophisticated patient in recent years. This treatment and the moment will feel entirely familiar—they exemplify our traditional model of psychotherapy.

The patient was a controlled, somewhat inhibited professional man in his late twenties who had reached a roadblock in his career because of performance anxiety and who was also aware of limitations in his capacity to love. Though externally successful, he felt a failure. (Could a case be more typical?) At the end of a session early in treatment he asked if I would not, as a small favor, write a prescription for a dermatologic preparation for his wife. I declined, and at the start of the following session, he recounted a dream.

The manifest content was simple: he dreamt that his insurance deductible for psychotherapy was $36,000.

He said he was aware that he had been upset over my hourly fee. In fact, his wife had from the first warned him that psychotherapy would be too expensive. When he then received a Major Medical notice indicating that my fee exceeded the "usual, customary, and reasonable" limit (a sum in line with the charge for therapy ten years prior), he had felt outraged and humiliated; although it turned out he had double coverage because of his wife's insurance, and in fact the therapy would cost him nothing beyond a modest deductible. The dream seemed to imply he was angry over having to pay anything at all for treatment.

I asked where the number 36,000 might come from. He thought for a moment and then said, "Oh, that's obvious." The number 36 for him had always represented the breast size of desirable women. In fact, when he was in high school, a flirtatious girl had once "inadvertently" let him find one of her bras, which happened to be size 36, and he had begun to pursue her only to be further teased and rejected. This episode fit well with other stories of humiliation at the hands of women, and other dreams of humiliation and even violence at the hands of men and women, which then came to mind.

The import of the "high deductible" dream and its associations is, I suppose, obvious, and in time I made or elicited from the patient a series of conventional interpretations. He felt threatened by women, he resented the therapy's putting him in conflict with his wife, he was competitive with me, he experienced the fee as a humiliation, perhaps even one which put him in a womanly position, and he had always felt himself to be rejected and his father humbled by his highly competitive mother.

In asking for the skin-lotion prescription for the wife, he had purposely requested a favor he knew I would decline, in order to experience a rejection the anticipation of which made him feel anxious and therefore "at home." And what of the nature of the favor? Did he think psychotherapy was useless anyway, since it would not bring him the flawless — and large-breasted — wife he imagined would make him feel fully masculine?

These interpretations made the patient visibly happy. He later said they made him feel close to me, and they gave him confidence that he was getting the hang of psychotherapy, which in his conception hinged on dream interpretation.

I don't mean at all to deny that these interpretations did what interpretations are supposed to do, namely, to unite present anxiety, past trauma, and current transference. Nor do I dispute that newfound awareness gave the patient relief through providing him conscious leverage over hidden self-destructive forces.

But according to the patient's account, the primary function of our exchange was support. To risk exposing himself and to be rewarded with a careful discussion of his inner life resulted in feelings of safe intimate contact and competency. By his account, the content of the fantasies and interpretations was secondary.

My own feelings were even stronger in this direction. I saw the patient as having used the opportunity to analyze a dream as a step in the male bonding process which was otherwise closed to him. He first asked, will you show me superficial love, but hidden contempt, as my parents sometimes did, by acquiescing to an inappropriate request (for the wife's skin lotion) and ignoring my anger? When I passed that test, he felt more at liberty to reveal, in the shyest and most intellectual way—through recounting the transparent dream—his lusts and fears. We engaged in an inhibited form of locker room banter, and for the patient it felt good to be in that position, accepted by and as one of the guys.

For me as a therapist, the task was one of maintaining the proper social distance, the right mix of admiration and suspended judgment, which is often the central issue in supportive therapy. The content of our interchange did matter, but only in this limited way: the subject matter (sex, power, and money) was the right one for men to use in bonding.

I present the vignette not as proof of anything but as a way of expressing how it feels to me as a therapist, namely that interpretation is less a specific tool for permitting liberation through insight than a condition of therapy, one which is used by both patient and therapist to many ends, and especially for the nonspecific fostering of comfort and self-confidence. While some children see a protective and unchallenging school environment as supportive, others feel supported only when they experience academic mastery; similarly, there are certain patients—often those for whom we would expect insight to be directly helpful—for whom the exchange surrounding interpretation is a prerequisite for a sense of security.

Indeed there are patients for whom interpretation is so comfortable that their participation in the process becomes a form of resistance to emotionally challenging self-examination. It may be that interpretation acts as support (though we hope it has other uses as well) even more strongly in high-functioning patients than in those who, like our bird-loving young woman, have evident intellectual limitations and rely on more concrete ways of interacting with the world.[3]

* * * * *

The role of interpretation has necessarily changed with a change in the social climate. Freud reported case after case in which interpretation effected growth in self-governance in a patient through growth in self-understanding. But in contemporary work—in my work, which I see as more or less mainstream—it more often seems that interpretation plays a secondary role to the development of the therapeutic relationship. If interpretation takes on its traditional role at all, [...] healthiest of patients, and then often late in the treatr[...]

In his well-known eulogy for Freud, W. H. Auden [...] he is no more a person/ now but a whole climate [...] whom we conduct our different lives. . . . "⁴ The clim[...] enced was powerful and stormy—he thought Freud's honest presence discouraged pride and even tyranny. Almost 50 years later, Freud is still a climate of opinion, but the climate is cloudier, the opinion more banal. We are prone to accept strong sexual or aggressive drives in ourselves; what Freud discovered about us is discounted, it has lost the power to take our breath away.

When I teach my section of the basic psychotherapy course for residents, I accompany Freud's "Miss Lucy R." case with a monograph about the dilemmas of the Victorian governess.⁵ What a truth-teller Freud was. Knowing what we do of the tenuous social status of the nineteenth-century governess, how daintily she had to walk the tight-rope of gentility, how narrow the line between failed governess and fallen woman, we must gasp as we read Freud's confrontation of Lucy: "I cannot believe these are all the reasons for your feelings about the children. I believe that you really are in love with your employer, the Director, though perhaps without being aware of it yourself, and that you have a secret hope of taking their mother's place in actual fact."⁶ The smell of burnt pudding, the smell of cigar smoke—it is not just that these hysterical symptoms have meaning, it is that their meaning is so danger-ous. They are the traces of impossible love, ruinous love.

Though there is plenty of pain in self-recognition in any era, and terror even in ordinary childhood memories for many who have been sufficiently abused, I doubt we often confront patients with anything whose ability to shock approaches the recognition of infantile sexuality in the self of the Victorian patient, or the Viennese equivalent. What once served to jolt someone into self-examination might today instead inspire a sense of relief in a patient, at the acknowledgment of his or her normality; today, to be shown to have unconscious aggressive and sexual fantasies is to be judged—thank goodnesss, at last—in the mainstream. The sense is less of being thrust out into the cold than of being drawn back into a familiar system of understanding and forgiveness.

So widespread are Freudian assumptions today—so ubiquitous is the "climate of opinion"—that when I use traditional psychodynamic con-

ιn work with someone who has in one way or another avoided .ounter with them, I feel less that I am introducing the patient to his unconscious than that I am introducing him to the modern world. It is his obsessionality or fearfulness or haughtiness which has allowed the patient to ignore not just aspects of the self but of everyday life, and the introduction of Freudian ideas serves less as interpretation than as a confrontation of character armor.

Most patients are quite at home with the dark side of dynamic conflict. To neither the bird-loving young woman nor the patient with the high deductible are his or her own aggressive impulses exactly news; it is the public sharing and mutual consideration of those feelings which drives the therapy. Or consider the patient who felt compelled to seduce her physicians; what is it we expect her to discover about herself that is more disturbing than the truths she already knows? She needs empathy over her fear of and longing for both self-destructive and self-respecting love. In how many modern novels does the hero in effect sleep with his mother and kill his father—or acknowledge impulses which are much worse?[7] Our patients are not so much pre-oedipal as post-oedipal, living in a world in which the oedipal truths are old hat.

*   *   *   *   *

A change in the role of interpretation has also necessarily accompanied a change in the focus of psychoanalytic work and theory, one which was already in progress, and in which, unbeknownst to me, I participated, during the period of my formal training. Although all schools of psychoanalysis still talk about interpretation as the central curative force, recent decades have seen a shift in emphasis away from the unconscious and toward attention to global needs and strengths of the person. (And this change is especially marked in the "sitting-up" psychotherapies derivative of those schools of psychoanalysis.) The movement is also, to my mind, away from magic and astonishment and toward commonsensical, widely accepted views of behavior.

The change began in Freud's lifetime, though the trend was in its early stages difficult to discern. Wilhelm Reich's character analysis, immediately recognized as brilliant in its own day, appeared merely to extend the thesis of unconscious dynamic conflict to issues of personality. But character analysis led more or less directly, as did certain of Freud's ideas in *Inhibitions, Symptoms and Anxiety* (1926),[8] to an analysis of common components of character armor, namely the defenses. Ego psychology flows from character analysis.

And when we focus on the ego's fixed mechanisms, some partly or even entirely conscious, we are working with habits and ideas much more in the everyday world, and much less exotic, than the specific and highly symbolic acute manifestations of the unconscious.

When shown how they habitually act, patients are more often hurt than astonished. And this move toward the ordinary is nowhere more apparent than in what we necessarily discover in examining the ego, namely its healthy parts, including the "conflict-free sphere of the ego." Conflict-free! Here we are, trying to do dynamic therapy, where dynamic means active unconscious conflict, and we find we can accomplish a good deal just by shoring up the part of the ego in which conflict is not an issue. We need the help of this part of the ego if we are to do therapy at all; we have no choice but to cultivate it.

Through attention to the fixed, the conscious, and even the healthy parts of the mind and character, the ego psychologists, Freud's direct heirs through his daughter Anna, have much to do with the changed role of interpretation. Their rivals, the object relations theorists, are in this regard more respectful of drive theory. They take the meaningfulness of unconscious motivation and extend it back further into infancy. But this shift in temporal focus in the end has a similar effect to the change in structural focus from id to ego. Early trauma determines temperament or type (paranoid, depressive) in ways that swamp the reflective ego; dynamic conflict remains useful as an explanation, but interpretation of conflict loses force and specificity as a clinical tool, so that the appropriate therapy of "pre-oedipal" injuries must emphasize character over conflict, containment and empathy over insight.

The third stream of contemporary analysis, self psychology, in its very name highlights the whole over the parts. In all three new psychologies, it is the integrity of the self which is at issue, so that support and the nurturing of strengths, as much as the optimization of anxiety and encouragement of independent discovery, become crucial to therapy. Self psychologists believe that supportive therapy, once scorned as second-best or considered drudgery by Freudians, is the most difficult treatment and the one on which a therapist should pride himself most.

Self psychologists stress the truth that humans are never entirely independent and at their healthiest require admiration from others.

To put the matter in a more conventional form, the new therapies, and especially the self and object relations psychologies, arise from work with more disturbed patients. It is not just that sicker patients appear clinically to require more holding. Oedipal issues concern rebellion; pre-oedipal issues are ones of holding anyway. The origins of oedipal issues are more amenable to being reached through memory and reason; pre-oedipal issues are reached through strong feeling and speculative reconstruction—if it is important to reach them at all. Since matters are so tumultuous, we may do better to leave the mess in the container alone and to focus on strengthening the container.[9]

And once we have settled on supportive therapy for the personality-disordered, we have affected our view of therapy for all patients. Analytic metapsychologies tend to rely on a spectrum theory of illness and health—there is really no one psychology for the sick and one for the well. Today all patients have variants of borderline and narcissistic personality disorders,[10] just as all patients once for practical purposes had variants of hysterical and obsessional neuroses. I don't mean to claim that this assertion is strictly true, only that therapists tend to develop a sense of core pathology and core therapy and that today's core pathology is in the ego or the self and the core therapy concerns the integrity of the self as experienced in the (necessarily supportive) relationship with the therapist.

* * * * *

I knew little of the history or theory of psychotherapy when I treated the borderline retarded patient who loved birds. But the considerations I have just discussed arose through praxis. For example, the patient was quite capable of day-to-day rage at her mother. The interpretation to her of her own anger lacked the power to shock. And today how shocking is it for daughters to discover they harbor resentment toward their mothers? What was hidden, if anything can be said to have been hidden, was the force and fury of the anger; and when that was brought to light, the patient felt more a sense of relief at being understood and accepted than a sense of discovery of the unknown.

The lessons of the modern analytic variants came to me also, in highly condensed form, through the repeated musings of a group psychotherapy instructor who had administrative responsibility for my overall caseload. He would ask me how things were going with various patients and then invariably say, in his strong Scots growl, "No one's the worse for a good experience." I liked this teacher, but I am sorry to say I do not think I accorded him much intellectual respect. Whatever we discussed would come down to the one sentence that guided his life as a psychiatrist: "No one's the worse for a good experience." And yet, of the adages I heard in residency, his is the one I have recalled most often in the years since.

When people say that supportive therapy is difficult, I think they generally mean one of two things. First, the patients who require the most support are uncomfortable to be with. To be an auxiliary ego (or, as in the case of the young woman who loved birds, a transitional father) for someone with uncontrolled passions is draining. Much has been written about this issue, particularly as regards work with borderline character disordered patients who in their neediness not only demand much from the therapist but also set their sights on the therapist to make his support role ever more emotionally involving and difficult. We in part identify character disordered patients by our discomfort with their inability to accept the parameters of the therapeutic relationship.

Second, support requires the acquisition of a degree of experience and judgment which the dynamic therapist sometimes can get along without. In "exploratory" dynamic therapy, the clinician has the advantage of being able to share his formulations with the patient and even develop them cooperatively. Interpretation usually depends on successive revisions of ideas by patient and therapist. In supportive work, the therapist more often is on his own, and as a result his formulations may remain inexact. The patient's feedback is largely behavioral and may be difficult to read or even purposely misleading.

Thus poorly armed, the therapist will have to make a series of decisions which involve the use of his own self in treatment: in setting limits; in allowing the patient to use the therapist transferentially to replace imperfect inner objects; in withholding the self so as not to overwhelm the needy patient; and generally in monitoring and regulating social distance in the therapy. Especially for the intellectualizing resident or therapist, these are much harder skills to acquire and practice than interpretation. And for the empathic student there is the problem of inhibiting his natural impulses in order not to activate the patient's potential for regression, dependency, and fantasies of merger.

These two areas of difficulty—the volatile patient and the difficult methods—overlap. The problem is in maintaining and applying professional skills in an emotionally turbulent environment that necessarily and appropriately encompasses the therapist.

But I think there is a third area of difficulty which is less often recognized, involving the mind of the therapist. A therapy of support is less planful than a therapy of interpretation. The concept of direction is inherent in dynamic therapy. We speak of reaching deeper layers of the self, of "peeling the onion," or of resolving the Oedipus complex. Interpretation has its directional strictures: interpret character before content, interpret negative transference before positive, and (according to a school of thought now less in favor) avoid interpreting the transference until it manifests itself as resistance.

Support has no direction. Our plan is to hold the patient—to strengthen the container—until the patient develops his own container-strengths or until the contents settle down. We do not know just how or when all this ought to happen.

Worse, we do not have a particularly cogent rationale for limiting our own actions. If support is necessary, why should it be only in this arena and not in that? Once we start giving advice on one subject, why not on another? Why not, for example, just introduce the patient with avoidant personality disorder to friends or guide him toward a job?[11] Permitting support as a first goal in certain therapies, and as a necessary element in most, opens a Pandora's box.

In supportive work, the therapist cedes great control to the patient. It may seem otherwise. The therapist is setting limits, perhaps implicitly commenting on the patient's behavior or sense of self, and so forth, and on the surface it seems that the therapist is taking responsibility for the patient's progress. But all this activity leads nowhere except, if we succeed, to stability. In supportive therapy, change arises in a more or less miraculous way, through the patient's suddenly feeling secure enough to move in a certain direction, perhaps one unanticipated by the therapist. It is this pathless quality of supportive work—the degree of blind faith it requires of the therapist—that makes it most uncomfortable.

[100]

Often it may feel that neither the patient nor the therapist is in control, that the external consequences of therapy bear little relation to the internal ones, that progress has nothing to do with process. The work may go well in the sense that the patient seems less at the mercy of terrible inner forces, but the various axes of hoped for improvement—symptoms, love, career—may change little. Or the patient may get better behaviorally without our understanding why.

This experience is unsettling for the therapist; it is the kind of thing that may drive us to consider ever more outlandish forms of biological diagnosis and treatment, or ever more aggressive forms of psychotherapy, so as to reestablish a sense of connectedness and control. Or, with less drama, it seems to me that a change within dynamic psychotherapy, away from interpretation of the unconscious and toward more supportive methods involving the self and ego, has played a role in making therapists more open to thoughts of alternative methods of case formulation and treatment. If I am right, it is not just neuropsychiatry and the growth of competing schools of psychotherapy, but changes within psychoanalysis itself, and within every stream of psychoanalysis, that have made us less and less loyal to the gold standard of interpretation.

*   *   *   *   *

My own work today tends to be highly exploratory, even in cases or in stages of therapy where I see the role of support to be crucial. But "exploratory" in my work generally means something less specific than it would in classical psychoanalysis. I may ask about the patient's concept of his symptoms, or remark on a pattern of interpersonal relations, or even examine transference reactions, in a way that remains pathless—without the hope that soon we will turn to oedipal material. Or I may onstensibly hammer away at oedipal material but only for the sake of having a good fight. The work has the quality of religious exploration by agnostics; we hope to learn something helpful for ourselves from the struggle, but we do not expect to find God.

Harry Stack Sullivan says somewhere that the most important thing a beginning resident can learn about himself is how he appears to others. Exploration in the sort of psychotherapy I find myself doing may lead to this end for the patient. Indeed, it might almost be fair to say that whereas my residency outpatient supervisor turned supervision into psychoanalysis, the corresponding error in my work is a tendency to act in treatment as if it were supervision.

Many practical reasons remain for attending to insight in treatment. There is an inherent dignity in the enterprise of attempting the analytic inquiry, dignity which is lacking in mere encouragement, admiration, and the like. (But there is no dignity at all in going through with a charade of a classical therapy for a patient who cannot tolerate interpretations.) And certain patients will always feel insecure in the absence of cognitive self-understanding. Even with quite ego-depleted patients, there are many instances when self-recognition can bring dramatic benefit. And for some patients, highly intellectual approaches offer the only chance of making contact. For the therapist, there are benefits in limiting the scope and form of treatment and in adhering to accepted rules, as there are in sonnet form for the poet.

But each of these reasons applies only more or less to each case; they make interpretation seem contingent, not necessary. At many moments and with many patients, I wonder whether my attachment to interpretation is not so much rational as sentimental, or rather, I wonder whether the exercise we are engaged in is not one of many possible reasonable choices, an arbitrary convention made useful by experience accreted around it.

In any interpretive therapy, interpretation takes on many functions, some quite distant from the function for which interpretation was developed. The therapist's use of interpretation for purposes other than insight can be as creative or resistant as patients' uses I have discussed earlier. The paleontologist and philosopher of science Stephen Jay Gould has written numerous essays on the ways in which physical adaptations originally selected for because of their competitive advantage in one situation come with time to be used quite differently, just because they are already there. The panda's radial sesamoid bone, first used in the wrist, becomes a makeshift opposed "thumb," not an ideal engineering solution, but a useful evolutionary outcome given the anatomy already present.[12]

Interpretation in therapy is an artefact which comes to hand in many ways. I have in mind, for example, the habit some therapists have of insistently repeating interpretations even in the face of patients' denials; the therapists mean to indicate that firmness and self-assurance are not vices. They may also be asserting power or revealing an aspect of their personality or reassuring the patient that they will not be fooled by superficial resistances. It is the manner of their interpretation that counts more than the content.

I often use interpretation in the engagement process, long before the patient can be expected to integrate the content of my speculations. For instance, I came once to treat a young man who had rejected or been rejected by a number of therapists, including some I knew to be quite kindly and tolerant, despite his appearing on first blush to be a "good therapy candidate." I interpreted to him in our first meeting that he seemed angry at his psychiatrist father.

He returned the next session to say, in an extremely intellectualized way, that my remark may have had some merit, and furthermore it made him disposed to like me because it had made him think, but he did not see how he could make further use of it. Also, he hoped I would be speaking a good deal because he could never come up with anything to say in therapy. And he hoped I had more interpretations in store because that one had not taken him very far.

He was then silent for a while. Rather than let bad turn to worse, I told him I thought he was challenging me from the start and looking for reasons to be angry at me. He still said nothing.

I then asked him why he was squinting. He said he had not brought in his eyeglasses. I said after last week perhaps he wished to keep things hazy with me.

He then said he had recently bought new wire-rimmed oblong eyeglasses which he thought made him look like a sixties hippie. I asked him why he had done this. He indicated he had contempt for students who were conventional, and so he had created a test to discover who would see that his act was "neat" and who would be so conventional as to criticize him and call him strange. I said not only did he not want to see me, but also he did not want me to see him as he was with others in the college community. Furthermore, I guessed he had contempt for me and imagined that if he had worn the glasses I would have found them odd.

I added that perhaps he was burdened with a good deal of contempt altogether. Since he had bought the glasses in order to express his contempt for conventional students, perhaps they were only seeing what was right in front of them when they expressed discomfort with his act. I sympathized with the insecurity in him which would lead him to alienate others. I continued to interpret rather vigorously.

When the student became angry at my taking the lead with such force, I accused him of having pushed me to talk with the express purpose of being angry at me whether I talked or not. He was just most comfortable when he could be angry at authority, and it was he who had created the situation at hand. Perhaps he had run across this problem elsewhere?

He laughed for a long while and got down to work.[13] It was many sessions before he fell silent again or accused me of talking too little; and I do not think my open aggressiveness put him off nearly as much as the covert aggression he attributed to others.

The functions of interpretation in this interchange are many—stimulating the patient's interest, making his anger concrete, letting him know I was not easily fooled and would not tolerate being trifled with, giving permission for anger and competition, blocking him from appearing odd, setting examples for ways of thinking about interpersonal problems, indicating seriousness, showing I would not be bound by false politeness or convention, protecting me from the stifled anger that undid other therapists, creating confusion, and others. Interpretation was just the tool that came to hand to induce this haughty intellectualizing young man into treatment. I was able to use it because to use it was expected, because I had been invited to use it—but we would hardly say that I used it for its usual purpose or in the way its developers would recognize. (The interpreting was not even "wild analysis" or "direct psychoanalysis," because its function was barely interpretation at all. Compare it, for instance, to my early encounter with the suffering trucker, to which it bears close resemblance in form but not intent or effect.)

This example is extreme, but it says something about the way I see interpretation. It is a particular implement with many uses, of which the imparting of insight is only one. I expect it to be present in exploratory therapy, but in what guise and with what importance, I would never want to guess in advance.

Despite this last example to the contrary, I see myself as an heir of the supervisor whom I so frustrated—in this sense, that I understand and maintain sympathy with the ideal of the dynamic interpretation. The residents I supervise are already a step further removed, some of them by habit more comfortable with family work and paradox than psychoanalysis, some of them behaviorists by training or inclination. When they become supervisors, their residents may be more truly eclectic, able to see theories and interventions with great neutrality, free of the wish that the reality of patients' needs and abilities were more in keeping with this or that beloved view of human behavior. Or, more likely, a new compelling paradigm will emerge to command new loyalties.

Often in therapy I become acutely aware of the contingent nature of the work. The patient and I have agreed to participate in a complex process based on a paradigm in which we both have imperfect belief. Interpretive psychotherapy contains the set of rules for action with whose variants I am most familiar and within whose strictures I can best understand the other. I do not know that I have moved far from the confused days of talking dynamics and enacting support, except perhaps that I have less contempt and more intellectual sympathy for the vague principle that, when all is said and done, no one's the worse for a good experience.

Just Good Friends

This was still early in my residency. A man in his late thirties was referred by his wife about a year after he had suffered terrible losses. First his mother had died suddenly and unexpectedly, and then his father, leaving the man in charge of the family business the father and he had run together. The wife said her husband was becoming isolated socially and was, through inattention, endangering the business.

He was not depressed, but he was markedly listless. A straightforward case of bereavement, then. I thought I knew what was needed: what could be more obvious? And so I set about my work; only the patient did not follow my plan.

He would not talk about his grief, and he would not abreact. He seemed to have neither the vocabulary nor the memories to describe his relationship with his parents, and his parallel childhood losses, if any, were shrouded in mist. Instead, he came in and talked about the business.

He did something like what good psychotherapy patients are supposed to do. He said whatever came to mind, without censoring his thoughts. Only what came to mind was whether this or that employee was floundering, what transportation costs were going to be this year, how his competitors were stepping beyond the bounds of fair play, and the like. Some days I felt I was conducting a branch of the local Rotary or Kiwanis. Now and then he talked about his marriage, always in grateful and contented terms: how good his wife was around the house, how lucky he was to have her.

I don't know whether these trains of thought could rightly be called free association. They were more like ordinary conversation, and he expected me to join in. What did I think of this or that development? And he was so ingenuous and direct in his questioning that sometimes I felt compelled to reply.

The treatment drove me wild. Try as I might to change his course, I could not get the bereaved businessman to address the topics he needed to grapple with, and if I insisted I ran the danger of being intrusive. But the patient seemed happy, and he thanked me sincerely at the end of each session.

I brought the case up with a wonderful, idiosyncratic supervisor, a man who had studied Eastern and "primitive" healing techniques and who believed in the mystical power of the healer within. This was the supervisor who had asked me whether I wanted to restore hearing to my deaf patient; I had been assigned to him by my favorite family therapy supervisor, Behnaz Jalali, who I suspect wanted to loosen me up a bit.

Did I like the patient? the mystical supervisor asked. Yes, of course, it was hard not to. I liked him and I sympathized with his hidden grief. Then, said the supervisor, I would not go wrong. He told me to play along and to trust my healing powers. If the man wanted to talk shop, talk shop. The most important element in this therapy, he said, was that I liked the patient. He needed to be liked, and I should not let his divagations disturb me.

And, sure enough, the patient got better. He left therapy with his energy restored, without ever having come to terms with his bereavement or his sense of fragility in a random world; but business and social interests were back on track. He and the wife would always be grateful to me.

I suspected that this man would sooner or later need to confront the meaning of his losses. But there was no arguing with the mystical supervisor; his prediction was right. The man had needed ordinary, general-store-porch conversation – nothing more.

I seemed to need more, though. I was not interested in having magical healing powers. For one thing, I think I felt it was too early for me to cross the oedipal divide. I had trouble with authority in others and I was not comfortable with it in myself, unless I could ascribe it to intellect and effort. Or, more simply, I wanted to have some sense of what was going on. I am not a mystic.

Well, patients just do get better sometimes, even when we do little. But then what required explaining was how the supervisor knew that placebo, if that is what it was, would work in this very case. Besides, it felt to me that I had done something, although not what I had at first set out to do.

To me, it seemed I had acted as a friend might: a particular sort of friend, one well matched to the patient, one open to emotional awareness and yet attuned to the patient's reluctance to talk directly about his pain.

This therapy disturbed me enough that I began in the back of my mind to keep track of therapies—they were not frequent, but when they happened they were striking—in which I achieved good effect with little effort and less help from theory. I did not want to start believing I had guru-like powers, but I did want to make sense of when less is more. I wanted to understand where this seemingly naïve healing came from.

*   *   *   *   *

Some years later, I began calling these treatments "rent-a-friend", an expression I first heard in Washington.

In the final months of residency, I worked at the interface of politics and science at the federal level in the Carter administration. Shortly before my arrival, the Senate Finance Committee, in its capacity of monitoring the Social Security Administration, had elicited testimony about the efficacy of psychotherapy, which was a covered service under Medicare and some Medicaid programs. The key recurrent phrase in the part of the testimony which was hostile to the mental health professions was "rent-a-friend"—shorthand for the accusation that the efficacy of psychotherapy was poorly established. Part of my job as a scientific officer was to counter that calumny with research evidence that psychotherapy works.

I later left the government, ran an academic hospital outpatient unit for some years, and then settled in private practice. It was there that I found myself, to an extent far beyond what I had anticipated, standing in a supportive role toward patients. As I considered how I felt about that posture, the expression "rent-a-friend" returned and troubled me. Was I no more than a hired friend for the psychically wounded? What did "rent-a-friend" mean anyway? The phrase is an oxymoron, the essence of friendship being, in the ideal case, indifference to recompense. The implicit accusation is not really that psychotherapy is no better than renting a friend—after all, one does not rent friends—but that rented friendship is just what psychotherapy is. And, of course, what one does rent is whores. That was where the phrase got its political punch.

The accusation is so threatening because in certain cases it seems we are hired friends. Here is a case I thought a good deal about:

A father called me to ask whether I would see his estranged teenaged daughter, an incorrigible delinquent. She was a bright middle-class young woman who in early adolescence had reacted badly to a family crisis and had gone on to misuse drugs, suffer abuse from boyfriends to the point where she was in effect prostituted by them to other men, undergo repeated abortions, and attempt suicide. I did not have time in my schedule for another acting-out borderline, so I told the father I would only see his child once, in order to advise whether she needed hospitalization.

She took an immediate liking to me. Something made me wonder whether the young woman's rage was not a confused and bitter response to unrecognized depression, so I started her on tricyclics (surely this was not the only true intervention?) and began to listen to her story, not just for one session but many.

Wanting to become an object of neither rage nor dependent love, I made myself little known except now and then to diffuse the transference. When on occasion things threatened to get out of hand, I quietly asked the patient whether she had not considered one or another practical course of action. She broke up with her boyfriend, put a new lock on her door, changed her phone number, and entered a course of study in which she moved rapidly to the top of the class. On graduation, she took an appropriate job and received promotions and raises.

I encouraged these changes (though never with such enthusiasm as to suggest they might be done for the sake of my approval), but I had no inkling of their origin. Borderlines are so notoriously hard to change, and this one had been a hellion. My role was—what? I monitored her progress, waiting for the moment when my professional skills would be called upon, the moment when her sham recovery would fall apart, when success would be intolerable and abuse required. The young woman continued to experience rage at others and to harm herself in small ways—she could still properly be labeled borderline—but the course of her daily life bore almost no resemblance to her self-destructive past.[1]

I did not meet with the parents, I ventured no dynamic interpretations and no paradox, I proffered no prognosis except a wrong one. I did not even see my work in the context of traditional models of supportive therapy. Supportive therapy can mean many things: the prevention of deterioration in otherwise helpless cases, the attribution of medical explanations to psychiatric disease in disturbed patients, and, most commonly, the use of dynamic therapy modified so as to diminish the degree of anxiety or frustration experienced by the patient. I don't know that I even provided much admiration or focused on her diminished sense of self. I had no explicit theoretical framework at all.

And yet discharging the patient was the farthest thing from my mind. I was "locked into" the patient, I understood that my presence was a requirement for her mysterious progress.

But this time, as opposed to the case in residency of the man who would not grieve, I did have some general sense of what was going on.

My insight into the process came from my experience of the treatment. To me, the therapy felt nothing like friendship. It was hard work. I found myself jumping, carefully or recklessly, from one posture to another to anticipate and counter the patient's impulses and expectations. I was like a log-roller, constantly readjusting to keep even a tenuous footing. The pace was too fast, balance unsteady, hard knocks always a threat. I suppose friendship may have this quality for people for whom any small loss elicits devastating inner states, but then my job was to move like such a friend while maintaining an intentionality always directed at the well-being of the other and without constant regard for myself.

Hans Sachs' famous reply to the rent-a-friend question of an earlier era was: "Ah, perhaps so, but where would you find such a friend?"[2] This answer seems to me essentially correct if one adds that the sense of the other being a friend is held only by the patient. To the therapist the experience has none of the gratification of ordinary friendship; any gratification is quite as professional and at least as hard-earned as that which one achieves through pharmacotherapy.

[111]

The nonspecific hypothesis of psychotherapy efficacy holds that therapeutic influence occurs not through the application of a discrete body of theory but through certain factors common to all therapies: respect, warmth, and empathy. But this dichotomy fails to encompass the sort of intervention which underlies the success of the rent-a-friend therapy with a borderline.

A good deal of what we do is neither specific, in the narrow sense of arising from a given psychotherapeutic school, nor nonspecific, where nonspecific means acting through the creation of expectancy, but rather a third thing which I might call "psychiatric" or, in the case of psychologists, nurses, or social workers, "professional." In the work with the borderline young woman, the most evident such skill was the maintenance of proper social distance with a patient in whom issues of isolation and engulfment were prominent. Psychiatric or professional skills are learned. They include expertise in patient management, familiarity with illness and crisis, judgment about ego strength and other non-nosologic diagnostic issues, and a host of other abilities related to our doctorly self-image and behavior.

Hope of these skills is a major reason patients turn to us. These qualities are not dogma-specific but neither are they innate nor restricted to the capacity to feel what the patient feels. They are the result, though rarely the focus, of professional training and experience.

At least this is how I comfort myself: rent-a-friend (this sort, anyway) is skilled work. There is nothing mystical about what the therapist does, nor does he require special healing powers. But the skills the rent-a-friend draws on are so much a part of us that we are scarcely aware of them when we put them to use.

This does not mean that the cures in these therapies are not magical; they are. The magic is this: the therapist sticks with the patient, and somehow this persistence allows the patient to alter her self-image, mood, and behavior.

* * * * *

But this justification may seem not to apply to every case of rent-a-friend. What about the bereaved businessman? Was I dancing this way and that to avoid a settled transference there?

Another therapy from recent years gave me some further purchase on

[112]

that case from residency. In this recent work, I seemed almost absent from the therapeutic process.

The patient was a mildly obsessional (anxious/dysthymic) man. He more or less conducted his own brief psychoanalysis in my office, with little more than a grunt or a nod of encouragement on my part, and achieved not only insight but substantial gains in his marriage and his career. He rented my time, but I had only to sit quietly for him to do his work.

At last there came a point at which the patient began to express anger at me. Yes, his life had changed for the better in remarkable ways, but how could I justify billing him when I did so little?

I felt the force of this complaint. And yet almost before I understood what I intended to do, I found myself making my first substantial interpretation: that the patient was experiencing me as his overly passive father. In retrospect I saw the earlier progress as based on my having taken on a role in the oedipal constellation. I had silently legitimized the patient's reclusive father over and against his intrusive and dominating mother, and this change in the balance of power had allowed him to examine himself and his hostility toward the mother.[3]

I had imagined that I had done nothing more than create a neutral arena, but in truth I also supplied a figure on whom to project. In general, treatments in which the therapist participates simply by "creating the setting" seem to me cases of the therapist's taking on a particular role as the other, namely the unintrusive other.[4]

There are, it seems to me now, many therapies in which the most important thing the therapist does is to assume a certain posture vis-à-vis the other. These two more recent cases, the one in which I felt like a log-roller and the one in which I was truly passive, define the range of this stance along one axis. There is, it seems to me, no comprehensive explanation for the effectiveness of these therapies of stance; or rather, there are a number of explanations which apply more or less in different instances.

I think, for example, of how I now sometimes behave toward divorced patients. After a divorce, a person may need to understand that he is acceptable even in grief and dislocation, and that the self which existed before the fights began is still discernible amidst the disorder. The therapist tolerates all aspects of the other and lets it be known that he sees the continuous self. We may understand this sort of treatment in terms of Kohut's mirror transference; what is provided is the gleam of admiration in the parent's eye.

Or consider the opening phase of work with self-punitive patients. There the temptation is to interpret the actions of the overactive super-ego early on, even before a therapeutic alliance has been formed. The danger is that interpretation will be felt as further punishment, which may drive the patient away or, almost as bad, ally him with the therapist through grateful masochism.

Often a better strategy is to empathize with the patient's suffering over his torture at the hands of his judgmental self. Indeed, it may be necessary to go far out of one's way to avoid being the "brilliant" parent who provided the superego energy in the first place. Sitting with the patient in pain and incomprehension may feel like the polar opposite of what a therapist should do, especially when many obvious interpreta-tions come readily to mind. It strains our definition of our role to avoid playing the therapist. And yet, without quite knowing why, we may find ourselves paralyzed and unable to interpret, which may be just as well. Mere "moral support" within the therapy hour may begin treatment on a sound footing and even obviate the interpretations one was so eager to make.

I think we recognize what transpires in such cases as a form of counterprojection, a refusal on the therapist's part to take on the role expected, and provided, by the patient. We are familiar with work of this sort from the teachings of Harry Stack Sullivan and Franz Alexander.

Of the "corrective emotional experience," Alexander writes: "The pa-rental intimidation is corrected by the more tolerant and sympathetic attitude of the therapist, who replaces the authoritarian parents in the patient's mind. As the patient realizes that his modest self-assertion will not be punished, he will experiment more boldly. At the same time he can express himself more freely toward persons in authority in his present life."[5]

Alexander correctly points out that as the model relationship is being enacted there can be a synergism between changes in and outside of the office. But it seems to me the changes must begin in the office. Only after the patient feels confident, because he has experienced the accepting other in the form of the therapist, does he have the wherewithal to behave differently in the "real world."

Some of these therapies, in which the psychiatrist assumes the role of a particular other and the change begins right in the office, have a mechanism of action so self-evident that it seems at once to defy explanation and to make explanation superfluous. I once treated a socially impaired patient who imagined no therapist could tolerate her, so that the chief active ingredient early in therapy was the existence of the therapy. Her first adult relationship took place right in the office, and the gentle, unintrusive doctor-patient script was just the right one for her, providing about as much of another person as she could allow herself. This was one instance in which I believed in the therapeutic value of paying for treatment; the fact that this patient could compensate someone for bearing her presence made the meetings possible for her.

Here to explain the mechanism of action we barely require even the notion of transference. We might say that I acted as the ideal parent, or some such thing, but I think it would be fairer to say that the treatment acted through the "real relationship," that is, through the patient's accurate appreciation of my concern and through our friendly social intercourse—with these *caveats*: first, I did not behave towards her just as I would on meeting her in the world outside the office. This "real relationship" is not the ordinary one between acquaintances or friends; it involves the maintenance of the therapist role. And second, she would not have been able to tolerate our interacting at all outside the therapetic setting. It was only the artificiality (the unreality) of that situation which made a "real relationship" possible.

We may now return to the case of the bereaved businessman and ask how the magic worked. Perhaps he caught the gleam of admiration in my eye (or, more likely, we enjoyed what Kohut would label an "alter-ego transference"). Or perhaps I created a corrective emotional experience by acting as a tolerant father in contradistinction to the judgmental one whose loss the son was ambivalently suffering. But to me it felt more that I acted as what Sullivan calls a chum. If anything tranferential occured, I was the good father his father really was, back for a few more weeks so that the son could chat with him a bit longer and come to terms with his absence.

Or we could say that the businessman came empathically to sense some yet more real relationship between himself and me—that he understood we both had difficulty crossing the oedipal divide, moving from son to father, and that the sharing of this struggle eased his transition. Perhaps this explanation sounds far-fetched. Perhaps they all do. These quasi-friendships, real enough in some respects, but tailored on the basis of our professional judgment or empathy and made possible because of the maintenance of a professional setting, seem hardly to require explication.

*   *   *   *   *

I might simply have said that all these therapies are troubling because we as therapists appear to be doing too little. But there are other therapies in which we equally seem rented friends but in which the disturbance to our sense of professional identity has just the opposite source: we seem to be doing too much.

Doing too much covers a host of sins. These include lending perspective or judgment (I cannot bring myself to write "giving advice"), recognizing and enjoying patients' successes, creating a forum for the discussion of concrete practical concerns, and, on a very rare occasion, even rising to action.[6]

I have in mind as an example a therapy conducted under an odd agreement I entered into when caring for a college student with family in a distant city. He had been treated there by eminent therapists whom the parents trusted more than they did me. When he suffered a minor break while on campus, I was asked to intervene in a limited role. Everyone wanted the student to pass his courses. No one intended for me to form a deep alliance—too much danger of competing with the real experts. Even changes in drug regimen were taboo: exam time was approaching and side effects might ruin the whole semester.

I wish I could write, "Never again," but I am ashamed to admit I agreed to this arrangement a second time with the same student when another crisis arose the following year. Once more, I encouraged, cajoled, set limits, supplemented judgment, advised on decisions, and smiled and became teary-eyed along with the confused young man. Rent-a-friend is just what I was, but not merely though my posture as a chum or a figure on whom to project a certain sort of transference. I did things; or perhaps I should say I substituted for those parts of the ego crippled by a psychotic process. Both times the young man passed his exams. The second time he recovered substantially and went on to succeed in his studies for a period without further treatment.

I think it is hard to spend much time in the business of psychotherapy without coming now and again to play this waiting game, hoping for an illness to run its course or for certain fears, of separation or competition or intimacy, to diminish in the face of success in the "real world" outside the consulting room. Sometimes we only try to keep the patient's head above water in hopes that the tide will carry him to happier seas. If we can buy the patient time, the healing elements of daily life—friendship, career success, the experience of putting together a few quiet months—will do their work. Paradoxically, treatment of this sort is less appropriate for the most unfortunate; we are counting on the environment to be benign.

We will no doubt classify these therapies as supportive and talk of supplying supplements to ego *lacunae* and the like. But I wonder whether we can lean even on this remnant of theory. These busy treatments sometimes arise with patients who seem quite healthy and whose egos are strong and relatively imperforate.

I think of therapies in which we help nature along with an expression of doubt or a mild social hint of precisely the sort a good friend might proffer: "Perhaps you come off as a bit urgent," said to an overanxious suitor. The effect of these comments is not so much insight as authority lent to encourage one action over another.

Indeed, the patient may already know he presses women too hard, or on the contrary he may be quite haughty about his social expertise and well defended against interpretations about his character. But if he can just this once exercise restraint, he may then find himself in a relationship which has its own softening effect on urgency or contempt.

These "friendly" comments are helpful not just for socially awkward patients. I use them for patients who have been well analyzed by other therapists but have somehow not managed to translate their insights into new behaviors. Here the new therapist lends social judgment or perspective in the hopes of helping the patient over a stumbling block and into a developmental role for which he is adequately prepared, if only he can get started. But whether we want to call this a case of supplementing an

[117]

ego function is hard to say—and if we do, how do we justify support in so healthy a patient? When therapists enter brief therapy as patients it is often for help of this sort. I once reentered treatment for just such a firm push and got it, with good results. I did not so much learn something new intrapsychically as begin new habits.

*   *   *   *   *

These therapies violate neutrality, a principle in which psychoanalysis and its admiring younger sibling, psychodynamic psychotherapy, are firmly grounded. Strictly speaking, neutrality means the therapist must resist the temptation to favor one side of a psychic conflict over another. Some exegists, beginning with Anna Freud, even demand neutrality as between psychic structures—avoid supporting the ego over the super-ego—although her father sometimes wrote that the therapist must ally firmly with the ego.

In the "too active" variety of rented friend therapies, we go out of our way to violate neutrality and, for instance, to encourage the id at the expense of the superego.

I once treated a professionally competent woman sorely handicapped by avoidant personality disorder with obsessional features, on the basis of abuse by one parent and neglect by the other throughout childhood. This patient was so meek and wounded that I found myself having to supply rage for her, and even sadness at times, mobilizing feelings toward her parents in the hopes that her emotional spectrum would broaden generally. This was a highly intelligent and introspective woman for whom traditional dynamic therapy might have been expected to work, but it turned out I had to encourage the development of an emotionally more vital person (that is, to act on behalf of her id and do battle with her punitive superego) before the therapy could begin.

To give a more common example: how often does it happen with obsessional, inhibited patients that as the affectless patient tells a sad story, the therapist tears up—and this demonstration of emotion (siding with ego and id against superego) allows the patient to realize he is depressed and then to feel depressed?[7]

Other rented friend therapies violate strictures against suggestion and seduction. We are a profession which contains schools of treatment with clear standards for productive work. Common to these schools is disdain for unfocused or merely kindly interactions, "seduction" or "suggestion," the false sirens tempting to therapists lacking in self-awareness.

Just what constitutes suggestion and seduction is a dicey matter. In my early training, and here I include my own psychoanalysis, almost any action on the therapist's part which strayed from the routine of silence, clarification, and interpretation was suspect, nor were all silences, clarifications, and interpretations beyond suspicion. That is, they might arise from the therapist's neurotic need for self-gratification, not excluding that doctorly infirmity for which Freud had disdain, *furor sanandi*, the self-indulgent hunger for cure.

Scruples about seduction, suggestion, and therapeutic zeal must go by the boards in these less defined therapies. There is too much action altogether for us to avoid using our self and our particular presence as therapeutic instruments.

In many rent-a-friend therapies, if we are to remain neutral and at the same time avoid the patient's rage, we will have to do a lot of work. If my log-rolling therapy with the borderline young woman was neutral, it was so only because I did not stand still long enough to allow the transference to mature. The fault was precisely that my actions were too energetically neutral, which is to say too zealous, too active, and ultimately, despite my neutrality, seductive.

So it is not just from outside the field, from the Senate Finance Committee, that we learn mistrust for rent-a-friend therapies. They break so many of our own most fundamental rules that it is difficult for us to be comfortable with ourselves in them.

I referred in the previous chapter to the extra anxiety inherent in the directionlessness of supportive therapy. More even than other aspects of modern eclectic psychiatry, supportive treatment is psychotherapy without maps. From our own theoretical vantage it is suspect, in practical terms it is difficult, and I suppose it is fair to ask why anyone does it at all. The persistence of support arises from the needs of patients, mediated by a doctorly posture which does not allow us to ignore the call of those needs.

At least it seems this way in my practice. I rarely enter a treatment aiming to rely on support; if an exploratory approach does not flow naturally from the patient's and my early conversations (and whether this happens is not just a function of diagnosis or ego strength), I look for a mechanism, a technique, a theory-driven tool which will give me purchase on the patient or the disorder, and only after we have danced a while do I content myself with this other ill-defined treatment. It is in this sense that I understand these therapies to arise from the patient as much as the doctor.

In the face of our own and others' hostility to the too-ordinary relationships in these therapies, I find little protection in theory. I grasp instead for some weak sense of what fits with what. For instance, if I am aware of working to stand in a certain posture toward the patient, I will not become too anxious if he takes some time in changing his behavior outside the office; and if I am actively suggesting and cajoling, I will not worry too much if the transference in the office has gone all to hell.

* * * * *

For me, the inner availability of these vague categories (therapy of stance *versus* therapy of concrete help, magic inside *versus* magic outside the office) helps alleviate the anxiety of loss of theory. Rent-a-friend therapies, in my way of classifying and justifying them, involve a disassembly of psychoanalysis and free use of the spare parts. Loose notions of transference and of psychic structures and their deficits dominate these explanations to myself, but the elements are used without regard to the rules with which they emerged and are mixed with other theories regarding generational boundaries, developmental tasks, differentiation of self, and the like.

The difficulty with supportive therapy, informed by bits and pieces of many theories and constrained by no overarching one, is that it is hard to keep within bounds. Even the relatively loose categories to which I have alluded immediately turn out to be too limited.

Some therapies seem to call for an all-court press. The work with the bird-loving borderline retarded young woman, recounted in the previous chapter, involved taking on a father role in many of its aspects—supplying admiration, ego support, and authority for judgment while monitoring the transference and social distance—and hoping for growth as much within the office as without.

Put differently, psychotherapy is that enterprise which always spills over its bounds—because the governing principle, for therapist as well as patient, is attention to reality. Reality is a funny word for a psychiatrist to use. What I have in mind is some ordinary, everyday way of seeing things—but then an adequate theory should surely encompass this point of view. I suppose what I mean is that there is no substitute for a psychiatrist's acting on his beliefs even when they contravene convention. Tendencies toward self-aggrandizement and self-gratification must always be monitored, but in the end there is no substitute for acting as one sees fit.

I think, for example, of a funny—but only in retrospect and in truth perhaps not ever—thing that happened to a medical school housemate of mine during her first psychiatric interview. She was assigned a man said to have marital troubles, and she interviewed him in front of a one-way mirror.

When she asked why he had come in, the patient answered with something about his wife and child and then "my foot." My housemate ignored this last crazy interjection, but it arose repeatedly as the structured interview—past psychiatric history, family medical history, and so on—progressed. Finally, after perhaps the sixth interruption, she asked the man why he kept mentioning his foot.

"I felt so desperate that before I came in here I stabbed myself in the foot," he said, pleased at finally being heard. As he removed his shoe, blood came rushing out, as did the supervisor from behind the mirror, and the man was whisked off to the E.R. for urgent care, having enhanced our appreciation of the need to hear the patient in an ordinary way, unfiltered by theory, plan, and fixed expectations.

There is no substitute for acting on what we see, hear, and feel.

I say this as advance apology for a final vignette on the subject of rent-a-friend, one which illustrates the strengths and dangers of bringing such ad hoc therapeutic camels into our professional tent.

A few years after residency, I served as director of outpatient psychiatry for a group of university-affiliated hospitals. I came to treat an overweight, awkward college student, the son of wealthy, renowned, and accomplished parents residing in the Midwest. He was inordinately, and of course ambivalently, attached to these powerful parents, who had never met his needs and whose achievements he could never match.

These cases are all too common; anyone who practices in a college town will have seen more than one student who fits this description. What varies is the degree of parental neglect, if any, and the extent and locus of the child's pathology. In this instance, both parents were narcissistic and had problems with alcohol, and the young man suffered substantial difficulty with identity formation. He was intelligent and imaginative, and he had succeeded in his course work at college; but he remained socially isolated and repeatedly engaged in immature, self-defeating behavior.

The moment I have in mind occurred during a school vacation. Therapy had gone well, and the young man had at last begun to form a life for himself away from home. For the first time, he had reason to remain in town over vacation time, working on a project away from the school.

The patient had medical problems and had recently developed an acute but poorly defined pain syndrome for which he was treated by internists about whose skill I was uncertain. In the middle of one night, I received a call from one of our affiliated hospitals; the young man was in the emergency room requesting pain medication. Did I think he was addicted and drug-seeking? This opinion was the one held by patients' internists, whom the E.R. doctor had already called.

A psychiatrist has mixed emotions in these circumstances. Whether or not he was drug-seeking, the patient had reason to be care-seeking. He was lonely and isolated and pulled by whatever forces in the "undifferentiated family mass" cause unhappy children to have trouble staying away from their parents. I said I thought the hospital would do best just to treat the medical problem at face value; we would have time to deal with its meaning.

The pain did not respond to large doses of sedatives and analgesics. The next thing I knew, I was awakened by a long distance call from the patient's father. He was considering sending a private plane to have the young man flown to a distinguished hospital near the family's home. The father was particularly concerned about the hint of drug abuse.

I said I doubted drug abuse was an issue, and I added I believed the problem could be handled here locally. I did not know how the father would respond; he was used to dealing with doctors more eminent than I. And in the small hours of a night in which the son was in crisis, I did not want to introduce issues of the young man's need for independence from the family. Despite my fatigue, I must have been persuasive; the father agreed to let the son be treated by an internist of my choosing. I next heard that the young man had left the emergency room in disgust and gone back to his lodgings.

The following morning I arranged for the patient to be examined by a top-flight doctor practicing in our city. When the father called me again, I was able to say that his son would see me that afternoon and go directly from my office to the new internist's. The father said he would call the internist later in the day to see how things had gone.

The problem was this: the young man did not show up for his appointment at my office. Nor did he answer his telephone when I called.

The question was what to do at this juncture.

I had a clear sense of what had happened. Far from being addicted, the young man had a normal tolerance to sedatives. He was now lying asleep in his room, knocked out by his treatment at the E.R. the night before. I also had a vision of what would happen next. The father would call and discover the son had not visited the internist. The young man would be rescued in dramatic fashion, and his small gesture of independence would be ruined, all because of the reasonable, but to my mind mistaken, judgment of various doctors.

Now, I know it can be said things should never have come to this pass. Perhaps I should have established a better relationship with the parents earlier, or arranged consultation with the top-flight internist sooner, or gone to the emergency room the night before, or been firmer with the E.R. staff, or dealt with the father differently on the phone, or discouraged the patient from remaining at school over break in the first place. On the other hand, I had believed the present issue for the patient was formation of an independent identity; I did not believe the parents could or should be drawn into treatment; and I had made a series of judgments each of which seemed reasonable at the time, and even in retrospect. Or rather, I suppose the point is that one just does find oneself in these situations, and the question then is what to do next.

The standard choices in this instance were to do nothing and let the patient take the consequences for his actions, or to call the police and have them rouse the patient and make certain he was not in danger. I believed either alternative would at best result in the parents' rescuing the young man; at worst, things could get very complicated. In the event, I did something the rankest beginner is told to avoid: I went to rescue him myself.

All my training told me to hold off. We know to beware of rescue fantasies, of competition with parents, of competition with colleagues, of urges for action, of special care for the the child of a V.I.P. family. These are our nonspecific rules, the general heritage we subscribe to. We know better than to act in certain circumstances; we know better than to act in certain ways.

To understand exactly why I made my decision one would have to know many more particulars: the diagnosis (not borderline), what I thought of the patient's past and present relationships with the parents, the symbolic importance of the stay in town, my assessment of the risks of dependency in the therapy, and my assessment of my own motives.

I chose to rescue the patient, and I considered this action a legitimate part of the therapy. I drove to his address, banged on the door until I roused him, directed him to the shower, and drove him to the appointment with the internist.

How could I have made this choice? Can I envisage Max—or any of my teachers—driving across town to throw a patient into the shower?

Believe me (writing that phrase I see I must doubt my credibility), I have treated dozens of borderlines in need of rescue without ever stirring from my chair. "No one can prevent you from killing yourself," I say. I treat patients with avoidant personality disorder without trying to find them friends. To the depressed, I say, "That must be hard to bear." To the repetitively self-defeating, I say, "I wonder why you put yourself in that position." But with this young man, I thought the experiment in independence was crucial to his recovery, and I did not want to see him pay a disproportionate price for his care-seeking.

The young man came to see me briefly at the end of the day. He had been diagnosed with a quite physical, quite treatable, quite painful medical condition, and placed on an appropriate analgesic regimen. He was able to complete his project in town and then continue at school.

Would I replace his parents? Would I be a friend? Would I rescue him always? These issues might have dominated subsequent treatment, but they did not. The patient was so used to having things done for him that my showing up at his door seemed less out of the ordinary to him than

[124]

it might have to another; his naïve expectation of entitlement to care may have been part of what made him seem a drug-seeker to the E.R. doctors and the first group of internists. And if I had to deal with hope and fear of dependency—well, we deal with these issues often enough anyway.

I see I have not described the prior therapy with the young man. Of course, it was of the rented friend sort, subtype "lending parts of the self" and "hoping for growth in the world." Though he appeared to trust me as much as he did anyone, the young man seemed not psychically built for exploration. I did something like interpretive work with him. I pointed out that whenever he saw his parents he became unnerved and began behaving in certain unproductive ways—that sort of thing. The interpretations related to external patterns more than to speculation about internal fantasy.

And this sort of therapy continued for some time after my having, more or less, thrown the patient in the shower. Then came a period of complaining on his part. Why did our work lack direction? Was there no more to psychotherapy than this? Always I replied by asking him why he did not bring more to the hours himself.

One day he ended a session with some bitterness. Why did I not, he asked, question him about specific incidents from his childhood like . . . And the example he gave was a story.

It concerned an event from early childhood. A friend was visiting, and they played together while the patient's parents were drunk and fighting upstairs. The friend's mother came to retrieve her son, and instead of calling his parents the patient—age five is what he said; must he have been older?—shut the bedroom door and ran to deliver the playmate at the front door. He spoke with the mother and said they had spent a lovely afternoon and would the boy please come again. But the friend's mother kept asking questions. And as she was about to leave she saw through a window the drunken faces of the patient's parents. So she came back in to see if she could be of help. The patient was mortified.

"How could she barge into our family like that?" he demanded, with more emotion than I had heard in our months of work.

It was, as I have said, the end of an hour, but I made the interpretation anyway: I was that mother, sticking my big nose into his family's affairs. As is often a case in these circumstances, the family placed a high premium on loyalty—a classic requirement for the double bind—and loyalty had even, in the son's mind, included proscriptions against his acknowledging his pain to himself or to me.

I was, I can tell you, delighted and relieved. And the degree of relief was for me an indicator of just how hard it is to be in the position of rented friend. It is never pleasant to face the negative transference, particularly not early in a therapy. But, to me at that point in the treatment, any evidence of symbolism and unconscious emotional forces right in the session was welcome. This is our bread and butter. We know how to do that work—where it leads and how it proceeds. What a relief to put rent-a-friend behind us.

I had been very much the intruder the afternoon I woke the young man from his drugged sleep. But I still doubt any other choice would have resulted in a therapy; nor do I think there was an alternative to the long period of support before our engagement. It was not just that the patient needed for me to demonstrate my *bona fides*; he had to experience a degree of independence, of differentiation of self on the basis of "good experience," before he could face the ghosts. It was the therapeutic effect of rent-a-friend that made more traditional therapy possible.

Rent-a-friend therapies provide welcome surprises of this sort. But for the most part I think they are the hardest treatments for us as therapists to bear. The popular accusations against our work are that it is soft, unscientific, nonmedical, of uncertain duration, and poorly differentiated from other helpful human relationships. Within the profession, our common self-accusations are of self-indulgence and soft-mindedness. We are most vulnerable to turning these criticisms against ourselves when we find ourselves in chartless terrain.

Conscious attention to this issue has made me less defensive about behaviors much more openly supportive or directionless than those which disturbed me in residency. There are occasions when acting as a rented friend is just the thing we ought to do. This role is often justifiable on dynamic, strategic, cognitive, and other grounds, even when the therapy is not recognizably of any of these schools. I mean, we see patients' dilemmas through fitting them to various templates (the way we "just understand" what a patient needs is not random), though the actions we craft for the situation at hand may bear little resemblance to those usually associated with the theory of mind under which we come to act. And because of who people are and what they need, sometimes what we will craft is a "craftless" relationship which, seen from the outside, looks more like friendship than like medical care.

Nor is it true that just anyone (a friend) could take this role. Rent-a-friend therapies rest on professional skills. Our judgment as to diagnosis, ego fragility, tolerance of intimacy, and gaps in psychic structure, and our skills in listening, modulating transference, and applying the hundreds of particular interventions in the psychiatric armamentarium—all these and more are called on in supportive therapy. When examined carefully, from the therapist's vantage, there is no mistaking it for friendship. If anything, I would guess rent-a-friend is an area where theory lags practice, where we know well what we are doing without being able to say in a systematic way what that is. These are precisely the circumstances in which there is plenty of room for legitimate doubt. How do we know we are not going too far?

What do we make of my more or less throwing my patient in the shower? Is it therapy or is it not? But even before we reach that question I think there will be disagreement as to whether it is out of the ordinary or not.

To some psychiatrists, such behavior is acting out on the part of the therapist, a form of self-gratifying behavior which indicates unresolved neurotic needs. This accusation is possibly accurate and in any event impossible to contradict. To psychiatrists from more active schools the intervention will barely merit mention. Why express self-doubt over engaging in the kind of rough-and-tumble the therapist should probably have started much earlier in the course of treatment, to move things along?

It is this sort of disagreement which makes the field of supportive treatments particularly hard to map. We cannot even agree as to whether we are in *ultima Thule* or very near home. It becomes difficult to distinguish routine treatment from charlatanism.

And yet if the demand to risk this danger arises from needs of patients, we are obliged to consider it, whatever unease the exercise may cause us. All of medicine revolves around the dialectic between theory and praxis, between the order of science and the messiness of the individual case. Though it concerns what seem the least technical and the least justifiable of our interventions, the question of whether to act as a rented friend is a thoroughly doctorly dilemma.

[127]

Is Empathy Necessary?

It seems it must be.

As patients, how would we experience a therapy in which we believed the therapist never felt empathy for us? Yet again to be mistaken, not seen, not recognized, not apprehended in the other's heart: how damaging to our sense of self-worth.

Some schools of therapy, and here I have most in mind self psychology, today promote empathy as the first and essential tool, the *sine qua non* of any effective human contact.

But before we go overboard, we may want to remember that not long ago empathy was the dirty secret of psychotherapy. Throughout most of the history of psychoanalysis, it was heretical to depend on the healing power of the interpersonal relationship. Traditional analysts recognized that superficial change could result from patients' feelings toward therapists, but "transference cure" was a term of opprobrium, an accusation of charlatanism. Deep psychic restructuring was the goal, and to rely too much on empathy—even Kohut said as much in his *Analysis of the Self*— was a sign of narcissism in the therapist, of the omnipotent fantasy that his love suffices for cure.[1]

Therapists have become increasingly aware of the power of empathy. Before the advent of self psychology, the role of empathy was attested to in such key ideas as Franz Alexander's "corrective emotional experience" and Carl Rogers' "unconditional positive regard." Though different, both concepts stand in contrast to the notion of insight as curative, both suggest that healing takes place through the experiencing of a new intimate relationship in adult life, namely the relationship with the therapist in the therapist's office.

Psychotherapy efficacy researchers in the fifties and sixties high-lighted empathy as a potent "nonspecific factor," an element common to all psychotherapies, and one which influenced treatment outcome more than the specific maneuvers to which each (self-deluding) school of treatment attended. Even mainstream psychoanalysis listened to this evidence, and today great attention is paid to the "healing alliance" and the "real relationship."

And while interpretation is still valued, not all interpretations are equal. Analysis of the transference, aided by the empathic phenomenon countertransference, has primacy. Merton Gill has said that if a patient comes to the office twice a week and sits in a chair facing the therapist, but the therapist bases the therapy on transference interpretation, that interchange contains the essence of psychoanalysis; while a five-days-a-week-on-the-couch therapy in which other sorts of interpretation predominate is not psychoanalysis.[2] Freud's early work—his cures through explication of hysterics' overdetermined symptoms—would not qualify.

In short, insight has passed its zenith and the star of empathy, like that of neurobiology, is on the ascendent.

Of the two alternatives to the curative role of insight, the rise of empathy has been less disturbing to psychotherapists, in part because we are inured to sectarian conflicts within psychoanalysis and in part because we have always valued empathy. At least it is so for me. Coming to experience what the patient feels was one of my first ambitions as a therapist. The devaluation of the intellectual functions of mind and of the analysis of trauma is disturbing, but it is partly compensated for by the pleasant discovery that something we have long loved is even more important than we had suspected.

But what of therapies that bypass empathy? Or worse, that bypass insight and empathy alike?

My own ideas about empathy were shaped by two treatments I conducted early in my residency training.

Both were family therapies. They are not profound work, but each is striking in its own way, and they were exciting to me at the time. The therapies are not equal children; I much prefer one, for reasons which are idiosyncratic but which I hope are also of general interest. I will present the cases in some detail, because I think the detail, as well as the contrast between the cases, may help illuminate the way we use the concept of empathy and the different sorts of faith we place in it.

*   *   *   *   *

The first case began when a strikingly beautiful young woman appeared at my office door. Her husband no longer loved her, and she felt suicidal.

I had the advantage of having read her clinic record before she arrived, and I knew that she had done poorly in individual therapy in the past. Schizophrenic, the chart said, probably meaning what used to be called "pseudoneurotic schizophrenia"—the patient looked healthy when you met her but deteriorated dramatically in the course of treatment.

The patient was seriously depressed by textbook standards, but then she had so many symptoms it was hard to know how to weight them. The mood was leavened by a charming histrionic style, and as a resident I liked patients who brought life into my practice. Oh, a male resident could come to grief over this one. At least I would not repeat the last resident's mistake; I would give her no chance to regress.

If only her husband still cared for her. Things had gone well in the honeymoon days of marriage, when the couple smoked dope and held open house for their friends. But then Wendy gave birth to twin girls, and as they grew Rick's ardor cooled.

Following the precepts of strategic family therapy, I used my impotence as my ally. Instead of giving her depression a name or alluding to the character traits which periodically got her into trouble, I agreed with Wendy. The problem was the marriage, and I could help her only if Rick would join the therapy.

He came, "for her sake." He was a dashing and overly smooth young man. "The tie that binds is not love but sadomasochism," a teacher of mine in medical school said repeatedly. At intake meetings this teacher would smile and mutter, in that deadpan voice which passes terrible judgment, "the perfect marriage." Wendy and Rick had a perfect marriage.

Rick confirmed his wife's story. Something's gone wrong with her, he said. She's become too responsible. He still liked to lead the laid-back life; she spent all her time worrying over the kids and the budget.

Rick listed the ways he liked to have fun, each more sexually threatening than the one before. He coached a woman's volleyball team, went out to drink at singles bars—and what he liked best was weeks alone in Las Vegas, where he was a big enough spender to have his own line of credit and a free room on the house.

Vegas, I said. I could see Rick shooting his cuffs and throwing dice. Where do you get the money?

He worked at his father's business, a furrier's shop. He turned his salary earnings over to his wife. But in recent years he had begun also to sell fur coats under the table at high season, around Christmas time, and this cash income, which just about equaled his salary, went into a separate gambling fund. So did the money he made dealing drugs.

Well, this is a classic circumstance in family work—the husband who has not quite married, who maintains two bank accounts and two lives. And the wife whose insecurity makes part of her prefer it that way.

I took my musings into supervision.

The supervisor was Behnaz Jalali, my favorite—a sparkling and creative therapist with a genius for crystallizing hard cases. And this was a hard case, I think, with risks of suicide, violence, and deterioration into psychosis. We were working with functional but fragile people whose dependency was by now most of what held their marriage together.

But beyond the potential for disaster Behnaz saw, as I did, an amusing aspect to the couple's dilemma. The wife was too responsible! We'd see about that.

The problem, Behnaz and I assumed, was that the birth of the twins had upset an equilibrium in the marriage. The husband's fear of adulthood had led him to ever wider and more dangerous exhibitions of his "independence." As he strayed, his wife's inability to stand alone made her more desperate, and consequently less attractive and more vulnerable. The question was how to strengthen her and at the same time induct Rick into fatherhood.

We decided on a paradoxical injunction.

At the next meeting, I told Wendy and Rick that the situation was grave and that I doubted they could do what was necessary to fix things up. (This is standard family therapy talk, of course.) Rick is right, I said. We have to teach Wendy to be less responsible and more immature.

What they should do was this: Rick was planning a gambling trip the next week. Wendy and he should go over his private books and see how

[132]

much he lost on average. She should then accompany him to Las Vegas and lose as much as Rick ordinarily did. Under no circumstance should she come back without having lost enough—her marriage and mental health hung in the balance, and she had to learn to be frivolous.

The intervention was calculated to explode in every direction. It had the form of carrying out Rick's demand that Wendy imitate his irresponsibility. But it would also give Wendy access to Rick's books and might in the long run either curtail the illegal earnings or bring the extra money into the family. (Certainly it would make Rick think twice before filing for divorce against Wendy's wishes.) It would force Wendy to find babysitting for the twins, with whom she was overinvolved and, indeed, teach her how to be less painstaking in a certain sphere. And it would make her sexually threatening again.

I liked the idea of Wendy in the casinos with a fistful of money to lose. She would give Rick something to think about.

A day or two before the trip, the couple returned and laid out their plans. Wendy would lose a certain amount of money—five or six hundred dollars.

I showed anger—a stance Behnaz and I had worked out in advance. Was that the best Wendy would do? Surely the correct amount was well over a thousand dollars. If the couple had decided on six hundred, I would have to accept that figure. But Wendy had better return without a penny of it in her pocketbook. And I ended the session.

Wendy came back cured. She had been unable to lose all her money in the casino, so she had bought an overpriced slinky dress and strolled about, looking in on the craps tables. Rick, poor guy, returned a few hundred ahead. And back in love.

The change in Wendy was striking. She displayed an assured, commonsensical style, leavened by sexual teasing, and she seemed able to enforce her demands in the marriage. For example, she came to realize how much it disturbed her that Rick would lie in bed while she fixed breakfast for the children; now she found the force to get him into the kitchen in the morning.

Wendy's confidence continued to grow. I did only minimal follow-up work. Wendy accepted further instruction in immaturity—she had always wanted to play jazz saxophone, and I encouraged her to take lessons. She began to sit in with a band that played singles bars. Rick began to spend evenings at home.

But most of the cure lay in our one crafted instruction: go to Vegas and lose money.

If anything, our intervention was too effective. Wendy flourished so dramatically that I began to fear for the marriage.

Over a year after treatment stopped, Rick called me complaining that Wendy wanted to leave him. He sounded paranoid and clinically depressed. He was now even more involved with drugs than in the past. He showed up once or twice, but he never really turned into a patient, and my last impression of the couple was that they were about to divorce.

Whether this outcome is desirable in a couples treatment of this sort is hard to say. In individual therapy we congratulate ourselves when a masochistic wife manages to leave a neglectful husband. In family therapy we tend more to wonder whether the marriage couldn't have worked after all.

About a second change there was less cause for ambivalence. One of the twins had been doing poorly—refusing to board the bus for kindergarten, so that her father had to drive her to school (presumably this was the point), and clinging to her sister when she arrived.

After Vegas, the child's school phobia disappeared. The cause of this recovery remained hidden. Perhaps the father's presence at breakfast had something to do with it.

As family theorists, we might say that the girl through her phobia had struggled to pull Rick into the family; once Wendy was able to do that job on her own, the girl was freed to mature. We might even wonder whether Rick had not in a subtle way—I never had frank abuse in mind—been using the girls for a sort of emotional sustenance that more properly needed to come from his wife. When Wendy again caught his attention, he was able to let go of his daughter.

Whatever the reason, the child blossomed steadily. A clear-eyed account of what went on might be: a girl was cured of school phobia and avoidant disorder of childhood by her mother's being sent to a casino.

This issue of empathy in this case is complicated.

To begin with a peripheral question: what do we make of the daughter's recovery? After all, I never met the daughter.

This is a common enough occurrence in family treatments. I have in mind, for example, cases in which a child has exacerbations of a psychosomatic illness in response to tensions between his parents. After evaluating the child, the therapist chooses to treat the parental couple, and when the marriage improves the child's illness abates.

If we want to attribute a curative role to empathy in these cases, we will need a new notion of empathy. After all, the therapist never sees or hears the patient in treatment. The usual empathic relationship between therapist and patient is entirely absent.

We can say that a strength of this approach is precisely that to succeed it need not induce regression in the child or disturb the child's image of his parents by interposing the presence of a stranger. So one can say that to exclude the child from treatment is in its own way an empathic act. More broadly, a family theorist might fairly say: the family, not the child, is the patient. The therapist and family are in an empathic relationship. Perhaps hidden here is the new definition of empathy. But what sort of empathy do we have in mind?

The question is even more striking in the case at hand. Behnaz and I were unaware of the daughter's phobia when we formulated our first intervention. Now, I don't think it was coincidence that the treatment worked out for the child; in diagnosing the family's structure we anticipated our learning of her trouble. But to say we were empathic toward her, or even toward the family in this regard, is stretching the concept. What we had was, I would say, something more intellectual than empathy, namely experience with certain sorts of marriages.

The distinction I am trying to make is, I think, the same one Kohut has in mind when he writes that intuition, and in particular medical diagnostic skill, is "not in principle related to empathy."[3] To collect, consider, and order details rapidly and then to relate them to prior experience or clinical lore is not necessarily a sign of empathy. We might understand and outline a case in this way and then say, "But I wish I could bring myself to feel something for the patient," or, "I wish I had a better sense of what the patient is experiencing."

As for detail, I wonder whether if we had known more about the child we would have done as well. Had the school called initially and said, "We want you to treat a little girl for school phobia," the best and simplest intervention would have been to send the mother off to lose money. But would anyone have been that smart?

The empathy we are familiar with relies utterly on detail. A dreamed word from a forgotten Greek epic, the look of a mother's hat, a trace of a smile at the thought of a child's war toy, a fleeting moment of despair in a long treatment of anxiety—these are the stuff of empathy. What is this new empathy in which information only obscures the picture?

Many a therapy generously extends its good effects to diverse spheres, and it is no doubt a mistake to put too much emphasis on the daughter. Looking only at Rick and Wendy, do we want to attribute a role to empathy in the treatment?

I think we want to say no. I did not sit with Rick and Wendy and come to understand the small distortions that betray the troubled workings of the mind. Even their relationship I apprehended only in broad strokes. Their time with me was almost all evaluation. The treatment consisted of a sentence or two—or else the treatment took place in my absence.

The key intervention was well tailored for Rick and Wendy, but I wonder whether we want to say it partook of the empathic. The tailoring took into account power relations in the marriage, and legal and financial realities, and that wonderful ego strength, sensuality. When a therapist is clever at dodging defenses and forcing a solution, do we say he is exercising empathy? I did not think so at the time. But before closing the discussion we might look at the second strategic family case, one in which the use of empathy was evident.

* * * * *

Jane was a young mother who was psychotically depressed, borderline retarded, and deaf on the basis of congenital rubella. She had recently been divorced by a somewhat more competent deaf man, and her break occurred after she and the children moved back in with her parents. She was referred from an inpatient psychiatric ward, where she had been treated with neuroleptics.

I began seeing her with a signing interpreter. Jane was entirely inaccessible. At the least suggestion of emotion, she closed her eyes and refused to look at the interpreter.

I discussed the story with Behnaz. She suggested I see the woman with her children.

To my surprise, the children did not sign. They had no way of communicating with their mother other than through mime and gesture. For her part, Jane would rap the table and make a gutteral grunt to get the children's attention and then point toward the area where the task to which she wanted them to attend could be carried out.

The children were largely being raised by Jane's parents, who had also never learned to sign. I saw the parents, and before I knew it I was doing family therapy, which seemed the only way to work the case if therapy was to be done at all.

For me, the key family member was the father. He seemed unsympathetic at first — in front of his daughter and her children, he dismissed the deaf as "different from you and me, doctor. They are stubborn, they are suspicious, they don't understand, *they don't listen.*"

I had already learned that the key for me in therapy often is coming to love the bitter parent. So I sat with the father and tried to gauge my reactions to him.

His overt contempt and rejection was accompanied by great protectiveness toward his daughter and vigorous warmth for his grandchildren. I came to perceive in him unexplored feelings of guilt, over having produced a damaged child. His iron-hard rejection of his daughter masked an injury to his self-concept as a parent — and paid her back for the hurt she had caused him.

The therapy contained a mixture of interventions, but I want to focus on what I believe was the central element: my work with the father.

He had been a farmer, but as the city encroached on his land, more and more of his income came from salaried work. This change was another injury. He had come from generations of farmers.

Beyond his muttered disparagement of his daughter, he was not much of a talker. I found I could engage him about farming.

So he and I talked about plants, vegetables mainly, and the cycle of the gardening year. We chatted about peas and how you can put them in the ground on a warm day in February and whether you have to pretreat them with fungicide or whether you can just plant them thickly in broad bands and accept what nature gives you. You will do well enough in the spring and, with the help of a little pea brush, have a row strong enough to support itself.

We talked about the feeling you get when a seedling breaks through the soil, and how much tending is enough and not too much. Some beds you turn over and never step on; sometimes you mulch and sometimes not. Some crops demand cultivating, some have shallow roots and do better without it. Nature has so much to say about how a crop will turn out.

This was metaphorical talk — hypnotic, Milton Erickson style talk — about good enough parenting and good enough farming, too. A man can have things turn out different from what he expected in farming and in parenting and still be a good man, a man full of valuable knowledge and sound instinct.

For weeks, all that happened in therapy was that the family came in and listened to the old man and me talk about plants. It was crazy work, but for some reason I had great faith in it. And the family showed up every time, even in deep snow.

Without a struggle, without the topic being mentioned, the father began to attend a signing class, and for the first time he encouraged signing in the grandchildren. Jane began to care for plants in her room, and when spring came she helped in the garden. She calmed down and was able to find a job outside the home. She was unmedicated. All sign of psychosis had disappeared.

And now the question I want to ask is: are these two therapies the same or are they different? Especially as regards empathy.

I ask in part because I was more comfortable with the second therapy than the first. And much of that comfort stemmed from my ability to use an empathic technique in reaching the father.

For the purposes of the treatment, I became that part of me which was closest to him. I experienced his grief in losing two identities, as father and farmer. I came to love the man, and coming to see the complexity of people we might otherwise dismiss is one of the great pleasures of our work. The therapy was one of approaching and stepping back, of entering into his world and taking distance from it.

In this way the therapy felt analytic. There was that familiar oscillation between experiencing the thing and examining it, even if the examination involved no interpretation and no resolution of the transference. The father came to understand that he was nurturant despite his having produced a deaf child, and the fact that he might have never put this understanding into words, nor ever heard it expressed in therapy, was irrelevant to the feel of the work.

I suppose I am saying something about dynamic therapies—that their essence never was insight nor transference resolution but this alternate use of empathy and distance, intimacy and objectivity, as a means of changing a person's story. And what appealed to me about my work with Jane's family was how closely it conformed to the model of more familiar therapies.

The therapy was comfortable in other ways. It had a nice pace. Change did not come about so fast that I mistrusted it. The family sat patiently for all the time that was needed for the father to repair his faith in himself—faith which was perhaps not terribly damaged in absolute terms, only so damaged as to be ruinous to the daughter after her divorce.

Might this not have been a therapy of meaning after all? Do we imagine that the therapy worked in any fashion other than the father's coming to understand that certain imperfections in the way things turn out in a man's life do not imply utter failure in him? The treatment had all the hallmarks of a cognitive therapy—a therapy of reframing meanings—except the appeal to cognition.

The therapy appeals for other reasons. The patient is so helpless. Deaf, psychotic, mildly retarded, rejected by her father. Listing the disabilities I am reminded of De Quincey's discussion of the number of commas appropriate to Milton's famous list of indignities in *Samson Agonistes*: "Eyeless in Gaza, at the mill with slaves." Jane's disabilities are more real, according to a self-righteous medical model, than those of "pseudoneurotic schizophrenia"; they cry out to the physician in us. Beware any psychiatric diagnosis containing the prefix "pseudo."

As I sat with the farmer father, healing seemed to come from within me. I had devised the treatment, I had formed the therapeutic alliance; it was I, not just as a psychiatrist but as a person, who was a gardener and could talk about plants; it was I who transferred confidence in my own nurturance to the father. And who would not like through his own powers to make over a father as more nurturant?

The appeal of the daughter's wounds, the congruence of the father's love of gardening with my own, even the family's and my mutual comfort with a leisurely pace of change and an appeal to the father's sense of dignity—these factors can all be seen as elements of an empathic treatment. For the moment we might want to say that what distinguishes this treatment can be summed up by the word empathy.

* * * * *

But how are we using the word empathy?

In a recent essay, Howard Book proposes a distinction between "empathy" and "being empathic."[4] Empathy is a preconscious, intrapsychic perceptual state in the therapist (Kohut called it a "mode of cognition which is specifically attuned to the perception of complex psychological configurations"),[5] while being empathic refers to therapeutic acts based on empathy. And this would be a nice distinction if we could maintain it.

But patients tend to apprehend when we have empathy, so that merely having empathy in therapy can be a type of action. (Think back, for example to my coming to appreciate the mother of the stubbornly mute young man in the chapter "Silence"; there was an instance where having empathy instantly became being empathic, without any further action on my part. Or think of what therapy is like if a patient comes intuitively to understand we have no empathy for him; there our perception or cognition becomes an act all too quickly.) Having empathy often becomes being empathic, in a way that is out of our control.

And as for acts based on empathy, well, what sorts of acts might these be? We may, on an empathic basis, come to understand that a patient needs medication; is prescribing medication, if that is how we come to the decision, then "being empathic"? Or would that depend on whether we acted in a kindly or authoritarian way during the process of prescribing? Assuming, which may not at all be the case, that it is through empathy that Behnaz and I arrived at the decision to send Wendy to Vegas, was that behavioral prescription "being empathic"? To Wendy? To Rick? To the avoidant twin daughter whom I had never met? (Surely a sociopath's heartless acts are not empathic, even if he pulls them off by using his attunement to complex psychological configurations.)

Book seems at first to want to distinguish kindness from empathy: "Empathy is often confused with sympathy, kindness, and approval." But then, in defining being empathic, he says it has a "positive valence" and

[140]

"results in the patient's feeling understood and soothed." Can acts which, on the contrary, rile the patient qualify as "being empathic"? I have heard it said that Franz Alexander's patients often left therapy angry at him, because he so firmly blocked their dependency. If so, was he being empathic, or not?

So here, to begin with, are two distinctions which are difficult to maintain and yet difficult to forsake: the feeling or cognition of empathy *versus* acts arising from that mental state; and, regarding empathic action, doing whatever is needed *versus* behaving with interpersonal warmth.

Leston Havens divides empathy into types depending on the part of the therapist which is engaged.[6] He distinguishes motor empathy, in which one takes on the patient's posture; cognitive empathy, in which one thinks as the patient does and can complete the patient's sentences; affective empathy, in which one feels what the patient feels or what the patient's feeling state elicits; and perceptual empathy, in which one sees the patient anew.

One might also distinguish empathies according to whether they are sympathetic or reactive—separating the depression one feels in the face of depressed patients from the desire one feels near hysterical patients. I mean, one may feel what the patient himself feels, as in the glow manics elicit; or on the contrary one may feel something quite different in response to the patient's urgent affect, such as the *Praecox Gefühl* elicited by schizophrenia or anger elicited by certain masochists. In one instance we are able to say, "I know how you must feel"; in the other, "I can see why people might respond to you that way."

Or is empathy something that goes beyond feelings in response to another's feelings? Is it a posture one takes toward another person, akin to civility or deference or respect? I remember a few years ago hearing Leston Havens and Hyman Muslin, the great teacher of self psychology, debate whether empathy is the central curative element in psychotherapy.[7]

Muslin held that one must always maintain empathy toward the patient.

What about an angry paranoid patient? Havens asked. Displaying fear or hostility in the room with a such a patient would be dangerous and destructive. So would any indication of intimate rapport with the other.

You misunderstand empathy, Muslin countered. True empathy for the paranoid patient is the maintenance of a respectful distance. Empathy is perfect courtesy. Empathy is doing the right thing for a patient.

But that makes the assertion that therapy must be empathic tautologic, was Havens' response.

The notion of empathy as tact or courtesy may be an appealing one, but we should recognize that we are using these words in a very unusual way.

To give an example (which happens again to relate to gardening): One morning I was dealing with some plants infested with mealybug, which shows itself through a white excrescence that appears as if from nowhere to cover stems and leaves. Later in the office a woman patient began quite neutrally to discuss an episode from her teenage years, and I found my mind drifting off to the infested plants. I could not understand why I was having such difficulty concentrating: mealybug can be dealt with. And then I realized I was experiencing a version of the sexual self-disgust the patient had felt when maturing, and I indicated I had a sense she might have felt dirty, and my speculation seemed to lead the right way.

This is a representative enough instance of the use of empathy in therapy. It can be called courtesy only if courtesy includes such things as letting another person know you are aware of her sexual self-disgust and are in fact currently experiencing it along with her. The ordinary use of courtesy refers to giving the impression that one is unaware, or almost unaware, of certain embarrassing aspects of the other. (In fact, it is only in defining empathy for the purpose of therapy that we would think of using the word courtesy to cover this interchange; in calling on the concept of courtesy, we are, once more, just saying that empathy is conducting oneself well in therapy.) And yet clearly there is some sense in which the speculation in this encounter *is* like courtesy, and also some sense in which a distant and unafraid stance vis-à-vis the paranoid patient is empathic.

A tricky notion to define, then.

* * * * *

To this list of difficulties we may now add another: when we say a therapy relies on empathy, what role do we have in mind for it?

Because empathy surely has some role even in the treatment I have been ready to label, to coin a word, anempathic.

To start with, empathy helped in diagnosing the patient. By her symptoms, Wendy fulfilled the criteria for major depression, but my empathic diagnosis was hysteria, a category useful to many working therapists, even though one no longer recognized by the prevailing diagnostic manual.

We do use empathy diagnostically, just as an internist might in attempting to distinguish somatization from multiple sclerosis. Empathy as a diagnostic tool is not unique to psychotherapy nor even to psychiatry; nor, it should be said, is it always the most reliable tool available. Before giving empathy too much credit for indicating that Wendy's depression was subject to influence, we might remember that a neuropsychiatric test battery would likely have reached the same conclusion. Even a good interactive computer program might have picked up a diagnosis such as "histrionic personality disorder." Diagnosis is a function for which empathy is useful but not crucial.

Therapists also rely on empathy in the formulation of treatment plans and specific interventions. Ericksonian hypnotists stress attention to the form of patients' inner metaphors—are they rural or urban, synthetic or analytic, romantic or dramatic? Hearing the patient's metaphors helps us formulate our own for use in the treatment. Empathy allows us to "speak the family's language," and here great exactness is required. We must tailor the plan to the patient.

But is empathy essential to this task?

Consider the work with Wendy and Rick. Isn't how the case worked like this: we know something about how couples function, the habitual pursuer losing status to the pursued. And something about hysterics and how they get themselves into masochistic postures in which they lose sight of their strengths. And something about sociopaths and the taste of blood.

And we have experience with stock marital situations. For example, we mistrust the couple's method of sharing money. A joint account for the family and a hidden account for the husband—the arrangement alerts us to the possibility that the marriage is incomplete in some more essential way.

We may have beliefs, too, about modern women and their need for, to use the dread word, assertiveness. We may know something about gamblers and what excites them.

To these we add a clinician's judgment of Wendy's capacity for regression and of the hidden dependency which ties Rick to the marriage. We consider Minuchin's concept of family structure, and we use the sort of analysis Jay Haley attributes to Milton Erickson, a view of the couple as having failed in a certain stage of adult development and family formation.[8]

In other words, we possess clinical wisdom and experience, and the way we combine information and beliefs determines how we devise a treatment. Do we want to call this gestalt empathy? But if so, we may have in mind an empathy that can exist free of emotion. The French use the expression *sensation en froid*, cold emotion, to describe feeling without its visceral concomitants, for example, an affectless pity. (Alexithymia, the presumed set of illnesses related to the inability to name or distinguish emotions, may if it exists involve something similar.) Do we want to admit the concept of empathy *en froid*? Is clinical wisdom the same as empathy?

To dramatize the issue, let us undertake a thought experiment. An incompetent resident interviews Rick and Wendy. He has no natural empathy for them, but he is able to elicit adequate diagnostic and factual information: Wendy has a histrionic character, Rick gambles and keeps separate books, and so forth. The resident brings this data to a supervisor who, irritated at the resident but aware of her responsibilities, uses her clinical wisdom to devise a paradoxical injunction which the resident successfully transmits to the couple. Do we want to say the intervention was informed by empathy? Did the supervisor have empathy for the couple? Well, yes and no—how far do we want to stretch the term?

And yet part of us does want to call the treatment plan empathic. Our clinical gestalt resulted in an accurate sense of the couple's gameness and their use of play, of the potential vitality of their response to sexual challenge and marital give-and-take. It would have been all too easy to do what the previous therapist did, to take Wendy's distress at face value and miss the point entirely. Do we want to call sinking into that swamp empathy?

Empathy can also come into play in certain aspects of the doctor-patient relationship, so that in this case we can say that Rick and Wendy experienced their doctor to be empathic and therefore were willing to accept his guidance. But here again empathy is a weak tool for the task at hand. Many patients obey surgeons they accuse of being cold and aloof.

Certainly charisma can have as strong an influence as empathy. If the Vegas intervention were—as in our thought experiment—created by one person and delivered by another, surely we can imagine any number of sorts of doctors-in-the-room who would elicit compliance. And would the strategy fail if the interacting doctor were unempathic?

These three uses of empathy—empathy as diagnostic tool, empathy as a basis for formulation, and empathy as bedside manner—confuse the issue of the centrality of empathy to therapy. None of these is what I take advocates to mean when they say that empathy is the essential ingredient in all therapy. What is lacking in the work with Wendy and Rick, and what makes us want to call it anempathic when we do, is the use of empathy as a direct force from one person acting on another, a force which changes the way the patient feels about himself. When we want to call the work with the farmer father empathic, we have in mind the power of mutually felt emotion in the minute workings of the intimate interactions of the therapeutic hour.

Those interactions were entirely matters of empathy: judging how openly to address an issue or how covertly, feeling the anger and the guilt and depression beneath it, thinking of plants lovingly enough and pragmatically enough, gauging the proper lengths of silences, titrating anxiety, knowing when to hold the attention close and when to let the mind wander, being right there with the patient's befuddlement, replacing pain with confidence. These tasks could not have been carried out by a computer or a test battery or a stiff-necked doctor or a surrogate for a supervisor in another room.

But I am not sure we can distinguish the empathic from the anempathic so easily.

In outline, the therapy with the deaf girl's family is just as structural or strategic as the Vegas cure. We can see the family according to a Minuchin-style analysis: the father needs to feel whole before he can let the daughter care for her children; in discussing the growing cycle with him, we are drawing an intergenerational boundary, nothing more. Or we can say, following Haley's Erickson, that the family failed a developmental transition, so that the father needs to become a father before the daughter can become a mother.

Empathy has a secondary, contingent role. If the mechanism of action of the therapy with the deaf patient is a strengthening of her father's self-image, strengthening which allows him to stop undermining the daughter, then we might have used any of a dozen means to make the father feel nurturant, and the success of the therapy—the restoration of dignity to the daughter—would have been unaltered. It is happenstance that the technique I used was empathic. If I had set the father to work on a difficult gardening project and later gotten the daughter to help him, the outcome might have been the same. Though it did not happen this way, we might have first analyzed the case structurally (without empathy entering into that analysis) and then decided whether or not to use "being empathic" in the sessions as the means of carrying out the strategy of empowering the father.

* * * * *

I think this is where we stand with empathy. Like insight, empathy is one tool among many. Empathy is not therapy; it is a technique. Empathy is not at the core of therapy, though it can be at the core of a therapy if we put it there. We can use empathy to make a patient feel competent, just as we might on another occasion use an antidepressant to make a patient feel competent. Our professional judgment, and no doubt our prejudices, will determine which treatment we turn to, but neither has priority.

Freud wrote more than once about the role of scientific revolutions in decentering key concepts. Galileo and Copernicus decentered the earth, Darwin decentered man, Freud decentered the conscious mind. In a smaller sphere, modern psychotherapies have decentered both insight and empathy.

And yet, and yet. I would not trust a therapist I believed to be anempathic.

I don't suppose it is hard to defend wanting therapists to have the capacity for empathy. Though any one case can be managed without it, it is hard to imagine a therapist showing good judgment time and again without the benefit of this particular mode of cognition in which one accurately grasps the other's complex emotional stance. While we might deny that, in order to devise an effective intervention, my supervisor needed to feel empathy for Wendy and Rick, we might find it hard to imagine she would be much of a supervisor at all if she could not often call upon an empathic appreciation of students and patients alike.

[146]

We demand of therapists even more than empathy – namely, we demand a critical awareness of their own empathy. This capacity is crucial for avoiding pitfalls in countertransference and other errors in monitoring social distance, controlling dependency, and the like.

But whether these capacities must be central, or even exercised at all, in every case is a more difficult question. Our insistence on the centrality of empathy – if we do insist on it – has an arbitrary, emotional quality, and while it is fine for doctors on occasion to be in touch with irrational forces, it is uncomfortable for them to obey them. We can save the notion of the empathic therapist, but can we save empathy as a touchstone of therapy?

Jung somewhere wrote that we need a different language for every patient. The two therapies, Vegas and gardening, are equivalent if we hold that empathy means something like "speaking the patient's language."

In the case of the deaf girl's father, how this works is evident right on the surface – we listen to his language, feel its force, and reflect it back to him. It is because the speaking of his language is both obvious and gentle that we are so quick to recognize empathy in the therapy and even to exaggerate its role.

With the drug-dealing furrier, to say that we speak his language recalls the Havens-Muslin discussion about courtesy. Sweetness and patience are not empathic toward the husband. The wife is already too soft and sweet; a conventionally "understanding" therapist would only reproduce her role and drive the husband away. To speak the language of gambling, action, and sexual threat is empathic for the husband.

But why must it be *his* language? Why couldn't an empathic therapy take place in the language of the wife? One answer is: that is just the sort of judgment therapists have to make; if you don't see why the husband's language has to come first, you don't have a feel for the couple. Another way to say the same thing is: you *could* do it in her language, but then you would be doing individual therapy. The marriage depends on the language of play. The therapy can be seen as a language class for the wife. In her distress, she has forgotten how to speak the language of the marriage. Once she relearns that language, she can go about her business.[9]

Both therapies induce change by using the family's language as a means of restructuring relationships; and both share the same formal structure (attention to intergenerational boundaries and family developmental tasks, carried out through altering the self-confidence of family members). In this sense the therapies are the same, equally empathic. But are we really willing to settle on this definition of empathy—empathy as apt speech?

Consider the case of successful therapies where we reach the patient enough to induce extensive change without ever coming to feel any kindred spirit. I occasionally treat a patient without making contact, and often as not the patient will get better. I find these cases immensely disturbing.

I once planned to write a column on this topic but found I could not—what if a patient came across the column and recognized himself in a vignette? How awful, to have had a successful treatment and later to discover your therapist never felt anything for you. I mistrusted any disguise, however thorough, I might give a case. I even worried that a patient might *wrongly* believe he was reading about himself. I could not take the risk.[10]

Which says both that I value something beyond efficacy (and beyond apt speech) and that I imagine patients do, too. Most patients want the old empathy. They want to know their therapist cares for them. Therapy differs from much of medicine in this regard. If a surgeon performs successful open heart surgery, the patient may be grateful without reservation even if he suspects the surgeon holds him in contempt. Few patients feel that way about their therapists—the contempt would hurt too much.

It seems we are stuck with distinct, though often co-occurring, sorts of empathy: empathy as apt language and empathy as emotional connectedness. And emotional connectedness itself has many meanings, ranging from feeling what the other feels, to understanding what is right for the other, to simply caring. (And when we say that a therapist must be empathic, which of these do we have in mind?)

If we prefer the treatment of the deaf girl, it is because we value an openly emotional form of empathy. And this may be so even though the outcome of the two cases—the family structure changed and the identified patient was able to get past a roadblock—is the same.

* * * * *

Through my disturbance over these two cases, I came to discover the strength of my attachment to empathy. I had told myself I had entered psychiatry to master a craft, but in truth I had also hoped to change the balance of forces within myself. To say I wanted to become a psychiatrist was, I understood now if I had not before, as much as anything to say I hoped my capacity for empathy (and wisdom) would grow. And so I found it disconcerting to discover the power of other therapeutic qualities, such as cleverness, to be at the heart of successful treatments, indeed a type of treatment for which I seemed to have a special aptitude.

As doctors, we had better be aware when we value process over outcome. We do not choose between surgical and medical treatments for ulcerative colitis on the basis of our sentiment for one or another process. It became important for me to understand the boundaries and limitations of empathy, because as a therapist one ought to be ruthless regarding one's own prejudices, and this includes scrutinizing what one loves as well as discovering the virtues of what one has held in disregard.

There may, of course, be legitimate reasons for favoring highly empathic treatments. We might believe that a hard-hitting, unemotional, radically brief therapy has little chance of finding the mark exactly enough. Subtle errors can lead to the sort of overbalancing that in the long term results in, say, Wendy and Rick's divorce. For power we sacrifice precision and control. (But do we ever have a very exact influence? Just because we can influence the course of a session, or head off an episode of acting out, do we imagine we have much say over whether marriages last?)

Or we might believe that directive therapies convey a pessimistic message about locus of control. More intimate therapies nurture the belief that cure comes from within the self. (Or they may only foster dependency.) I say this in the way that I might say I prefer a kindly or stimulating way of teaching young children in school even in the face of evidence that harshness and regimentation produce better measurable "outcomes." I would say, reading and arithmetic are not all children learn in school.

Therapies implicitly teach something about life—how we size up problems and how we might do it differently—as well as promoting change in symptoms. But once we have taken this tack, we are on the verge of acknowledging what critics of psychotherapy allege, namely that much of psychotherapy is "advice for living," burdened by the therapist's particular philosophy and sense of the zeitgeist, and divorced from science.

The arguments favoring the primacy of empathy are weak at best. We cling to empathy, if we do, in the face of effective anempathic treatments.

There is, of course, a final case one can make for keeping the therapist's needs in mind. Efficacy, we hope, depends in part on the genius of the therapist. We want him to work where he is most comfortable working, where he will be best inspired.

I do not mean that therapists should be hedonists or take advantage of patients to fulfill their own needs; on the contrary, they should examine and hold suspect any gratification they experience. Rather, I have in mind something like what Carl Whitaker must mean when he says, as he does repeatedly, that a requirement of good therapy is that the therapist get better. This might just be Whitaker's way of admitting he will not do his best in a therapy that bores him; Whitaker is most inspired working at the limits of his own tolerance for craziness, almost entering the patient's insanity and thus stretching his own stability and humanity.

It may even be that appreciation of the therapist's active struggle—a sense the patient has of having "gotten to" the therapist, of having transcended the routine and reached a disturbing, not entirely controlled part of the other—is a requirement for the efficacy of empathy in certain therapies. The deaf girl's father "got to me"; he sensed that we both struggled with the issue of distant fatherhood and loss.

In the absence of that commonality (if Wendy had decompensated, I would only have gotten irritated with her), it was better with Wendy and Rick for me to enter quite differently into their struggle. It is precisely issues of this sort which can never be approached in efficacy studies and which in practice determine which tool we choose for which treatment.

To put the matter differently, issues of efficacy arise for the therapist in terms of power and impotence. These family cases gave me a sense of power.

Power is something we want. But we do not want it just any way. We want it on our own terms.

Once after I gave a lecture on the mind-body problem in psychiatry, an analyst approached me from the audience and said I should talk about the irrational anger psychiatrists feel when patients get better in the wrong way. He had in mind an episode from his training. After working with training case "on the couch" for some time, he threw up his hands and used an antidepressant. The patient got better (and it is interesting the patient did not get angry at the analyst-in-training), and instead of blaming himself or his teachers or feeling gratitude for the drug, the therapist felt hatred toward the patient. How dare the patient have applied to be a control case when his problem was biological? Meaning also, how dare the patient through his recovery have challenged the analyst-in-training's world view?

In a similar way, I think I found my work with Wendy threatening. In curing her (of schizophrenia! of depression!) so quickly and efficiently, I felt a great sense of power. But I was left off-balance.

Should my other patients recover this fast? Does the power to cure imply an equal power to harm? But most of all: has the need for empathy disappeared? It was important for me to redefine empathy in such a way as to include this case and make me comfortable with my newfound potency.

In contrast, work with Jane filled me with confidence. That empathy came from a part of myself to which I was glad to attribute power. If one's nurturance is a strong force, well fine, there is no need to be ambivalent about that.

But I found — and this is a funny discovery for someone in the midst of residency, eager to master a craft — that I was less willing to acknowledge the power I could develop through cleverness, play-acting, and prescriptive psychotherapy. I evidently did not trust certain aggressive forces in myself.

I began to understand that I would have to learn to trust these forces, because counterbalancing the permission for the psychiatrist to take into account his own strengths is an obligation to cultivate strengths in diverse areas and to bring to the treatment whatever he has to offer. I had in a sense entered psychiatry to nurture my empathic side rather than certain critical faculties. These cases helped me see that I needed to develop not only the parts of myself I prized, but also those I had hoped to ignore.

*　　*　　*　　*　　*

These two therapies no longer seem as distinct to me as they once did, and this similarity is not attributable only to the structural resemblances I have already discussed.

What they have in common is their coherence as stories. The narrative or story is a concept modern theoreticians have used to engage a number of paradoxes in psychiatric work. The notion is that much of what goes on in insight-oriented therapies is the agreement of patient and therapist on a new story about the patient's life. The concept is common enough (and deconstructionist literary criticism is sufficiently popular) that sophisticated patients now come in talking of this or that "narrative" in their lives.

The concept of arbitrary narrative frees psychiatry from a defense of the scientific validity of such concepts as the Oedipus complex. But it leaves in place another difficulty: is it true that just any story will do?

Samuel Novey wrote years ago about the utility of "opening out" psychoanalysis and having the patient return to his childhood haunts and test the accuracy of his reconstructed memories.[11] But surely verifiability is not a prerequisite for cure. This difficulty, of course, precedes our decade. Once Freud, in the Wolf Man case, began creating speculative histories, the door was opened to paradox and doubt.[12]

For me, one strength of the notion of story—changing the patient's appreciation of himself—is that it redefines the problem of empathy.

I think it is clear, without belaboring the point, that the stories which helped Wendy's and Jane's families were appropriate to those families, so that I need not, for instance, have worried about pace as if the choice of pace were all mine. Some people are ready to change quickly if they are moved forcefully enough. For Jane's family, slower progress was appropriate to their narrative; the treatment moved from dormant winter to fertile spring and summer, mirroring the growing season. The pace was an integral part of the story.

Nor does it seem crucial whether the story be told in words, or

[152]

through play-acting, or through a participant's being asked to walk through a new role.

Pacing the story right is an element of empathy. Using or avoiding what I have called the old empathy (displaying caring) is a part of empathy.[13] Speaking the right language is empathy and good story-telling.

Once therapy — even pharmacotherapy at times — is seen as a form of joint storytelling, distinctions among different forms and uses of empathy seem to fade away. Moment by moment, we understand patients sometimes mostly through affect and sometimes mostly through cognition, and we respond with sympathy or firmness, and these responses are to greater or lesser degree informed by scientific knowledge or experience, but all of this action is subsumed under a more general aesthetic judgment, a sense of what fits and what does not in a given case.

As for our viscerally favoring one or another type of treatment, we may find that to us as craftsmen it is of minor importance whether our feel for the subject is most manifested in the definition of the topic, the plot outline, the details of the dialogue, or the narrative voice. We are in any event creators — in therapy, joint creators — of the work, and if it is good work there will be enough of our selves in it. Nor is there any requirement that we rely only on our capacity for kindness; our humor and dry intellect and, yes, aggression will be welcome as well.

Does this *deus ex machina*, the story metaphor, save empathy? If we can still say empathy is crucial to therapy, it is because we have been willing to stretch its definition. It is crucial only if we make it crucial.

Empathy is seductive for us as therapists. For those raised or temperamentally endowed to love closeness, it triggers the right reward-giving chemicals in the brain, as performing surgery is said to do for those whose stimulus-seeking tends toward action. I wonder whether one of these addictions may not be as dangerous — as distorting to good practice, and as productive of misplaced pride and contempt — as the other.[14]

I still love empathic treatments. But with time I have come to find empathy, like interpretation, drugs, strategy, experience, diagnosis, and all the other important elements, to be only one among many tools of the trade.

When It Works

And yet, it works. Despite the limitations of each element of theory and technique, we manage to devise successful treatments and to practice with a sense of mastery.

Insofar as we are not just fooling ourselves, this confidence stems from our own experience of engagement in a powerful, empirically based discipline, one rooted in lore and wisdom which transcend theorizing, really transcend the written heritage altogether. Our confidence arises from the examples of mentors and from what we read, which may be in developmental psychology or philosophy as much as therapeutics,[1] and most strongly from what we do. What we do nowadays is nowhere written down; it would take an anthropologist to tell us what we do.

The sense is one of being a bundle of skills and of beliefs, some of which are quite simple and down-to-earth. For example, we may believe that depression causes, and antedates, divorce as often as divorce causes depression, and this belief may dominate our approach to certain clinical situations; this sort of belief can be common to psychiatrists and yet unconnected to any particular body of doctrine.[2]

My own sense of belonging to a guild, and of having absorbed many useful beliefs and skills, was strengthened by a therapy which I began early in my second year of residency. The case called on diverse aspects of the profession, and in the end the interventions worked, although just where the success lay was hard to say. It is perhaps ironic, but I think not untypical of these formative encounters, that the case was one which I at first undertook with quite a different motive than curing the patient and in which, when I did finally have to face the patient for her own sake, I experienced hesitancy, awkwardness, and uncertainty as to the goals of treatment.

I became aware of my patient early in the course of a liaison assignment to a continuing care unit of a general hospital.[3] To be more precise, I became aware that I needed to make her my patient.

The ward specialized in the treatment of people requiring instruction in self-care—ostomy patients learning to cleanse their wounds and apply their bags, stroke victims learning to walk, and the like. As a second-year resident, I had been asked to revitalize a psychiatric liaison role there. Shortly after my arrival, I noticed conflict among the staff over the care of a "special patient."

She was a woman in her early twenties who had just had one leg removed below the knee because of vascular insufficiency caused by relapsing polychondritis, a progressive autoimmune disease involving destruction of cartilage throughout the body. The wound was healing poorly, and, knowing that the patient would likely die in the coming months, the staff was divided about further treatment to assure optimal "quality of life." Some sided with the internists, who believed the wound would not heal and that a more proximal reamputation would result in earlier hospital discharge, though with greater disability. Others sided with the surgeons, who wanted to wait for further healing to avoid reoperation. This unusual standoff, in which the internists favored surgery and the surgeons favored medical management, made my clinical nose twitch.

In addition, the doctors were trying to lower the patient's pain medication, but the nurses seemed unable to comply with the orders; no matter what the doctors wrote, somehow day after day the actual total dose remained the same.

I had a tenuous position on the ward. The nurses, social workers, and physical therapists were aware that the working group needed some help, but so far the doctors had given me only the simplest of consultations, mostly requests to evaluate the psychotherapeutic medication needs of agitated patients. I decided to earn my spurs by helping the special patient, Julie. The problem was that I had never seen her.

The rounding team did not enter Julie's room, for fear of disturbing her, since she was in great pain from the surgical wound site when awake. And Julie's mother was such a vocal critic of any perceived insensitivity to her daughter that it was thought best for the ward attending to see the patient privately. When I asked to be brought in, the attending said the mother would be enraged by any suggestion that her daughter was not normal. If I upset the family, caring for the patient would become impossible.

One of the skills we were expected to develop as residents was the ability to analyze and enter into organizations. Not every residency program considers this skill to be psychiatric, but ours did, both because of our mandate to manage therapeutic milieus on inpatient psychiatric units and because of our loyalty to the community mental health movement, in which consultation is a key function. The paradigm for our liaison work was the management of wards disrupted by borderline personality disordered patients with the capacity to polarize organizations through acting on their own intrapsychic "splitting."

So I began as if I were dealing with a ward split by a borderline. I talked at team meetings in a general way about the difficulty of working with attractive, young, suffering and dying patients, and our identification with them, and their need for clarity and firm boundaries—but to no effect. I realized I was in danger of stereotyping myself as another ineffectual shrink.

Instead, I looked for a different strategy. I consulted with the head of the consultation/liaison service, and we decided to meet the staff where its own conflict was most obvious. We offered to hypnotize the patient to see whether she could learn to control her pain and use a lower dose of analgesics. I courted the doctors by addressing the medication issue and the nurses by acknowledging Julie's pain. The offer to hypnotize was particularly powerful because cartilage loss had left Julie deaf.

In this way I got to meet the patient.

Julie was a frail and pallid young woman with a saddle nose deformity and a nasal voice which resulted in part from cartilage loss and in part from deafness. She had the Pre-Raphaelite angelic quality common to certain dying children, but as I got to know her I found she had maintained a forthright sense of self and a corny sense of humor which made her seem disturbingly familiar and normal. She had no personality disorder at all, but it was easy to see how awareness of the implacable illness in this young woman had disturbed the staff.

Julie was mildly depressed but without thought disorder or cognitive impairment. She was glad to talk to me. And far from objecting, the mother was relieved that a psychiatrist had been called in.

The young woman's story was extraordinary medically and in every other way.

Julie had been a healthy, active girl until age 12, when she suffered a viral syndrome with fever and joint tenderness, followed by recurrent ulcerations of the mouth and nose. Soon other symptoms came and went: chest pain, weight loss, invasion of the soft palate. In time, a dermatologist diagnosed Behçet's Disease.

By age 15, Julie was spending more time at home than at school. She worked with a "home bound tutor." She was hospitalized repeatedly for leg ulcers—sterile abscesses on the basis of peripheral vascular disease. She spent her last year in public school at age 16, where she was teased because of facial distortion she suffered in response to high-dose steroids.

The next year the hearing in her right ear began to deteriorate. An NIH consultant said he believed Julie had her own unique disorder, a relapsing polychondritis with vasculitis. Before she was 19 she had lost all hearing.

Somewhere in those years, an expert warned Julie's mother that the girl would enter a period of depression, mourning the loss of her hearing. In fact Julie remained vital, maintaining friendships, intellectual interests, and even sports activity, at which she excelled. Julie took speech therapy and signing lessons, and without missing a beat she graduated from high school. After a brief period of visual impairment, possibly due to steroid-induced changes in intraocular pressure, she went directly on to a college for the deaf located on a university campus. Because of the mistaken prediction—the expert's blindness to the daughter's unique strengths—the mother turned some of her rage onto the helping professions. Julie's father developed an alcohol problem, private binge drinking, and mother and daughter grew even closer.

From 19 to 21, Julie had what she called her "three good years." She took classes for the deaf but associated freely with hearing students. She had her first boyfriend and her first sexual experiences. She learned to drive and had her own car.

One of her great pleasures was a job as resident advisor for deaf students. Her fortitude inspired others. A friend wrote Julie's mother that she would have dropped out of college were it not for Julie's example.

Julie adapted her aspirations to her disabilities and settled on a course of study as a medical technical photographer. Meanwhile, the disease flared again, and Julie returned to the family. She remained a leader for the younger children. She was particularly close to her next younger sister, whose sloppiness she criticized and whose clothes she helped to select.

At age 21, Julie was hospitalized on different occasions for iliac artery occlusions, buccal ulcerations with difficulty swallowing, arthritis, fever, anemia, and finally for further peripheral vascular disease requiring major surgery — bilateral femoral bypass grafts. When she happened serendipitously (can that word be used here?) to be in the hospital building for a checkup, she became nauseous and was found to have acute aortic insufficiency, secondary to cartilage disease of the ascending aorta. She underwent emergency aortic valve replacement.

Later that year, she required external iliac endarterectomy with regraft to the prior bypass graft. And finally, after a year of almost constant hospitalization, the leg was amputated below the knee, and Julie was referred to the continuing care unit in anticipation of her being fitted with a leg prosthesis.

So here we had a remarkable — heroic in a certain use of the word — young woman in physical pain and less able than usual to maintain hope; a struggling father; and a mother involved, perhaps overinvolved, if we are brave enough to make such a judgment, in the daughter's care. And of course the other children, some of whom were suffering in their own ways. And the many nurses and doctors coping imperfectly with untenable options.

In the evaluation phase of this encounter, I had already learned a thing or two: it is not only disturbed patients who disturb wards. Resistance to consultation attributed to patients or their families often resides instead in the medical staff. And those with spirits stronger than our own may nevertheless require our help.

Because it seems, on telling the story, that despite the patient's resilience, we can think of things we might do. But what are these things? Do we consider individual or family dynamic therapy, or cognitive, or behavioral, or systems theory, or a particular developmental approach, or biological treatment? One answer is, no, none of these comes to mind. None meets the enormity of the problem or its many facets. Or to answer differently, yes, we consider all of them, and would like to know more about the girl's cognitions and her unconscious fantasies and her early history and her illness behavior and her role in the family and on the ward, and the mechanism of her pain and depression, and a dozen other things—and similarly for the mother and father and the doctors and nurses. Isn't it mostly that we will hope to involve ourselves in some way and see what happens? Isn't this the sort of case, if it is a case, that from the start makes us aware of our many diverse skills and our lack of a comprehensive schema to unite them?

After informal evaluation, I presented hypnosis as a talent Julie might have and which she could develop to give herself control over pain. As I had hoped, this approach appealed to mother and daughter, and Julie agreed to go to the consultation/liaison chief psychiatrist's office even though the transportation would entail pain. Julie was able to lipread sufficiently well to understand the induction, and she was hypnotized without difficulty with her eyes open.

She proved able to "remove herself to a warm beach" so as not to feel pain. She was instructed to practice the induction and then to use it before dressing changes and whirlpool treatments when the wound pain was most severe.

I maintained contact with Julie around her practicing self-hypnosis. I let the conversation stray into related areas, such as her medical progress and her frustration with the illness, but for the most part we stuck to the task at hand. I would have said at the time that my standoffishness was a requirement imposed on me by the ward doctors: under no circumstances was I to increase Julie's anxiety.

But if I were honest, I would have added that Julie's illness and the prospect of her death unnerved me as much as they did anyone else. She had a charm which drew me in, and at the same time she had death written all over her. I think it best to say from the start that one of the potential disadvantages of technical eclecticism is that it allows us, if we are inclined, to choose our interventions dishonestly while telling ourselves we are doing our duty. Here I was able to shield myself from the pain of intimacy with a dying young woman. Although it is also true that if we maintain a degree of self-observation, these resistances will not last forever; we could equally say that our liberation from exaggerated requirements of empathy and engagement with the unconscious allows us to enter relationships in a way which is more comfortable to doctor and patient alike.

I could see that Julie got only modest relief from the self-hypnosis, perhaps because for her the hypnosis was a way of maintaining contact with me, and I was so little engaged around her central needs, such as her fear that she would never leave the hospital. But from my point of view, the hypnosis had always been meant to treat the staff, and in this it succeeded.

The doctors and nurses were able to agree to reduce analgesic medication while at the same time making whirlpool debridement treatments more regular. To the staff's relief, Julie's wound began to granulate in, and it became clear that immediate reoperation would be unnecessary. I was accepted as a full member of the rounding team—and no one remembered that it had ever been otherwise.

With my encouragement, a nurse specialist developed an on-ward work program for Julie. Julie filed papers and organized data. This activity let the staff see her as more able and less special. She was discharged after a hospitalization of two months, a shorter length of stay, I suspect, than she would have had without my intervention. I did not expect to see her again.

A few weeks later, Julie was readmitted via the emergency room, for sharp back pain. An x-ray revealed increased dilatation of the thoracic aorta, and it was feared she was dissecting an aortic aneurysm. She was placed on a high-dose antihypertensive regimen. Since the past aortic valve replacement had demonstrated the quality of the tissue of Julie's aorta to be poor, the surgeons decided not to attempt to repair the aneurysm.

I visited Julie informally during her brief stay on the surgical intensive care unit. The family seemed not to want to involve themselves in outpatient psychiatric treatment.

But within weeks, I heard from Julie again. The continuing care unit nurse specialist, whose clinic monitored Julie's progress, said that Julie had begun to experience terrifying nightmares at home. She had signs and symptoms of a moderate depression of the sort we used to call endogenomorphic, with prominent biological features however seemingly evident its psychic causes.

Even at this late stage, I almost declined the case. I reviewed Julie's chart, and it seemed likely to me that the nightmares, and possibly the depression as well, were attributable to a recent increase in dose of one of her medicines, propanolol. It required a strong faith in the biological model to entertain this thought. This was Julie's dream: a person held a tiny person in her hand; the tiny person broke into pieces and crumbled like paper, or someone tore the skin off the tiny person.

Now this dream sounds concretely related to Julie's situation—loss of body parts, debridement, the tissue-like quality of her aorta—but I had heard similar nightmares, centered on distortions in body size and integrity, from patients on propanolol. (This question is interesting and I believe unresearched: do particular medicines induce characteristic sorts of dreams? I mean this in the sense that when a patient has a hallucinatory sensation of ants running over the skin—"formication"—we suspect withdrawal from alcohol or a related drug.) I suggested to the nurse specialist that she recommend a change in the patient's antihypertensive regimen.

But I must have been willing to get my feet wet as well, because I also volunteered to visit Julie at home, where she was virtually bedridden because of the slow-healing wound, generalized weakness, and postural hypotension due to the high doses of antihypertensives needed to keep pressure off her aorta.

I had in mind dynamic psychotherapy, and my initial question was how I was going to make the transition from my hitherto (inadequately) supportive role. I found Julie in the living room, lying draped on the couch to which she was moved once a day. (As I write these lines, I associate this circumstance for the first time with that of my great-grandmother, who lay dying on the dining room settee during the months my father was in the sanatorium and my mother and I stayed with my grandparents. It is quite extraordinary to see what draws us to the work we do—and hard to see how we can ever honorably abandon attempts to remain aware of the unconscious.)

Julie's nightmares had stopped when the propanolol dose was lowered, but she began our meeting by recounting the recurrent dream. I said it must be difficult to have no sense of how the disease or medicines would affect her next.

She took this flat comment as an opening and complained that the hypnosis had only given the nurses one new way to ignore her pain: "hypnotize yourself." I acknowledged how enraging this must have been, but I also said it might have been hard for the nurses to attend to her, since she was at once so vital and so ill. I said I had experienced similar difficulties.

This approach is on its surface not psychodynamic, not unrevealing in the "tabula rasa" style. But it was my way of clearing the decks, of allowing the patient to settle old scores and move on to the work. I would maintain that this self-exposure can be seen as more truly psychodynamic than neutrality would have been. What appears to be self-exposure can be understood as a transference interpretation: you see me as untrustworthy, and this impression will hinder your entering treatment. It also modeled a degree of frankness which would be necessary if we were to do quick-enough therapy.

Julie responded as we hope patients will, not by acknowledging the implicit interpretation but by elaborating on it. She told a series of stories about people on the ward or at college who were insincere. I said she might have been angry at my minimal involvement with her on the unit, and she might now be afraid that my interest in her would prove to be insincere or fleeting. She responded by praising the nurse clinical specialist, who had been attentive and helpful. I took this reply to be an expression of hope, which is to say positive transference, and I seized the moment to offer regular therapy at home, which Julie accepted.

I would say, by the way, that this dance was the dance of engagement which we do all the time without thinking about it, but which beginners sometimes fail to do at all. Knowing the steps to this sort of dance is one of the things I have in mind when I refer to uncategorized professional skills.

With the offer of treatment, Julie's mood changed markedly. She talked happily about what she enjoyed doing, for example, drawing. She directed me to a folder on a bookshelf and selected from it a self-portrait, drawn from such an angle as to emphasize the deformity of her nose. She said she sang songs in dreams she could no longer sing in life. I took her to be saying she wanted to continue to live productively, although she had extreme, even exaggerated, if that is possible, fears about her limitations and others' ability to tolerate her. She wanted me to know her losses were great, but also to recognize how much of herself she had maintained.

So "therapy" had begun. But I think it is important to remember how entry had been made through a medical problem, the propanolol side effect, and how even access to this technical problem had to be earned through attention to ward liaison issues and to a technique for entering the family without enraging the mother. Before recognizable psychotherapy began, I had cause to act as ward consultant, family therapist, biological psychiatrist, and, though someone else did the initial induction, hypnotist. What is interesting is how little these roles impeded the transition to conventional therapy, even though I had begun by disappointing the patient and causing her pain with a use of hypnosis that was as much focused on my own needs as hers.

Nor had the need to attend to family issues disappeared.

Like it or not, I was doing family therapy. The living room had no door. During the therapy hour, family members breakfasted and dressed and rushed guiltily by. Even the living room was never fully ours. On its periphery it housed guinea pigs and hamsters and class projects, so that I could not help absorbing information about the quality of family life. Inevitably the therapy lacked privacy. Even if I had talked only to Julie it would have had the effect of "family therapy with one person," piquing the curiosity of other family members and raising fears and hopes that the identified patient might change.

After the first session, the mother asked me how things had gone. Rather than involve her in the daughter's therapy, I asked her how she was holding up, and she began to tell me about her serious hobby, vegetable gardening. This was right up my alley, and so we began a weekly ritual of discussing plants.

The talk was straightforward, and I learned a good deal from the mother, who was a true master gardener. I was not weaving metaphors in an obvious sense; metaphor was inherent in the topic: the mother had nurturant qualities, the daughter's illness was not punishment for any of the mother's imagined failings. Still, the choice of topic and the way I internally interpreted the mother's talk and guided my responses to it was such that I found myself in a second, Ericksonian therapy which went on before or after the daughter's sessions. (Another meaning of my talk with the mother was the message conveyed by my sincere interest in her: she was not, as a few caregivers had implied, and as her husband perhaps implied by his retreat to drink, a menacing ogress. She was a caring mother, and her caring sometimes led her into conflict.) Neither treatment, I came to believe, was possible without the other. Or we might say both distinct "therapies" were part of one family therapy, though this is not how we usually conceptualize family therapy.

I was not unmoved by what I touched. At the end of the second session, I noticed a book of photographs of Africans on the coffee table. The photographer was Leni Riefenstahl, and I asked Julie something about it. We discussed what it meant that Hitler's propagandist, who had filmed *Triumph of the Will*, could produce beauty and also what it meant that she had turned her attention to blacks' bodies. Insofar as the talk was integrated into the therapy, it had to do with inner and outer beauty — with the meaning of Julie's distorted self-portrait. The conversation also touched on Julie's hope her own photographs might be a lasting and redeeming product of her life.

Driving back to the hospital, I found myself seized with anguish — not an anxiety attack, but a sense of the awfulness of life, its unfairness and ugliness and its terrors. I pulled off the road into a wooded area and let my thoughts collect.

What I came to realize was that I had translated Julie's decomposition into the fear of my childhood, a Jewish child's angry fear of Nazis. I understood Julie partly through my own early nightmares.

The anguish was for me a reliable sign that we had engaged in dynamic therapy. I think it interesting that the reverse transference did not emerge earlier, when I can equally be said to have been treating the patient, and when I had extensive exposure to the terrible physical degradation her disease caused. The early treatment was by this marker anempathic or unengaged.

I think on the day I had to pull the car over I had been annoyed that, while I had extended myself to enter the fearsome parts of Julie's world, she, by displaying the Riefenstahl book, had shown insensitivity to my own life, though of course rationally I understood she knew nothing about me and owed me nothing. And at the same time I felt remorse for having used Julie to earn my spurs on the continuing care unit, and having done it in a way that made me symbolically, in my own night-mare, a torturer.

I have always suspected that one of my deep motivations for becoming a psychiatrist had to do with my childhood outrage over torture; in treating Julie I was doing just what I had set out to do but also, in my method of entering the case, betraying my ideals. Once I understood the terror it did not recur.

The core of my further work with Julie was cognitive and psychodynamic. The illness was undermining her self-worth and identity in different ways. She cared most about schooling, and now she feared she would never return to college. She felt other people would not want to touch her because of the deterioration of her body, and she often wished her brain could be put in someone else's body. She had difficulty maintaining her sense of role in the family, particularly when she became jealous as her younger sister began to surpass her in social and sexual experiences. She felt guilt over the jealousy. She had difficulty with her faith and was angry at God. At times she also felt an objectless guilt, saying it was as if she were being punished in this body for sins she had committed in other lives.

Much of the therapy involved validating the reasonableness of these feelings. We also covered some of the ground reached in many ordinary therapies with young women this age regarding jealousy, anger, rivalry, and identity confusion and the way these mingle with gratitude, ambition, love and desire. As weeks passed, Julie's depressive symptoms resolved.

The continuing care nurse and I had discussed ways of restoring or reinforcing Julie's sense of competence. (Julie said that at college she had felt not like a deaf person but like a hearing person who could not hear; now she wanted to be not like a dying person but like a living person who happened to be dying.) The nurse recruited an art therapist, and despite a series of further complications of medication and disease, Julie resumed her drawing.

Meanwhile I felt moved to use myself in a peculiar way. Julie had pride in her ability to teach signing, so I arranged, through the signing interpreter who had helped me with the psychotically depressed deaf mother, for Julie to co-teach a class in her living room. But exacerbations of the illness made this approach impractical, so instead I asked Julie to

[166]

teach me signing. We ended each therapy session with a brief period of language instruction in which the patient became a teacher and the doctor a student.

I had already used some elementary knowledge of signing to supplement our usual means of communication in therapy, which were lip-reading and written notes. Now I became very slightly more fluent. But the main purposes of the exercise were to prevent Julie from being stripped of her skills as a teacher and to control her fear of dependency. She was relieved to have something to give me.

Perhaps we can see my assuming the student role as cognitive or behavioral therapy ("What makes you say you have lost all your talents?") carried on through a concrete metaphor. Or perhaps this act had the effect of blocking a dependent transference. Or I may have wanted to diffuse an erotic transference and countertransference implicit when the therapist is the only man from outside the family who enters the life of a young woman, whom he sees loosely clad lying before him on a couch in her own home. Whether it was a perfect intervention or not, the signing lesson was a strong element in a complex therapy that seemed to work.

Some four months into our series of meetings, Julie experienced an episode of sharp back pain associated with difficulty swallowing, and she was rehospitalized. I saw her throughout the hospitalization and took on a limited liaison role on her new medical floor. Julie suffered a rapid downhill course which included tracheal collapse requiring permanent tracheostomy. Although suffocating and air-hungry, she at first refused the operation because it meant she could never swim again.

Even during this final hospitalization, Julie was rarely interested in discussing dying. Throughout the treatment, I had felt a sense of artificiality when I tried to raise the subject. My work with Julie caused me to lose respect for some of the popular helping-profession works about thanatology. More broadly, this case made me doubt whether a special discipline was required for treating the end of life, although, as Julie's last days may be said to show, I may have missed the main point altogether.

Julie was angry that she would die, and until very late she held on to the hope, shared by some of her caretakers, that she would recover enough to return to college. I did not share this hope, and I made my opinion clear without forcing it on her.

In her final days, Julie understood she would very likely die, but by then she was more concerned about pain medication than she was about death. (At another level she had been aware all along that she would die soon.) She was not reconciled to dying, and two days before the end she went through a brief and terrible panic lasting minutes when she begged not to be allowed to die. I did not feel at all bad about a young woman's wanting so strongly to live, though I wished I could have spared her the panic. The terminal event, either more central tracheal collapse or bursting of the aortic aneurysm, occurred while she was sedated.

Six weeks into the individual therapy with Julie, I had asked her mother during one of our garden walks whether I might not sit down with her and her husband. The next week we shared a pot of coffee in the kitchen before Julie's session. Although I had often been in his house as he left for work, this was the first time the father talked with me at any length.

He complained about the complex insurance forms he had to fill out and praised his wife's ability to care for Julie. He tried to give an impression of extreme incompetence, as if he could barely earn a living while his strong wife carried the family on her back.

I thought I understood pretty well (not least from my old Penthesilea fantasies) what the father was talking about and to what position he had retreated under the terrible stress of his daughter's illness. I complimented him on his special talent for dealing with his wife and with doctors diplomatically. I speculated that he must use this talent at work as well and must be a good administrator. The father brightened up and said that this was the one talent others had identified in him, although he did not see it himself.

By the next week, the parents were using the kitchen meeting as "therapy," and it became difficult to break it off and give their daughter proper attention. The mother considered the father alcoholic. Under stress or when feeling particularly good about himself he occasionally went on benders, and drunkenness was the one thing she found most insufferable in people. She was afraid he would resume the more serious pattern of alcohol abuse that had occurred about the time Julie became deaf. The drinking was making the mother consider divorce after Julie died.

For his part, the father contemplated quitting his job when Julie died and moving his family to a part of the country where there was less East Coast pretense and less opportunity to drink. However, there was little logic in this reasoning, since the father did not drink socially. When he binged, he drank alone.

The father had never been able to leave his middle-level job in his father's company. He said he continued there only to keep up the health insurance for Julie, and he was extremely bitter that a change in the policy meant that coverage for Julie would end after another year. However, he also knew she would almost certainly not live another year. He was fighting this matter out with the insurance commission.

Both mother and father struggled with the problems of Julie's siblings, who the parents worried were receiving too little parental attention and who were experiencing school and social difficulties. The mother felt barely controllable rage at schoolchildren who competed too vigorously with her children or who were cruel or unkind.

My involvement with the parents moved far beyond facilitating Julie's treatment. I intended to help them with their own pain and to allow them to function more effectively. (I believe this involvement also helped me to function more effectively, and to bear the loss of Julie.)

To this end, I conceptualized the mother's aggressiveness toward doctors and sometimes toward her husband as a manifestation of her grief and her anger at her daughter's illness. She was being a good mother, although sometimes one can be almost too good. (I did believe she was an extraordinary mother, and believe it even more strongly now that I am a parent.) Likewise, I explained the father's withdrawal as a way of coping with his wife's rage and his own sense of helplessness at his daughter's illness. This sense of incompetence had roots in his family of origin. Husband and wife needed to be able to fight and also to commiserate with each other and to reform an attachment that now existed as an exclusive bond between mother and daughter. Both had to be able to grieve.

I used multiple techniques. These included sympathetic listening with relabeling (for example, of the father's skills and faults); explicit interpretation (of the mother's displacement of her anger); and techniques of the Minuchin and Haley schools, including paradox (encouraging an exaggeration of the father's supposed weakness and praising the father for being such a gentleman that he would use his weakness to hold the

family together) and assignment of tasks (requiring the mother to pro-
voke an argument and lose it). I even turned to coaching of the Murray
Bowen sort, focusing on the father's relationship to his parents.

During the course of the therapy, the father's binge drinking de-
creased, disappearing except just at the time of Julie's final hospitalization, which he nevertheless handled well. The mother dropped her talk
of divorce. Both parents were able to devote more concern to children
other than Julie. And Julie and her father were able to talk more openly
to one another, although this change was the least marked.

The family coped well with Julie's death. The nurse specialist and I
attended the funeral. After the service, the parents asked if I would be
resuming my early morning visits, and I agreed to continue.

The remaining therapy concerned bereavement and a restructuring
the family without Julie. Julie's mother blamed herself for feeling angry
at her other children for not taking on Julie's leadership role. The father
felt hopeless at his job; he no longer had reason to stay, but he seemed
unable to move.

Shortly after Julie's death, the family took a vacation, something they
had been unable to do during the long period in which Julie was dying.
The ostensible purpose of the trip was to clean out a family house that
had been left unattended after the death of a relative. The housecleaning
seemed a displacement of the cleaning they could not bear to do in their
own home. If so, it was an effective one. Afterwards, the parents were
able to let the younger children wear Julie's clothes and to discard some
of her effects. Finally, a child moved into Julie's room; the child stripped
the walls bare, repainted them, and changed the furniture.

I suggested tasks to let the parents feel they could turn outside the
family. First they took walks together, later they accepted invitations
from neighbors, then they began to look seriously for new jobs locally.
Our breakfasts took on an informal quality. It was no longer clear where
ideas originated, whether from me or the parents. The father drew up a
resumé and began to seek new employment. The mother contacted the
licensure board of the profession in which she had some training and
began to seek out course work needed for her to take a professional job.
By the end of the therapy, the parents found themselves less irritated at
those around them who were concerned with "trivialities"; they were

even able to forgive some neighbors they felt had let them down during Julie's illness.

When I said good-bye, the mother gave me a hardy potted plant, which I have to this day. We talked by telephone now and then for some months.

I purposely let the therapy degenerate and fade away in this fashion because I wanted to leave the family with the impression that they had barely been in treatment at all. They were a strong and healthy family faced with an unbearable misfortune, and their final proper relationship to me was not one of doctor and patients.

* * * * *

This therapy had a profound effect on me.

Any therapy with this young woman and her family would have been a moving experience, and perhaps we can imagine what it would have felt like to work more intensively from one or another single point of view. But it felt to me at the time that my patchwork quilt of a treatment had special standing, as if no other plan would have succeeded.

One had to treat the ward and the family to reach the young woman. By the same token, would any therapist have been acceptable to the parents who had not known their daughter and struggled with her care? The effect of working in this fluid way was not just to convince me that eclecticism was possible but to make me believe that in many circumstances no school or dogmatic approach would be adequate.

There is a longstanding debate within psychiatry as to whether medical model psychiatric care of patients can be integrated with psychotherapy in the hands of one person. And in certain regards, Julie's case underscores pitfalls in integrated care. The transition from liaison psychiatrist to individual therapist involved a touchy transfer of allegiances. (More broadly, the engagement with Julie made me keenly aware of the ethical difficulties inherent in certain liaison strategies.) And, if we think only of the individual dynamic work, once I had advocated hypnotism for Julie it was that much harder to establish a working alliance. Once I had attributed the nightmare to drug side effect, the dream content was almost unusable in the psychotherapy. But perhaps this is only to say that in negotiating complex combinations of systems one has to attend to boundaries and transitions. These are technical problems.

The global impression this treatment left on me is that the integration of models of care is a necessity, a *sine qua non*. To touch an isolated family or to reach the core problems of a troubling patient one has to take any means of engagement that comes to hand, and one has to expect the problem of "entry" to recur repeatedly. (To be concrete: imagine a skilled psychotherapist from a nonmedical tradition who immediately identified parental marital dysfunction as central to this case. Would such a therapist gain entry to the ward, family, or individual systems? Well, only if the therapist had a broad systems point of view to begin with.) To enter the ward, the family, the individual soul will take every skill we have; and sometimes we will wish for more skills yet. Working with Julie I came to believe that technique, where technique includes improvisation and living by your wits, is not an impediment to intimacy but a prerequisite.

I suppose we are bound to ask whether this case was not too atypical to have any significance in our thinking about psychotherapy, in the way that one might dismiss a certain judicial conclusion by saying, "Hard cases make bad law." But before grappling with that problem, perhaps we should ask what sort of case this one was altogether.

Certainly it was a case where the patient's embeddedness in different systems was apparent. To reach the patient, I had to think about the ward and the family, and not just initially but often. I had first to address the explicit issues on which everyone agreed—the pain and then the nightmares—before I was allowed to grapple with Julie's guilt over her anger at God and her sister; and I had to show I understood how special Julie was, and feel how terrible it was to lose her, before I could ask how the parents were contributing to their own isolation.

But put this way, the necessary steps in the therapy sound quite ordinary. I mean, don't all therapies contain these requirements? We continually earn our right to take the next step, we repeatedly judge what many systems require or will allow. The only special aspect of this case is that the steps are so distinct; the cards are fanned out for us to see.

I think we might also say that this treatment was special because it belonged to a certain genre, although once this is said it is less evident what that genre is. True, this was a "therapy of a dying patient," but it was not one where the patient was asking to be put at ease with death. (I have treated a number of people near death, and very rarely have I found coming to peace with the fact of death to be the central issue. People have all sorts of individual goals and problems which become starker and more pressing when they know they will die.)[4] We could say equally that this was a treatment of a traumatized healthy patient, or of the stressed or bereaved. All these labels apply.

But in asking myself what this treatment felt like, I concluded it was a therapy of handicap or of rehabilitation. Julie already knew deafness, a handicap among the hearing, and I came to understand that for her dying was a handicap in the world of the living. A separate burden beyond pain and medication side effects, awareness of imminent death interferes with normal activity, changes power relationships, vitiates ego strengths, and heightens anger, regret, and the sense of difference. It also constitutes an ongoing loss and thus acts as an ever-present stimulus for depression. As do blindness, cardiac disease, and chronic schizophrenia, dying requires adaptation beyond coping with the symptoms of the disability.

Cognitive and dynamic interpretations are important elements of a therapy of rehabilitation. So is attention to aptitudes, much in the way that bolstering of ego strengths while seizing the moment to encourage insight is a standard technique for crisis intervention. Indeed, this course of treatment can be seen as a series of interventions in response to a subacute crisis; the aptness of this point of view is evident when we think about the parents.

Any therapy that focuses so strongly on ego strengths will rely on the so-called nonspecific effects of psychotherapy, and these were no doubt important here. Julie made clear her gratitude for my traveling to her home and for my speaking with her parents. I never made any effort to interpret the positive transference. I hoped that, in addition to what therapy had to offer directly, the mass of interventions would provide encouragement for Julie to apply to dying the strengths she had used in adapting to deafness.

But once again, isn't this mixing of cognitive and dynamic work, with attention to ego strengths and tolerance for support as an element of treatment, just what we do in many cases today? Isn't rehabilitation an apt model for much of therapy?

I think we can also ask whether there was an indication for treatment at all in this case. Julie was never very depressed, the father was not very alcoholic, the mother surely bore no diagnosis. Beyond my helping adjust the propanolol, it might just be this way: a young psychiatrist got involved with a family and had a moving experience which he used intrapsychically for his own purposes. This objection is unanswerable, and I was aware of it at the time. It only made me question the concepts of diagnosis and indication. I mean, if there wasn't cause for a psychiatrist to work with this family, what is our job?

*   *   *   *   *

If anything, it seems to me that what makes this case atypical is the ponderousness of its eclecticism. It has a house-that-Jack-built quality: here first is the hypnosis, and then the propanolol, and so forth.

For work I was doing on psychotherapy efficacy, I once tried to make formal sense of what people meant by eclecticism. Certain Freudian psychoanalysts consider themselves eclectic when they succumb to a passing Kleinian thought. Here eclectic means something like tainted or, to be more neutral, altered. A treatment becomes eclectic when it deviates from a rigid standard.

Other therapists consider themselves eclectic if they treat different patients with different methods: dynamic therapy for psychologically-minded college students, interpersonal therapy for depressed spouses, cognitive therapy for rigid, emotionally shallow patients. Here the therapist is eclectic, but each treatment is kosher, meat or dairy but not both, and each according to its proper rules. Modern psychotherapy trials attempt implicitly to validate this sort of eclecticism-as-choice, asking which treatments are best for which indications.

Some therapists divide the course of a treatment into stages. Thus a marital therapy can move into individual treatment for one spouse and then into group therapy when interpersonal skills become an issue. Here discrete treatments are linked together *seriatim*. The work with Julie and her family was largely of this sort. More subtle serially eclectic therapies may use different approaches in different phases of therapy: cognitive therapy in the engagement phase, dynamic in the middle game, and so forth.

But it seems to me that most ecelcticism is not of these three sorts—variation, selection, or serialism—but of a fourth more fully integrated type. In this fourth eclecticism, the admixing occurs within the therapist. He has absorbed the theories and techniques of different schools,

[174]

and what he and the patient produce is a tailored therapy, one which arises broadly out of psychiatric theory but may not be justifiable in terms of any one school, and one which weaves seamlessly together the therapies it integrates.

*   *   *   *   *

Just after residency, when I was working in the government in Washington and seeing a few private patients during the evenings, I cared for another dying patient in a way that seemed to me more seamlessly eclectic than the work with Julie. The eclecticism was still serial, but the series melded more completely.

The patient was a well-to-do housewife in her forties who declined to undergo adjunctive chemotherapy for a surgically treated cancer on the grounds that hair loss, or any other modest disfigurement, would repel her husband and bring an end to her already shaky marriage. She was referred to me in part because she was depressed but also because her decision seemed irrational and almost suicidal. But her only goal in therapy was to stay married—in truth, to die married.

A white Southerner from an established family, she had in her one act of rebellion married a man of "mixed blood" against her father's warning ("All colored men are unfaithful"), and even now, 25 years later, she could not afford for the marriage to fail. She gave me all the evidence I needed to be sure her husband was carrying on an affair under her nose, but she herself maintained doubts. The husband, who had lost both parents young and seemed unable to tolerate the thought of now also losing a wife, had said he would divorce her once the doctors declared her well, so she saw no rush to be treated further for cancer.

There are cases where tempo is a dominant consideration, and this was one. I wanted the patient to be able to make a free choice regarding further cancer treatment, and my notion of what "freedom" entailed encompassed challenging a number of powerful defenses and unexamined assumptions.

The husband was planning a business trip to Montreal, and he had said the wife could accompany him, but only if she promised not to cry and nag. She badly wanted to go, but how could she?

I began by using this opening to institute antidepressants—to make her a more fit companion for her husband.

I also scrutinized her request to be in shape to accompany her husband without crying. Just how did she expect the husband to act, and what would make her cry? We anticipated that he would work all day and then break his dinner date with her in ambiguous way, leading her to wonder whether he was intentionally ignoring her or even carrying on an affair. The more we talked, the closer we came to letting reality creep round the denial.

Finally, I suggested to the patient that she accompany her husband but also bring along a girlfriend and thus have a companion with whom to enjoy days and nights of planned activities. (I may have had in mind the work with Wendy and her gambling furrier husband; I wonder if in both cases I did not like the idea that the husband would pay for the response to his overbearing posture.) The patient would travel with her husband but expect nothing, thereby avoiding disappointment and tears.

She returned from the trip with substantially more confidence, and the therapy moved from a strategic to a cognitive phase. Why was she unassertive? Why was her self-esteem so tied to the continuation of an unhappy marriage? What did she feel she lacked? Where else might she find what she needed?

She soon remembered that her father had maintained a "back street" sort of mistress for years, in a way that was apparent to the children but ostensibly invisible to his wife. With the return of this nearly repressed memory, the patient led us into a traditional psychodynamic therapy. I put it in this way because I think it is important to remember that it is not only the therapist who determines the theory underlying treatment; the patient has a say as well.

Two related themes emerged in the dynamic treatment. The patient began to reconstruct the history of her marriage in a new way. Time and again she let slip details that showed her husband had been philandering throughout the relationship. The wife began to remember mysterious occurrences: a tuxedo returned from the cleaners when she could not recall having sent it out, odd letters and phone calls, strange names mumbled in the night—the usual details.

At the same time she began to reexamine her perfect childhood. She had been raised in taffetas and crinolines and had been encouraged to display an inordinate horror of dirt or sexuality.

She began to recount past dreams in which the cancer appeared as dirt. Could it be this way: that she saw the cancer (and her husband's infidelity) as a just punishment for having recognized her father's imperfections and for having disobeyed him in a sexually provocative way — dirt for dirt? Past and present became more complex and more understandable.

The patient progressed in therapy, but not fast enough in the real world. Understanding did not lead to action. Should I begin to give advice? Her pain recurred and another biopsy was scheduled. I called Behnaz Jalali and asked what to do. She gave that most crucial supervisor's comment: it sounds like you're doing fine.

Sure enough, the patient returned the next session with news. Her husband had asked what she wanted for Christmas, and she had replied, "A blank check to redecorate the bedroom." Then she had added, "I've had enough of your threats to leave. Since I will never be able to bear seeing you pack, do it while I am in the hospital for the biopsy, and be gone when I return."

This paradoxical command — asking the husband to leave when it would be most shameful to do so — came purely from the patient. To my mind it was the perfect moment of assertiveness, beyond any I could have suggested. To make her demand, the patient had to be able to risk what she feared most, that she would be left to die alone.

I also see the moment as more truly eclectic than any of the work I had so far done with her. The patient had internalized the prescriptive behavior I had modeled at the start of the treatment and was now able first to use the progress she made in the cognitive and dynamic work to analyze her husband's motivation and her own and then to craft an intervention.

The patient had recurrent cancer. We entered a period of wildly eclectic treatment in which the patient took the lead role, free associating when she felt confident and trusting enough to do so, plotting strategic interventions when they seemed called for. At one point we even used hypnosis and self-hypnosis to diminish pain and to aid in mastering social phobias the patient discovered had been making her overly dependent on her husband.

There are certain theoretical reasons why this shuttling among schools of treatment should not work. Dynamic therapy in particular seems to have a privileged position. In order for the patient to project cleanly onto him, the therapist needs to reveal few of his prejudices and to display neutrality toward the patient's conflicting urges. It seems we cannot direct the patient through behavioral prescriptions (thus violating neutrality), or share part of ourselves as is often done in strategic work, and then return to doing dynamic treatment.

The imperative for us to avoid contamination unarguably applies to certain patients. Therapies may fail, or languish for months, because of a comment that reveals too much of a particular aspect of the therapist, or even because of an inadvertent social contact between therapist and patient. Patients and therapies can be exquisitely delicate; and perhaps it is true that the "deepest" therapies do require the near-disappearance of the idiosyncratic traits of the therapist.

But therapy can flourish in many soils. In medical school I spent some fall and winter months with Milton Mazer, the psychiatrist who established the community mental health center on Martha's Vineyard, an island which comprised almost all of the poorest (in terms of year-round population) county in Massachusetts.[5] There is no anonymity on a small island. The therapist's patient will also be his plumber and school board president, and with one psychiatrist and one plumber and one school board in a town there is no avoiding these multiple roles. Mazer taught that therapy is possible in a small closed community; and of course the early psychoanalysts, who taught, summered, and raised children together while treating one another in analysis, knew much the same thing.

Even in the strictest of school therapies, our patients see us in many roles: counselor, physician, bill-collector, interior decorator, consumer, citizen. Families function this way, and much of what children learn is to tolerate and even appreciate each other and their parents in different capacities. The ability to shift frames of reference is one of the demands of modern life, though of course it is a relief, as in some therapies, largely to be free of this demand.

Some patients can tolerate therapists' shifts from neutrality to action and back, and certain circumstances push us into testing this capacity. I find now that I not infrequently distort a dynamic therapy by asking a patient whether he or she has considered a certain odd-sounding course of action or by recommending a behavioral solution to a symptom.[6] If the patient who has asked for advice does not follow it when it is given, then that behavior can itself become the subject of scrutiny. In many therapies patients are able without the need for explanation to distinguish therapist roles and tailor their own actions accordingly. The work with this dying woman obsessed with the integrity of her marriage was of that sort.

She went on to have both chemotherapy and disfiguring surgery. As she had feared, the husband left. But the wife felt some recompense in the knowledge that she had conveyed to her children the message that life is good and worth fighting for. She held her ground, and within months the husband returned, without a mistress. He helped nurse his wife for the remaining months, and she died as she had wished, with her family intact.

Just before the end, I lost all track of the theoretical underpinnings of the treatment. I was visiting the patient at home now, in her newly redecorated bedroom where she lay too weak to be transported, and she told me whatever last things she wanted to say while I admired her fortitude. (I admired the husband's fortitude, too. They had both found bravery.) This almost atheoretical caring seems to me also a part of psychiatry, that and, of course, providing a setting in which a person can say what she thinks. After the funeral, the husband, who at times had seen me as a hidden adversary, cooking up plots against him with his demanding wife, wrote me a brief and touching note, thanking me for letting him see his wife in a new light.

* * * * *

Despite their focus on death, these therapies were joyful for me. Beyond the sense of being in touch with the patients and families, I felt I had healing skills to put to use. These skills were part of me. I did plot out certain interventions: for example I gave thought to the pros and cons of using hypnosis with the cancer-ridden housewife, who I feared (wrongly, as it turned out) might have substantial capacity for regression at the wrong moment. But for the most part I did not have to plan; I knew with confidence how to act. Or if I did suffer self-doubt, it was in comfortable measure.

There is, of course, an idiosyncratic aspect to the satisfaction that accompanied these early feelings of mastery. Perhaps it was precisely standing steadfast in the face of death that appealed to me. Emotions related to my early years—when my father disappeared mysteriously to the sanatorium and my mother and I went to live in her parents' apartment, where my great-grandmother lay dying on the dining-room couch—may have contributed to my tenacity in these cases and to the pleasure I subsequently took in them.

Certainly these therapies were not aesthetically pleasing. They were full of jerry-rigged solutions to problems and plagued by false starts and half-successful interventions requiring revision. The success of their outcome is subject to question. Perhaps Julie should have become reconciled to death, perhaps the dying wife should have done without the futile surgery for her cancer. In conducting these therapies I at times lacked conviction regarding the aptness of certain discoveries or choices the patients made, and perhaps a longer, less frenetic treatment would have resulted in greater clarity. But there was so little time.

No matter. I had the sense of being a craftsman.

The particular craft into which I had entered was eclectic psychotherapy of the integrated variety. I was not, finally, varying a therapy, nor choosing among discrete therapies, nor moving from one therapy to another as crises arose or progress took place—at least not merely these. Rather, the many therapies I had studied were deconstructed within me, and I was able to turn their elements into new therapies to match the patients and families at hand. And I think this is how most therapists practice.[7]

To put it differently, when I say that skills resided in me, I have in mind a belief about the locus of eclecticism.

Most of the literature on eclecticism is written by researchers initially trained in the theory of a school or dogmatic psychotherapy, often a behavioral-cognitive approach.[8] By eclecticism these researchers mean the successful melding of common elements of seemingly conflicting theories of mind. The melding may be through referring to a higher order theory or through specifying an algorithm for combining approaches. In effect, these writers end in creating one more school, their own, to add the list of contenders. In considering themselves eclectic, rather than school, therapists, they ignore the truth that all schools (which is to say ways of delimiting and combining theories and ways of delimiting and combining techniques) are eclectic in origin. Freud combined theories of child development, neurology, and physics to create psychoanalysis. And we see Freud continually searching for technical interventions to match the reality at hand: nasal surgery, hypnosis, free association, the setting of termination dates, attention to the death instinct.[9]

To me the researchers' approach feels wrong. Practicing eclectically does not feel like applying a theory which is outside over there. The eclecticism is close to us, or in us. Yes, an anthropologist might discover an unacknowledged pattern and rationale to our behavior, but insofar as our experience is a guide, eclecticism is how we do without theory or how we cope pragmatically with many theories. I mean, what feels truer is that we have many tools and are free to use them as we wish, in line with certain vague strictures of the profession. Eclecticism is not what in theory we should do, it is what therapists just do, creatively.

Sartre said somewhere that jazz is like bananas, it is meant to be consumed on the spot. Eclectic psychotherapy is like that. It has a heritage, models, and patterns. But it cannot be done without improvisation.

*   *   *   *   *

I have said that eclecticism just comes to hand or springs from the patient. I would like to give a more mundane example—nothing to do with death or crisis this time—to show how I see this to be so.

Not long ago I found myself engaged with a woman patient in a moderately successful therapy which relied on cognitive and behavioral techniques, with some family-of-origin coaching, to none of which I had encountered resistance. I was planning a three-day weekend with my family, and as a result I had to reschedule the patient's Friday appointment for Thursday. She came, but from the moment she entered the office she was sullen and uncooperative.

I asked what was wrong, but without result. Was it the changed appointment?

Finally the young woman acknowledged she was angry because I was taking my son skiing when I should be seeing her. It turned out that on her way in she had noticed that a ski rack had appeared on my car. But the reference to a son was more mysterious. The only child I had old enough to ski was a daughter, and the patient had once seen a photograph of my children and was generally aware of their ages.

I asked what she meant, and she replied, "But I have no conscious fantasy about your children."

I said she did have a conscious fantasy—that I was taking a son skiing.

What she had meant to say was she had no unconscious fantasy, a claim which now seemed unlikely.

She then said that when she saw the ski rack she had remembered an occasion when she had surgery delayed because a doctor in the community had taken time off after his wife gave birth to a son. She realized now that she had conflated the episodes.

But I knew well that the surgeon in question had only daughters.

This second discrepancy was hard to ignore, and we were led to considering the patient's jealousy of her brother and his role in relation to their father—in short, to a very different psychotherapy.

What struck me about this session was how small a role I played in the choice of modality. Perhaps someone could have resisted exploring the comment about a son, but only someone with greater forbearance than I have.

This sort of episode makes me doubt the feasibility of systematizing eclecticism, and also to doubt the argument that patients cannot tolerate our mixing treatments. Patients are a mixture of needs. The question is how much discipline we ought to exercise in ignoring certain needs. Well, some discipline. For example, we do not allow regression in every patient. But to the extent that our method relies on immediacy, we will want to be free to follow where patients lead and to act on our understanding.

*   *   *   *   *

When I depict eclectic psychotherapy as the skillful use of tools and concepts associated with diverse theories of mind, I do not, through stressing the primacy of techniques, mean to imply that such treatment is more mechanistic than school or dogmatic approaches. Instead, when I say eclectic I suspect I mean something not distant from what others call existential. The main tool of therapy is being there with the patient or, to put it differently, listening. But being there or listening for psychiatrists necessarily entails simultaneous awareness of possible theoretical perspectives and interventions. We listen as a musician might listen to music, at once passively and with a critical ear and with a mind open for alternative possibilities. We are existential, but we are existential professionals.

Hellmuth Kaiser epitomized existential psychiatry in a script in the form of a play about two psychiatrists.[10] Into the office of a Dr. Terwin comes a Mrs. Porfiri. She is the wife of a psychiatrist who is depressed and drifting toward suicide but who will not accept treatment. Mrs. Porfiri belives Terwin is the only psychiatrist likely to agree to do what she has in mind: go to see Dr. Porfiri as his patient. Terwin assents to the crazy plan, and much of the rest of the drama consists of dialogues between Terwin, the apparent patient, and Dr. Porfiri, the "real" patient. Of course both characters have the traits and feelings of doctor and patient.

The dialogues are Kaiser's attempt to define the essence of psychotherapy, psychotherapy stripped of form and convention. For Kaiser, psychotherapy is listening, which is to say focused attention accompanied by communication characterized by immediacy.

At one point Terwin complains that Porfiri, in the therapist role, is not listening. Porfiri asks what Terwin imagines is preventing Porfiri from listening. Terwin answers: "Your preoccupation with therapy. What I mean is: You are obviously under the urge to do something— oh— *therapeutic!* —no matter what you feel or how you feel. You are keeping yourself, should I say, protected or at a distance from what I am saying, so that you can manage not to take it in, not as you would take in an ordinary telephone message or the question of your neighbor when he asks you whether your electricity has been cut off . . . "

Dr. Porfiri becomes agitated and blurts out, "Excuse me—Why are you talking to me in this way? No, that's not what I wanted to say."

Dr. Terwin responds, "Are you sure? I rather got the impression that was exactly what you felt like saying, while at the same time you seemed to feel you shouldn't." What is unique about psychotherapy, according to Terwin, is that people are not selling each other anything nor coming to an agreement about resolutions; rather, they are saying what they feel like saying.

It is almost, if not quite true, to say we are with Kaiser: all we do is listen and respond with immediacy. But today the listener, if he is honest, is burdened and strengthened by knowledge of nosology, epidemiology, natural history of disease, genetics, stages of child and adult development, psychopharmacotherapy, hypnosis, schools of psychotherapy, and the like. And he will have the hope of specific cures beyond the power of the setting, the alliance, and the spontaneous human relationship.

It is not possible to consider the roles of theory and technique at length as I have done and claim to be in entire agreement with Kaiser. (This is what is sad about being so laden with this new biopsychosocial profession—we do lose immediacy.) But I wonder whether the more important part of Kaiser's message does not lie in the structure of the drama. Psychotherapy can be conducted through quite unconventional actions, in fact by a man in another man's office in the posture of his patient. All that matters is what the situation requires. So that asking to be taught signing or sending someone gambling or rising toward the patient with arms extended is psychotherapy, that effective medical technical intervention.

Indeed, rather than saying eclectic psychotherapy is existential, we might equally call it medical and mean much the same thing. Plato, not always an admirer of the medical arts, nevertheless in the *Statesman* uses the physician to epitomize the professional who, though he can sum up his craft in rules, is master of those rules.[11] The doctor cures in a way that is sensitive to circumstance and is not bound rigidly by past prescriptions.

As craftsmen we have skills but we act as circumstance dictates. That is, we act in accordance with the reality principle: we try to see clearly and not lie to ourselves, least of all by hiding behind our own strictures. We are a guild (and this is the only sort of guild worth belonging to) whose rules include the injunction to disobey the guild's rules. These eclectic cases with the two dying patients mattered all the more to me because I understood them to be instances in which challenging convention did not place me over and against the profession but firmly within it.

Ambiguous Profession

What Is Psychotherapy?

There are definitions, of course. But how can they encompass backrubs, silence, injunctions to gamble, asking for instruction in signing, identifying nightmares as a drug side effect, chatting about gardening, throwing a patient in the shower, doubting the identity of a mythical amazon, rising with arms outstretched to embrace a violent paranoid woman?

Most attempts to define psychotherapy rely on intent and theory. Backrubs and silences are not therapy when they occur as a matter of course, independent of theory and without intent to cure.

Perhaps the most catholic definition is the one developed by Lewis Wolberg after taking into account 36 more parochial attempts by eminent psychoanalysts and psychologists. Wolberg writes: "Psychotherapy is the treatment, by psychological means, of problems of an emotional nature in which a trained person deliberately establishes a professional relationship with the patient with the object of (1) removing, modifying, or retarding existing symptoms, (2) mediating disturbed patterns of behavior, and (3) promoting positive personality growth and development."[1]

This is good as far as it goes. Theory resides in the adjectives "psychological," "trained," and "professional," and intent in the words "treatment," "means," "deliberately," and "with the object"—although it may vitiate the definition to include throwing someone in the shower as psychological means. Aren't we finessing the whole issue unless we bravely go back and define psychological?

But let us turn first to the question of intent. For it to be psychotherapy must we mean it to be that way?

I think, for instance, of a woman psychiatrist who came before the largely male medical staff of our local private mental hospital to argue that premenstrual syndrome is not a psychiatric illness. Her stance was political—women should not be burdened with a psychiatric label for a common variant in biopsychological functioning—but she presented a scientific argument as well, based on her own research. The details of the work matter little for our purposes here.[2] Suffice it to say she excluded from her sample, even if they had perimenstrual exacerbations, women who met standard criteria for depression, anxiety disorders, epilepsy, migraine and the like and was left with a cohort of less generally ill women who suffered a 60 percent worsening of symptoms, largely difficulties with mood or irritability, in the 10 days before menses for at least two monthly cycles.

These women filled out weekly reports on their symptoms and came as a group to the psychiatrist's clinic office, where they discussed their problems with one another and asked the psychiatrist questions about their symptoms. They were helped in concrete ways—encouraged not to make irrevocable decisions on their most irritable days and so forth—but medicated if at all only minimally. The psychiatrist's findings were that 80 percent of these women recovered (in the sense that the variability of their symptoms over the course of a cycle dropped below 60 percent) during the course of the study, without a need for progesterone, diuretics, antidepressants, or anticonvulsants. She concluded that once you exclude diagnosable illnesses, what remains of "PMS" is a self-limited normal variant.

After discussion with the speaker regarding what constitutes a psychiatric disorder, the medical staff settled on a simple question: does PMS respond most often to treatments most usually given by psychiatrists? And with regard to the presenter's own research: hadn't her patients improved because she treated them with psychotherapy?

But no, the speaker, replied, you misunderstood me. I didn't do psychotherapy.

Did she or didn't she?

The staff argued: you ran a therapeutic support group, supplemented by individual counseling. If this condition remits spontaneously, why did your patients show up in the first place? One flattering questioner alluded to the speaker's thoughtful and compassionate presentation of self. She could not have helped doing therapy with her suffering research subjects.

The speaker replied, when I do therapy with patients, I do very different things from what I did here. The PMS sufferers just chatted with each other while waiting to speak with me. I asked them for clarification about their symptoms, and I gave them practical advice and information and encouragement. If I had wanted to do psychotherapy, I would have done something quite different, withholding myself in certain ways, letting the group process develop, and so forth.

Perhaps it is best to steer clear of the questions of whether premenstrual syndrome exists and whether it merits a psychiatric diagnosis. I want simply to ask, was the researcher doing psychotherapy?

There are many ways to approach this question. One way is to dodge the issue by asking, for what purpose do we want to call it psychotherapy?

Let us imagine (my mind wandered in this direction as the dialogue at the meeting progressed) that the researcher set up shop in our town and advertised herself as doing psychotherapy for PMS — and then the medical staff discovered all she was doing was passing out rating forms, having patients chat with each other, answering certain questions, and providing information and advice. The staff might then protest that she was misrepresenting her treatment. She didn't do psychotherapy at all, or she was very bad at doing it. For the purpose of getting a certificate or diploma in psychotherapy, what she did would certainly not be considered adequate.

On the other hand, if the researcher were helping to conduct a controlled trial of psychotherapy and hers was to be the placebo or "no treatment" condition, we might say she was doing too much. Her actions would likely obscure the effects of the active treatment. For these purposes we would want to say she was "doing psychotherapy." This is a common occurrence; often we read reports in which a placebo treatment appears to produce results (early studies in which meditation groups were used as a control condition sometimes had this outcome). Indeed, so effective are some of these interventions that in their famous meta-analysis of psychotherapy outcome studies, Smith, Glass, and Miller included "placebo therapies" as a category of active treatment.[3]

So what the researcher did might be psychotherapy for some purposes and not for others. But this is as much as to say that a person can be doing psychotherapy without intending it.

And this conclusion comports with observations we have made earlier. Consider the time I consulted to the nurse-clinician over the nightmares of the young woman dying of collagen-vascular disease. In attributing the patient's symptoms to propanolol, I did not intend to be doing psychotherapy; indeed, it may be I was trying to avoid having to do psychotherapy. But because of the context in which the intervention occurred, it turned out I was doing psychotherapy after all, namely, creating the conditions for the establishment of trust, by reassuring the patient I would attend to her suffering without overinterpreting symptoms she considered physical and involuntary. In other contexts this same intervention — attributing symptoms to medication — would have remained entirely within the nonpsychotherapeutic medical frame.

To return to our by now largely hypothetical researcher: what about her interaction is psychotherapy?

Well, her behavior meets some of the criteria of the stock definition. She deliberately established a professional relationship with patients; it seems fair enough to call these research subjects patients and to call the relationship professional.[4] She had the intention, along with other intentions, of changing maladaptive behavior patterns, for instance by advising the women not to make irrevocable decisions when irritable. Wolberg uses the conjunction "and" to demand that therapy attend all at once to symptoms, behavior, and personality; but surely that part of the definition is too exigent — many therapies are aimed only at one of the three targets.

Isn't the key question whether just giving encouragement and advice constitutes psychological means? Perhaps it matters how the advice is given.

In order to say whether she was doing psychotherapy we might want to know more about what the researcher does when she is with the patients. Let us imagine she wants only to do research on PMS. But as we watch her, we note that she, all unintending, acts as a seasoned psychotherapist would, skillfully maintaining just the right interpersonal distance, reassuring anxious women enough to allow a return to better functioning but not so much as to induce overdependency, nonjudgmentally asking unassertive women exactly why they assume they must continue to allow themselves to be mistreated, encouraging mostly recovered patients to enjoy the satisfaction of teaching coping skills to newcomers, interfering with malignant patterns of group formation, and so forth. I think then we would say she was doing psychotherapy, and doing it on the basis of her professional training. And we would say this whether or not she contravened any particular rule of psychotherapy—even such an important one as having an explicit treatment plan in mind.

When Roy Schafer wrote of "the analytic attitude," he was in truth outlining a complex set of technical maneuvers as well as defining a type of intentionality toward patients.[5] But in a simpler sense there is a psychotherapeutic attitude, characterized by acceptance, neutrality, abstinence, insight, empathy, proper social distance, and the like, which a person may bring to many situations and which may be therapeutic.

At a recent professional meeting, Michael F. Basch, the self psychologist, reported what he called an "unintentional psychotherapy" in a taxicab with a troubled cabbie. The hack began the ride by attacking Basch for being a rich doctor. The weather was snowy, and, uncomfortable at being at an angry man's mercy on slippery roads, Basch tried to mollify him. Through empathic responses, Basch was able to maintain a proper distance, ally with the cabbie, and finally to compliment him on his real skill as a driver. When Basch happened to take the same cab a second time, the hack told him how the memory of their first conversation had raised his self-esteem and helped him avoid a needless brawl in a bar. Basch characterized the encounter as a therapy utilizing alter ego, idealizing, and mirror transference to produce a transmuting internalization.[6] Even if Basch is a quick thinker, this was a therapy short on plan or intent. It began as mere self-defense. The question is just which interactions governed by the psychotherapeutic attitude ought to be called psychotherapy.

We may now wish to retreat and more closely specify "psychological means." But we know this business is tricky, since backrubs and silences alike turn out to be psychological means. You can't tell what are psychological means just by looking at them.

Imagine quite a different scenario. When we observe the researcher, we find she behaves toward the patients as, to use a stereotype, a gruff surgeon might. Then we would want to say, she is merely acting in her capacity as an investigator and is not doing psychotherapy.

But what if after acting gruff she then said, I was trying to do psychotherapy after all? We might say, well, you didn't succeed. And if she answered, but I had the object of helping, we would say, the means you used weren't psychological (or, you did not display the psychotherapeutic attitude). But then she might convince us they were, if she had some rationale for having been peremptory, and then we might come to agree with her. And in this case we might be tempted to say her intentionality mattered after all. But I think then we would do better to say we had learned something new about psychological means (and the requisite attitude), and it is only happenstance that we learned it from her; had we learned it from someone else we would just have recognized sooner what she was doing. That is, we would have recognized her actions as falling within the tradition of psychotherapy.

But then let us imagine she had no psychological intent but was just a gruff person who happened to do well with patients. I have in mind a story from the early days of cardiac care units. One CCU had extraordinarily good results, and when researchers went back to try to account for its success, it turned out all the difference was due to the patients of one nurse, a forceful woman who told those under her care that no one could die while he was hooked up to a cardiac monitor. This was an effective intervention, and one we might even seek to replicate in a modified way. But I don't think we would want to call just having acted in this way, without any more specific theory or intention, psychotherapy. So that for an interaction to qualify as psychotherapy we might require more than "cure through 'psychological means'" alone. The plan and intent matter after all, not just the means.

It seems we are in a mess. Since the time of Wittgenstein, we have been less surprised that attempts at definition lead us into messes. We expect less of definitions. For many concepts, the thing just is what we know it to be. If the definition fails, it is the definition which has failed, not the elusive concept.

Regarding psychotherapy, it may seem the mess is growing because of the multiplication of genres. Historically, psychotherapy begins as psychoanalysis, which seems definable, and then behavior therapy, which also has discrete theory, rules, and methods.

This observation may lead us to wonder whether it would not be better to define psychotherapy genre by genre, and then define the whole as the collection of genres, the way we might want to postpone defining the concept of "game" until after first understanding checkers, cricket, blind man's buff, and the like.

There are, it seems to me, at least two problems with this approach. First, in an eclectic era the genres are no longer so definable as they once were. Let us say we have set out the rules for dynamic therapy (as efficacy researchers do in treatment manuals) and then we have an instance in which the therapist rises out of her chair to embrace a violent patient who has moved to attack her. Is the therapy in, or out? It is the nature of modern therapies not to obey rules, for the therapy to take place at the boundary of the rules. The denial of this truth—a truth which seems to me central to therapy, the way the ability to make and use new words and phrases is fundamental to language—is part of what I find disturbing about attempts to validate and compare psychotherapies by creating training manuals which define what is and what is not proper to a given genre.

Second, therapies multiply in the spaces between established school therapies, and this dynamism also seems to be an essential and not contingent part of the nature of psychotherapy. Merely grouping existing genres would omit most of what day-to-day psychotherapy is. And this method has an additional political and practical problem: when something new comes along, how will we know whether it is a psychotherapy?

Nor will it avail us to spread out the genres and ask what is common to them. When I mentioned Wittgenstein just now, I had in mind the way he attempts to define language by first defining games, comparing the language game (*Sprachspiel*) with chess (*Schachspiel*). He is teaching us that denotative definition will not do for this sort of concept.

Wittgenstein writes:

Consider for example the proceedings that we call "games." I mean board-games, card-games, ball-games, Olympic games, and so on. What is common to them all?—Don't say: "There *must* be something common, or they would not be called 'games'"—but *look and see* whether there is anything common to all.—For if you look at them you will not see something that is common to *all*, but similarities, relationships, and a whole series of them at that. To repeat: don't think, but look!—Look for example at board-games, with their multifarious relationships. Now pass to card-games; here you may find correspondences with the first group, but many common features drop out, and others appear. When we pass next to ball-games, much that is common is retained, but much is lost.—Are they all 'amusing'? Compare chess with noughts and crosses. Or is there always winning and losing, or competition between players? Think of patience. In ball games there is winning and losing; but when a child throws a ball at the wall and catches it again, this feature has disappeared. Look at the parts played by skill and luck; and at the difference between skill in chess and skill in tennis. Think now of games like ring-a-ring-a-roses; here is the element of amusement, but how many other characteristic features have disappeared! And we can go through the many, many other groups of games in the same way; can see how similarities crop up and disappear.

And the result of this examination is: we see a complicated network of similarities overlapping and criss-crossing: sometimes overall similarities, sometimes similarities of detail.[7]

Psychotherapies are like that. I am not thinking only of distinct genres, but even, say, Freud's psychotherapy and Reich's, and Klein's, and Sullivan's, and Winnicott's, and Semrad's, and Havens'—which are from one vantage point all of the same school, or a limited number of schools, but for which different rules apply with overlapping and criss-crossing similarities. And we can see how the similarities extend to cognitive and behavioral and hypnotic and the eclectic therapies as well.

Therapies have what Wittgenstein calls "family resemblances." In families, it is not that there are explicit rules or generalities that will apply to every family member in terms of build, features, eye and hair color, temperament, developmental lags and so forth, but the resemblances overlap and criss-cross. Games form a family; so do therapies.

Well, how do we recognize that something is of a family? We just do. Of course, we may have doubts and may be convinced or dissuaded. Any particular rule may not apply, and any particular intervention may occur, and still that member may be recognizably of the therapeutic family, that is, may properly stand within the therapeutic tradition.

Consider the seemingly simple rule that a therapy must have a plan of action. This requirement is built into a number of the definitions cited by Wolberg ("'Psychotherapy is taken to mean the informed and planful application of techniques derived from established psychological principles . . .'"; "'Psychotherapy is a planned and systematic application of psychological facts and theories . . .'"; "'Psychotherapy in its broadest sense is the systematic effort . . .'"; and so on).[8] But when we think of this requirement we may wonder about all the "just good friends" therapies in which systematic plans are so hard to come by, as well as all the spontaneous gestures in therapy which upset plans but make the treatment work.

So we are left relying on such vague concepts as "family resemblance" and "tradition." I believe this is just how we understand what psychotherapy is. (Think again of the hypothetical researcher and the issue of whether we will accept a certain interaction as a placebo, before we know whether it "works." Think also of our opinions about "fringe therapies," and why we put that label on certain new treatments and not others. Our labeling of something as therapy has first to do with what it resembles and only later with efficacy. We might even admit as reasonable usage the phrase "an ineffective therapy"; if someone talked about an ineffective therapy we would understand what was meant.) We know a good deal about what ought to inform a therapy; we require that it accord both with our clinical experience and with a body of professional knowledge, developed within psychiatry and psychology and elsewhere, about human interactions. And yet the field of psychotherapy is impossible to encompass in any strict way. Practitioners keep pushing the envelope.

Certainly the field is not what we imagine it to be when we think of it most simply. I have in mind the notion of psychotherapy I had early in my training. I understood it to entail a human relationship with definable rules: the patient is in the office with the therapist, they share the goal of understanding symptoms through exploration of the unconscious mind, and so forth. Corollary rules relating to the therapist's conduct and inner state could also be specified: the therapist makes certain that each session is of the same fixed length, he reveals little about himself, he attempts to maintain an empathic rapport with the patient, seduction and support and explicit instruction are kept to a minimum—we could make a long list.

There is a sense in which these rules still remain with me. But as a definition of psychotherapy they are wrong, not just a little wrong, but wrong in every particular aspect and wrong globally. They do not even do very well in defining a particular school of treatment.

If this image depicts where we have begun, then we are now in strange territory. And the territory is difficult to map, because it is the nature of this land for the terrain to change as we walk it.

This difficulty leads to anxiety. I do not mean that as psychiatrists or psychotherapists we are anxious because we do not have the use of a comprehensive denotative definition of psychotherapy. (Of what do we have such a definition?) I mean that it is difficult to practice in a field in which it seems anything is permitted and in which simultaneously, because of patients' needs, much of what is permitted is in fact demanded. It provokes anxiety—and hope and excitement and titillation and shame and a number of other emotions—to practice in a profession where needs are so great and our ability to define limits is so weak.

*   *   *   *   *

Not long ago at a psychiatric meeting I attended a discussion group on the topic "boundaries and psychotherapy." Without having given the matter much thought, I assumed the participants would attempt to apply modern theory to the usual nuts-and-bolts "boundary issues": whether to accept gifts from patients, when to set an end to interminable analyses, how to act if your patient runs into you naked at the sauna in the local gym.

Boundaries are a standard item for discussion in psychotherapy. For the patient, psychoanalysis is a Garden of Eden with but one rule: you can say whatever you want so long as you withhold nothing. This injunction to associate freely is a boundary the patient inevitably, not to say immediately, transgresses. Given how clever and self-protective humans are, the rule is impossible to obey except in ways that are inauthentic and themselves liable to interpretation. It is the crossing over of this boundary, labeled resistance, which allows the therapy to progress, through its interpretation. Ours is a business of boundaries and boundary-testing.

But at the meeting, the discussion rapidly turned in another direction.

One woman therapist was treating a man who had earlier in life raped a number of women and was now implicitly threatening her around issues of termination. A male therapist had in treatment a child molester about to be appointed a school nurse. The stories became more and more violent and lurid. The group began to rally round the threatened therapists, giving advice on how to bring in the police, suggesting how many therapists ought to be in the room, and so on. We were discussing the transgression of boundaries all right, but in a near-hysterical fashion, as if we were all routinely engaged in an enterprise of the most dangerous sort, surrounded by enemies ready to ignore the most basic human limits. The issue was not understanding the role of boundaries in theoretical terms, but saving our hides.

I have treated dangerous patients, and I know how uncomfortable certain therapy situations can be, but the experience the group was discussing had little to do with the feelings I experienced in my daily work. And I wondered, how did we get here—and so fast?

I asked this question to the group.

Boundaries are part of everyday treatment of ordinary patients, I tried to say. Boundaries are our meat and potatoes. We teach students about boundary issues—money, time, gifts, requests for special treatment, questions raised in the last minute of the session, termination issues, contact outside the therapy hour—right from the start, and with good reason. If we attend only to boundary issues and ignore the rest of what goes on in treatment, we will still do pretty well; whereas if we attend assiduously to the presumed content of sessions and ignore boundaries, we will certainly fail. Psychotherapy is that game where attention to the boundaries is the essential activity. The historical origin of psychotherapy is the testing of boundaries by Breuer's hysterical patients. To understand boundaries, we have no need to turn to the most extreme examples.

But my reasoned (so I felt) plea to discuss the core of our trade fell on deaf ears. Within minutes we were once more immersed in mayhem, molestation, and murder.

One distinctive voice, an academic psychiatrist, tried to make use of the discussion of death to turn the meeting in a political direction. He told the story of a psychoanalyst who considered it as much a sign of resistance if the patient did not within a reasonable time mention fear of nuclear annihilation as if a patient failed to mention sexual anxiety. Where did the boundary between medicine and politics lie, and was there room for such idiosyncratic, but on their own terms inarguable, beliefs?

And what, he wanted to know, did the group think of therapists who held patients in their arms and encouraged regression to infantile states in the treatment of schizophrenia? And of therapies in which all sorts of intimacies were encouraged, under supervision? This was a respected, thoughtful psychiatrist speaking.

These comments threw the group into a frenzy—only the energy was not directed at the academic psychiatrist. Rather, he was pointedly ignored, and the discussion returned with even greater vigor to the need to control patients. Soon the group was comforting a psychiatrist who had to deal with a supervisee who, there was reason to suspect, was a seducer of teenage girls and who was about to rotate through the adolescent unit. At least I think this was the issue; in retrospect it hardly seems possible that in a group this size there were available for discussion so many instances of imminent danger from those under our care.

One or two other participants attempted to guide the discussion to a more theoretically interesting plane, but to no avail.

I tried to puzzle out the process. The message from the group was that we feel threatened and in need of greater control over others. This is a common theme in psychiatry today. We do feel threatened by insurers, malpractice lawyers, legislators, health economists, professionals in competing specialties, and a host of other "enemies." The resulting sense of vulnerability may make it hard for us to discuss any issue from a posture other than the paranoid.

But I thought the response to the academic psychiatrist was particularly telling. He had said to the group, it is not only patients who threaten boundaries but psychiatrists. (Indeed, although the ostensible focus of the group's agitation was patients who overstep what is reasonable in therapy, much of the discussion had to do with psychiatrists' temptations to breach the rules of confidentiality and certain other aspects of the implicit doctor-patient contract.) Regarding our own actions, we have no consensus as to what is acceptable and what goes too far.

I was not aware that therapists were still creating wombs for schizophrenics, but I had heard of past instances of this work and knew that certain leaders in the field had done it in their youth. The truth about this business is that we are often at an impasse: we know perfectly well what conventional treatment is and also we have a strong opinion that it will not work. So we are obliged to face the boundaries we have set for ourselves and decide whether to challenge them. We must ask whether can we can flout individual rules and still remain within some broader professional strictures, ethical and technical. With his extreme examples, the academic psychiatrist had brought explicitly into the discussion this particular anxiety—the one caused by the truth that we, as much as patients, are tempted to defy limits.

I came to wonder whether the group was not itself resistant and avoidant—of the ordinary implications of topic at hand, boundaries in psychotherapy—and whether our focus on the lurid did not express our feelings about the topic as a whole, namely that it entailed danger and the threat of craziness.

Sometimes it seems that everything is permissible. At one time, it was understood that the therapist revealed as little of himself as possible. This posture came to seem to have an ethical as well as a technical dimension. But almost from the start the rule was transgressed. We read that early analysts summered and studied together in colonies; therapists and patients knew one another intimately on many levels. We learn how the interpersonal therapists found it was necessary to reveal enough of the self to block certain harmful distortions on the patient's part. And we find that in family treatments it is crucial that the therapist show the parts of himself which mirror the style of a weak family member. We may even be encouraged to take on a false persona in order to reshape the family. So that this simple and clear rule fades to nothingness, and we run the gamut from anonymity to play-acting.

There are no certain guideposts.

Indeed, it is difficult to think of a proscribed action at the verge of treatment which may not also, in some therapy, be considered a therapeutic intervention. In terms of actions the field has highly elastic limits.

We live daily with the difficulty in delimiting the field. We do not know where we may tread, or, which is almost the same, we suspect we may tread anywhere. Some days we revel in our freedom. But there are also times when we project our fear of the chartless world outward and perceive threats from our patients which borrow their force from unacknowledged impulses of our own. Or, in the case of patients who are dangerous, we may feel so accustomed to our own sense of "boundary ambiguity" that we fail to set clear limits where they are desperately needed. (Do we really need to debate whether to alert the residency supervisor when we believe a resident under our supervision may present a risk to patients?)

I broached this speculation. To little avail. Later in the day two or three colleagues approached me to say their thoughts had been similar. But the group ended still debating the management violent patients of whose threat to society only the therapist is aware.

*   *   *   *   *

A serious, and to my mind troubling, response to the messiness of the field has been a sea change in psychotherapy efficacy research.

I know that this statement implies an odd theory about the etiology of research. Surely research topics arise from scientific opportunity or public health need? Or, at worst, from political pressures?

I worked for a time in the relevant part of the Federal government. I was "Acting Director of the Division of Science of the Alcohol, Drug Abuse, and Mental Health Administration," an eminent division which at that point, not long before it was dismantled, contained me and a secretary. I served just when the mania for efficacy evidence was at its height, so I am aware of the economic, political, and scientific pressures which helped mold the field. But I think the direction of the existing research effort would have been hard to change had there not been a consensus within the profession that things were out of control. Too many therapies had come on the scene, and the possibility of charlatanism had become too great. We had to know what was in and what was out.

One convenient way of defining psychotherapy would be via efficacy. We could say, psychotherapy is what works—if only we could say what works.

This effort has moral dimensions.[9] As doctors we need objective evidence that what we do can help patients. The question is what we count as evidence. In terms of number of studies, the broader question—does psychotherapy work?—is one of the best researched in medical technology, and the answer seems to be yes. While I was in the government, the Congressional Office of Technology Assessment concluded, on the basis of meta-analyses, cost-offset research, and the body of individual studies extant, that psychotherapy is an effective treatment.

But we are talking about an unbounded entity. What is it that works? For years, researchers, usually carrying out small scale studies of the process of psychotherapy, tried to answer this question by looking for the active ingredient in psychotherapy. Was it the factors specific to the various therapies (interpretation, behavioral prescription, and the like) or, as was often argued, nonspecific factors, such as empathy and creation of expectancy, common to many therapies?

Suddenly, in response to pressures within and without the field, the great emphasis turned away from process research and toward straightforward outcome trials, modeled on the safety and efficacy trials for drugs required by the Food and Drug Administration under the Kefauver-Harris Act. Nor were we content with seeing whether individual treatments worked for individual indications; the field moved immediately to comparisons of competing therapies for given indications, the so-called "horserace" trials of psychotherapy outcome.

To me, these trials constitute a curious phenomenon which requires explanation, much as the insistent discussion on patient violence required explanation in the seminar on boundaries in psychotherapy. It is as if we had agreed to imagine we could define as complex a field as psychotherapy with the crudest of research designs.

The expertise that goes into these studies is extraordinary. At different university centers two therapies are operationalized and defined in manuals. Then methods are developed for training practitioners in these therapies and for rating whether what they do conforms to the manuals. And then entry criteria and outcome measures are defined, patients are recruited, and it's off to the races.

But the overall research design is fatally flawed, something the field has known from before the time the trials began. This is "as if" research. We act as if this were a way of answering all the field's questions at once, only we know in advance that the results are likely to be uninterpretable. We have sacrificed the reality of proper research design for elements of the form.

To consider one problem: we are comparing two "drugs" without knowing their active ingredients (or how to purify them), or their mechanism of action, or their dose-response curves. A pharmacologist intent on testing such compounds would risk abbreviating his academic career.

Imagine, to choose a non-random example, we are comparing interpersonal therapy (IPT) and cognitive-behavioral therapy (CBT) as treatments for ambulatory depression, and let us say IPT performs better than CBT. What does this mean?

Well it may mean that IPT works better than CBT for depression. Or it may mean that the length of treatment chosen in the particular trial favors IPT over CBT. Or it may mean that the training manual for CBT ties therapists' hands more than the manual for IPT, and that therapists do better when given more leeway. Or it may mean that the training program for IPT is better than that for CBT.

Let us say, for the sake of argument, that the success of a therapy is largely determined by the confidence of the therapist. If the training programs have different effects on confidence, then the trials are really comparing training programs, not therapies. Unfortunately, the situation may be more complex. It may be that for one therapy, say CBT, confidence in the therapist is crucial, but for the other, IPT, the efficacy is unaffected by the manner in which interpretations are presented. Then even if we produce rating charts to take therapist confidence into account and find, say, that both training programs produce low levels of therapist confidence, we will not discover the real reason for differences between the interventions. One horse can run hobbled, the other can't; we do not know how they would match up unfettered.

It is easy enough to poke holes in this sort of research, the question is how it came to be funded. One answer is that the field was disingenuous in a certain way. These trials are not really outcome studies but pretexts for gathering large amounts of data on psychotherapeutic encounters which will then be analyzed in terms of process using other approaches. Another is that these trials are political window-dressing, a way of saying to those who would scrutinize us that we are making a substantial effort to police ourselves.

But I wonder whether we cannot adduce an additional motive, one closer to home, which relates to another flaw in the studies' research design.

To explain this flaw, I would like to imagine what would happen if (as is not the case) these studies showed that neither therapy worked for depression. How would the field respond to this evidence? Would we, and ought we, to stop treating depression with psychotherapy?

The answer is, it depends on the quality of the evidence. I think we would argue, correctly, that what goes on in these research trials bears little relationship to what we do in our offices.

Swiss psychiatrist Christian Müller made this objection when asked to comment on a large comparison trial which appeared to show once and for all that psychotherapy had no role in the treatment of schizophrenia. He wrote: "I have in mind some examples in which prolonged work with patients whose schizophrenia is running a protracted course has produced completely tangible results, not only in the therapist's subjective assessment but also as measured by objectifiable parameters in the patients—such as integration into sociocultural life, work capacity, sense of well-being, and disappearance of symptoms. How can we reconcile these isolated successes in frequently desperate circumstances with the results so clearly demonstrated in the present study?"[10]

Müller answered his question by saying the well-designed study necessarily omitted the question of *indication*, and wrote even, "It seems to me quite clear that the indication for an intense modified psychoanalytic treatment cannot be based on purely logical and rational criteria." The decision whether a doctor will, as Müller puts it, bind the destiny of a very disturbed person to his own is based on unquantifiable factors of countertransference, timing, the therapist's feelings about his status within his institution, and the like. "For the conclusion of a valid therapeutic contract between an analytical therapist and a schizophrenic patient, there must be a very great freedom of choice." And this objection rings true. We do not expect to be assigned just any schizophrenic patient and marry him.

This same truth, along with others, holds for the outpatient studies of treatment of depression. We do not in ordinary practice randomly assign patients to interventions. By and large we do not treat patients according to the strictures of training manuals. We do not even always attempt to remain within the bounds of a particular school of treatment, and when we do our actions do not conform to the denotative rules defining that treatment.

Indeed, the whole concept of manual-guided treatment, if the manual succeeds in tying therapists' hands, runs counter to the essence of the therapeutic relationship.[11]

At the start of the *Philosophical Investigations*, Wittgenstein has us imagine a language meant to serve as a means of communication between a builder and his assistant, or a tribe of builders and assistants. The builder calls out the words "block," "pillar," "slab," and "beam," and the assistant brings him the appropriate stone. This enterprise looks a bit like a language, but it does not allow for the play, the constant change, growth, and humor, which is essential to a language. It contains all of language except its essence. It is only a slight exaggeration to say that manual-guided treatment resembles psychotherapy in the way that the block-pillar communication resembles language. What happens if in the midst of therapy gamma for indication Q the therapist feels the need to rouse the patient from bed and throw him in the shower? Which defined therapies allow this intervention and which do not?

Perhaps something about the illness being treated in the horserace trials has blinded us to their inadequacy. Both IPT and CBT hasten the amelioration of ambulatory depression. On a certain level this result is pleasing and surprising. Depression has biological features and sometimes genetic underpinnings, and here we find it responds to psychological interventions. But in another sense this trick is rather like reaching into a magician's hat and pulling out not a rabbit but a satin lining.

Ambulatory depression is a condition which generally remits spontaneously and which appears to be related in psychic terms to issues of loss, isolation, and low self-esteem. Any of a number of human interventions which offer adequate support or instill a new sense of competency will likely hasten the remission. This is an important, even life-saving, accomplishment, but technically it is no great trick.

Because researchers have chosen an easy target illness, they have been able to affect it with treatments which appear to be definable technologies. And this appearance is, I think, the major, and intended, outcome of the horserace studies: the creation of the illusion that psychotherapy is more "scientific" than in practice it can or should be. (Just think of the mass of indications for treatment mentioned in the essays in this book. What resemblance do they bear to uncomplicated ambulatory depression? How often does it happen that patients enter our offices complaining of uncomplicated ambulatory depression and asking to be treated merely for the symptoms of that one episode? Well, it happens, but that simple indication for treatment is hardly representative of what we see.)

For political purposes and, on a bad day, for purposes of our own morale, it would be convenient for psychotherapy to have the form of a medical technology. And the hope of this illusion is, I think, the deepest reason for our enthusiasm for evidently flawed research.[12] Certain psychiatrists want all of psychiatry to be a scientific (I might say scientomorphic); and since there is still no substitute for psychotherapy in the care of patients, they would prefer for psychotherapy to be like all other medical technologies. But to treat psychotherapy as a science is to lose psychotherapy altogether.

If psychotherapy is a medical technology, it is one where more of the technique rests in the doctor than the instrument or protocol, or where all three are inseparable. If we are to test psychotherapy, we should first rely on our sense of what psychotherapy is and be certain that the gist of what we do in practice forms the basis for the trials we undertake.

For the moment, we are stuck with a number of minor indicators of our work's efficacy, including that most tricky form of evidence, our own experience. In relying on private evidence, we risk self-deception, but this risk is perhaps no worse than the likelihood of public scientific self-deception. Doctors practice empirically, where, paradoxically, "empirically" often means in the absence of clear rules and clear evidence. There are some anxieties you just have to live with.

* * * * *

"However he may get it, mastery—not a full mental catalogue of the rules—must be the therapist's goal. He must get the art of psychotherapy, in all its complexity—the whole tradition and all its technical options—down through the wrinkles and tricky wiring of his brain into his blood. Not that he needs to learn the literature first and practice later: The two processes are inseparable. . . . Mastery is not something that strikes in an instant, like a thunderbolt, but a gathering power that moves steadily through time, like weather."

When we think about particular cases, isn't that more how psychotherapy is—an art, informed by tradition and technique and synthesized in the instance at hand in the brain and blood of the therapist? The quote, of course, is a trick one. I have taken it, with four word changes ("therapist's" for "writer's," and so on) and an omitted reference to Melville and Shakespeare, from the chapter on "Aesthetic Law and

Artistic Mastery" in one of the novelist John Gardner's last books, *The Art of Fiction: Notes on Craft for Young Writers*.[13]

For me, understanding psychotherapy begins with the acknowledgment that it is an art. This belief may be wrong. Psychotherapy is unarguably a practical medical trade of which we demand efficacy, and if it were demonstrated empirically that artless therapy is as effective as artful, we would be obliged to change our minds and characterize psychotherapy differently.[14] But in the absence of that evidence, a practitioner's sense of what transpires is a fair starting point. Doing and teaching the work, it feels like an art and a craft.[15]

When we say a medical subspecialty is an art, we run into the issue of the "art of medicine." I have never had a clear understanding of the meaning of that phrase. It may refer to the way in which medicine, which is conceived of as a "hard" science like applied microbiology, is skillfully applied, so that the "art" part of medicine is bedside manner, common courtesy, masked coercion, and the like. It does not seem to me that psychotherapy is an art only in this limited way.

Or perhaps "art" refers to certain, but not most, things a doctor might do, for example diagnosis; we might agree that in all of medicine diagnosis is an art (and in this field there is computer art as well). There is an art to putting together information to arrive at the right conclusion, just as there is an art to designing research projects. Here art means a skill, and not just any skill but one which calls on intuition and pattern recognition. This use of the word art is closer to what we might mean when we say psychotherapy is an art, but it does not quite go all the way.

When we say psychotherapy is an art we mean something more immediate and comprehensive. It is like art as art is commonly understood—painting, poetry, musical composition, dance—a practice informed by aesthetic sensibility, tradition, attention to the medium at hand, and the humanness of the artist. This similarity to art goes some way toward explaining our paradoxes about intent. As a rule, art should be planned and orderly. Art is governed by as much theory and technique as we please to specify. But often the plan and order are only vaguely developed in the artist's mind, and sometimes a complex work will seem to rely more on spontaneity than tradition. There is even "found art," just as there are things which occur between people quite divorced from formal therapeutics which we might wish to call psychotherapy.

No doubt it would be fair to build an analogy between psychotherapy and musical performance or dance. All are learned in a certain way, not just from a book but through observation, historical study, and practice under supervision. But I would prefer for now to stick with Gardner's book and see how well we can make the case that psychotherapy for the therapist resembles the creation of fiction.

I like the paragraph about mastery, quoted in altered form above, because it gives a sense of what I mean when I say psychotherapy does not exist far from the therapist, in rules which are adhered to, but inside the therapist. Gardner is quite explicit about art residing in the person of the artist, and I want to take the liberty of quoting him on this point at length, because I find what he says so applicable to the locus of psychotherapy:

> On reflection we see that the great writer's authority consists of two elements. The first we may call, loosely, his sane humanness; that is, his trustworthiness as a judge of things, a stability rooted in the sum of those complex qualities of his character and personality (wisdom, generosity, compassion, strength of will) to which we respond, as we respond to what is best in our friends, with instant recognition and admiration, saying, 'Yes, you're right, that's how it is!' The second element, or perhaps I could say *force*, is the writer's absolute trust (not blind faith) in his own aesthetic judgments and instincts, a trust grounded partly in his intelligence and sensitivity—his ability to perceive and understand the world around him—and partly in his experience as a craftsman; that is (by his own harsh standards), his knowledge, drawn from long practice, of what will work and what will not.[16]

Perhaps we might ask for more self-doubt or humility, and also the ability to hide his admirable qualities at times, but in the main is this not an equally good description of the authority we seek in the ideal therapist? It is the requirement of this authority or mastery which I sometimes think is threatened by the ease with which we can reach or change people given new psychotherapeutic techniques.

I should admit also that part of what draws me to Gardner's teaching is his description of the troubling beginner, an aspect of myself I have not kept hidden in these pages. He writes: " . . . nothing is more natural to the young and ambitious writer than that he try to find a voice and territory of his own, proving himself different from other writers. Such a young writer is likely to take advice from no one, and though the fact may exasperate his writing teacher, the wise teacher knows it's an excellent sign, and gives the young writer his own head. . . . "

Gardner's emphasizes the need for seriousness even in one's earliest work, and he does not mean only that the enterprise of writing is serious but that the apprentice must take his own instincts seriously from the start. Gardner quotes Robert Frost: "I never write exercises, but sometimes I write poems which fail and call them exercises." When we teach therapy we are teaching independence. It will do the resident no good to try to please the supervisor; once with the patient, the resident must do what he believes will work. To act otherwise is to betray himself as a doctor. But this does not mean the resident can do just as he pleases; his actions must "make sense"—recognize the real constraints of the medium (I mean the patient's style, needs, and strengths), take into account which techniques work together, reflect thought about the training he has received. But the only adequate practice is work which is "for keeps," which means rules are in jeopardy from the start.

And likewise: " . . . art has no universal rules because each true artist melts down and reforges all past aesthetic law. To learn to write well, one must begin with a clear understanding that for the artist . . . aesthetic law is the enemy. . . . Invention, the spontaneous generation of new rules, is central to art. And since one does not learn to be a literary artist by studying first how to be different from literary artist, it follows that for the young writer, as for the great writer he hopes to become, there can be no firm rules, no limits, no restrictions."

This is, I suppose, what I find at the heart of the "art of psychotherapy," its simultaneous dependence on a tradition of rules and requirement for disobedience and inventiveness, its making of aesthetic law the deity and enemy—so that in a sense oedipal tensions remain part of psychotherapy, however well analyzed the therapist.

If mastery and spontaneity are the first two elements of psychotherapy, a third essential aspect is awareness of genre. Genre is central to storytelling. An artist does not set out to express himself, Gardner insists, he sets out to write within a genre—yarn, ghost story, or realistic story. But as soon as he starts, the artist begins to vary or meld genres or to create a new structure. (Think of Melville, or Conrad, or Italo Calvino.) What matters is that he maintain the "fictional dream," the continuity of tone, pace, and symbol that holds the reader in the tale.

Psychotherapy strikes me as an art of this sort. The great therapists—Semrad and Whitaker in recent years, or Freud and Jung—subserve their experience and humanity to a particular approach to therapeutic interaction, but only so far. They work in genres and constantly transcend them.

And this is why it is not true that "just anything" counts as psychotherapy. What occurs must make sense within the genre. When we read a ghost story we do not expect it suddenly to turn into serious moral fiction—except, of course, that it does when Henry James is writing. Ultimately, we will rely on something like an aesthetic sensibility to determine whether a piece remains within its genre, and whether it meets other tests of coherence, necessity, or greatness when it does not.

That and the patient's response. Awareness of genre is both a technical skill and part of the sensibility which contributes to the therapist's authority. We know the rules of dynamic therapy and, in a different way, we know whether the patient can tolerate the admixture of a behavioral prescription or paradoxical injunction. What fits may be unconventional, but if odd it will nonetheless do for the therapy something similar to the maintenance of the "dream" in fiction. It will further the story or heighten the tension without tumbling the patient out of therapy altogether. In some therapies we can act as flamboyantly as we wish; in the case of orthodox psychoanalysis, to offer the least hint of personal idiosyncrasy will suffice to disturb the dream.

In identifying psychotherapy as an art, I do not mean to undermine my earlier arguments that it is a technical enterprise. All arts are crafts. Gardner lists the skills a beginning writer must master: first syntax, diction, and sentence variety; then the genres; then the continuity of tone, pace, and symbol necessary to maintain the fictional dream. In learning therapy, we begin with courtesy, empathy, respect, the ability to elicit a history and do an unobtrusive mental status exam, fluency with simple clarification, interpretation, and confrontation, and also invisible basic knowledge concerning human development, theories of mind, nosology, and pathology; and the styles of mentors and the theoretical schools; and then issues of choice of approach and of timing and tone, necessary to make the whole cohere.

Mastery primarily means mastery of technique, where in this case by technique we may mean something more than the judicious use of particular interventions or even adeptness with the broader professional skills. The technique inheres in listening and in deciding upon which path to follow: character or content, theme or overtones, depression or anxiety, rage or love, commission or omission, word choice or tone of voice, symptom or transference, tradition or innovation. The existential moments in therapy—the errors, lapses, and leaps—are, if all is going well (and sometimes even in the absence of intention), fully informed by technical considerations.

As in certain well-crafted short stories, the technique at the highest level is invisible, but it is nonetheless, or all the more, present.

There are, of course, enormous differences between psychotherapy and art. The goal is cure, not beauty, although if we say that the goal of fiction is to move people in certain ways, we will be able to cling to our analogy a bit longer. And the medium—people—acts on us almost as much as we do on it, and on itself more than we do. The creation of the object of art (and is this the therapy or the changed person?)[17] is a mutual act.

But even when we move from the therapist's solipsistic point of view to take into account the patient, notions of mastery, spontaneity, and genre may be of use.

One way of understanding the continual changes in Freud's rules of analysis is to see them in this light. I think, for instance, of the the Wolf Man case.[18] Freud had previously relied on the patient to supply his own impetus for cure, and he had demanded that within the analysis there be the illusion of timelessness or eternity. But with the Wolf Man, Freud came to see that certain patients can use the rules of free association as a form of resistance, and he evolved a variant therapy to integrate the needs and skills of these difficult patients into the genre.

Equally interesting is the sort of artist the Wolf Man was. He used the tools at his disposal, namely the rules of the genre, to continue to express his character and illness. He turned compliance into resistance. It is this creativity in the patient that guarantees that psychotherapeutic genres must always change. Any static rule will become an obstacle to cure. In this sense, therapy is the peculiar art in which two participants, each attempting to act within a genre and each attempting to influence the other, are always stretching rules and striving for originality.

*   *   *   *   *

The problem with this definition by analogy is that it, too, may feel not quite right.

It may feel wrong for a number or reasons. After all, psychotherapy is not exactly an art or a craft; it does have scientific (or social scientific, or educational) qualities which I have downplayed. Even considering it as an art, much of it takes place well within the confines of known genres, far from boundary-testing or innovation.[19] I take these objections—that psychotherapy is in part a science and that as an art the scope of its originality can be confined—as understood and worth discussing further. But here I would like to consider two ways in which the analogy between psychotherapy and writing fiction seems wrong in terms of the day-to-day feelings of a practitioner.

First, we need to acknowledge that patients are even more active than we have taken into account, so that the art of psychotherapy often feels more like ballroom dancing or, to be honest, like the art of prize-fighting, or of the bullring, than literary composition. It is not just through resistance or aptitude that patients influence the shape of treatment, but through specific activity which can be more or less explicitly directed at affecting the genre.

I do not have in mind only "client-centered therapy" or "the customer approach to patienthood," abused terms which in their original meaning referred to a negotiating process in which the therapist's expertise, including his evaluation of the patient's wants and needs, played the major role.[20] I am alluding instead to the constant interplay of patients' behavior and our, and their, conscious and unconscious awareness of many possible forms of interaction.

I have already given two simple examples of this sort of interaction: the episode (in the prior chapter on eclecticism, "When It Works") involving the woman who was angered by my taking my son skiing when I should have been seeing her; and (in the chapter on technique, "Pièce de Résistance") the detour in the cognitive therapy of the anxious patient who could not give up his symptoms because of guilt over his son. Patients' behavior continually determines the genre of therapy. In work with more volatile patients, interactions of this sort can take place minute by minute, so that the shape of treatment is determined by an odd *pas de deux* with two sometimes competing choreographers.

Staying therapist-centered, I suppose we could compare such incidents to what happens when a sculptor encounters an unexpected seam in a stone and is forced to modify his vision to incorporate what nature provides, but this analogy fails to resonate with our sense of the resourcefulness of patients in creating their own treatments.

A more extreme view of this circumstance is that the art in the therapeutic encounter resides from the beginning in the patient, who has after all created a complex self, while something quite reactive—creative only in a secondary, interpretive way—is required of the therapist. The therapist is primarily a critic of the work of art, and the limitations of his criticism are inherent in the genre at hand. Roy Schafer says something along these lines when he writes:

> . . . the analyst is in a position analogous to that of an informed reader of literature, one with what has been called interpretive competence. . . . Competent readers recognize the genre, the historical period, the formal constraints and opportunities of one or another type of literature. They do not approach a Cavalier poet, a Romantic poet, and a Symbolist poet with the same expectations, nor do they read in the same way a lyric, an epic, and an occasional piece, when all three have been written in the same tradition. In clinical analyses, too, the patternings of expectation vary from analysand to analysand and from context to context, and varying with them are the forms and degrees of analytic activity.[21]

Schafer and other modern theorists try to encompass the many variants of psychoanalysis by saying that, at the core, analyst and analysand together come to create and agree on a narration regarding the patient's history, or rather a parallel series of narrations, one lesson of psychoanalysis being the possibility and necessity of multiple points of view. And surely one could describe all therapies, even those in which the therapist takes a more evidently active role, in terms of such a collaboration.

The notion that therapy is art may feel wrong for a quite different reason: most of day-to-day therapy seems artless and blundering, and it is psychotherapy nonetheless. It abounds in error.

Therapists' errors are essential to empathic diagnosis. When we are aroused by the hysteric, we take on a posture toward the patient which is ordinarily unacceptable in the physician. Likewise when we are depressed by the depressive. (Or when our mind wanders to mealybug infestations.) These mistakes, when taken into account, lead to the treatment plan.

Countertransference in the narrow sense—those perceptions in the therapist elicited by the transference—is error. We intend to see the patient without distortion, but repeatedly we fail. Our vision is clouded by the patient's expectations—judged by ordinary standards we truly misapprehend—and catching ourselves in this error is the basis for much of our work.

Our interventions are almost always a little bit wrong. The hallmark of a good interpretation is imperfection. "No, not like my father—but what you say reminds me of something I did with my older brother. . . ." This correction is, we are taught, the sign of our interpretive accuracy, or rather the aptness of our inaccuracy. Our works are not like Beethoven's, in which not a note could be changed; on the contrary, every one of our notes must be improved on.

We routinely say the wrong thing. Our speculations put us at risk by exposing our imaginative processes. Time and again we demonstrate to patients the right to be wrong. For some, this lesson, usually couched as willingness to take risks or make commitments, is central. Those patients most like ourselves, the obsessionals, are cured when they can better tolerate imperfection.

Error is a building block of our trade, a truth which makes it hard to call our structures art.

I once treated a woman with poor self-esteem who early on said she wanted to take flying lessons. Why didn't she? I asked, and, somewhat to my surprise, she did, with great satisfaction.

She then began to struggle with why she had never completed her graduate degree in social work. Each year she filled out the form to reapply, but she never mailed it in.

Why not just do it? I asked—and the therapy took a turn for the worse. How could I have failed to see the difference between flying, which was liberating, and professional school, which represented her parents' wishes? She now saw me for what I was, conventional, judgmental, and so forth.

I had made an outright mistake. But would we have reached her anger so readily if I had not? The meaning of the difference in the two choices (flying *versus* schooling) was revealed only through the patient's response to my empathic lapse. This is just how we work, piling our errors on patients' errors, lurching from one correction to another, composing a symphony of error.

There are perhaps too many examples of messiness in psychotherapy for our comfort. The sense of being lost characterizes the craft; one of the early lessons for students is mastering the anxiety that comes with the formlessness of the work. In time, we come to discount the everyday sort of error; the inexact or even mistaken interpretation is familiar to us. We turn our own slips of the tongue and even lapses of memory to good use.

But there is further messiness yet. Sometimes we try to stop doing psychotherapy only to find we cannot. We step outside the bounds, believing we are no longer doing psychotherapy, only to find we are doing it to great effect.

I had such an experience with a woman who made a move to "terminate psychotherapy prematurely." She began to deteriorate, and since I would not have the time to do psychotherapy, and since the need for action seemed urgent, I stepped out of role (not without irritation) to advise her concretely. Her response to this empathic failure was to integrate my move into the therapy:

She was a woman who had come to me unhappy in her marriage. In the past, she had engaged in intense, ambivalent relations with men with whom she became obsessed after they left her. She managed at last to marry a man who loved her, but after the wedding she faulted him for his lack of sexual sparkle, even though she had once found him especially "good in bed." Though she saw him as kind, creative, and energetic, she could not help attacking him.

At the start of treatment, it had become apparent that the patient's carping reproduced her mother's dependent and undermining relationship with her (the patient's) father. I had carried out a Murray Bowen-style coaching effort,[22] in which I encouraged the patient to spend time alone with her father. She discovered his admirable qualities and was then able both to take some distance from her mother and to enjoy her own marriage.

All went well until the husband was reassigned to a more senior job in a distant town. The patient was halfway through a year-long project in her own job, and she decided to let the husband set off without her. She would enjoy six months of separation and then rejoin him.

But suddenly she experienced a terror that her husband, who showed every sign of being unswervingly devoted, would leave her for another woman. She renewed contacts with a firm whose offer of work in the new town she had just refused. They agreed to reconsider her for the job, which would begin in a few weeks, but they would not be able to give a definite answer until just before the work got under way.

I was about to leave on vacation. If the patient were offered the job and accepted it, our therapy would end abruptly. Just at this point she began to display blatant narcissism in imitation and parody of her mother. Narcissism had always been part of the daughter's style, but its expression had been muted; it had appeared as a sort of appropriate grandiosity, a confidence in her intelligence and attractiveness.

But now she began to talk in therapy of how lucky the new employers would be to get her, how good she was in bed, how all men admired her breasts, and so forth. On visits to her husband, she criticized him for not being more enthusiastic about varieties of sexual experimentation which she knew he considered unappealing. This grandiose and demanding aspect of her personality became so prominent that I began to lose sight of the progress she had made and the very real strengths she had always had.

It made sense for the patient to rejoin her husband; still, by changing her schedule, she was managing to avoid resolution of the emotions of termination. I was afraid she would experience me as she had the old boyfriends, from whom she parted so painfully, and suffer the vulnerability common to certain partly analyzed patients.

But she would not discuss the end of treatment and instead plunged into vigorous worrying about choices in job and romance—should she stay here and have an affair?—worries colored by her newly exaggerated self-centeredness.

Three sessions before probable termination I stepped beyond my usual bounds. I was concerned the patient would leave therapy in her current state without having the way she appeared reflected back to her, and that she might thereby lose job, marriage, and self-regard all at once. Forsaking my therapeutic style, I ventured, in my most teacherly voice, that she had started to display narcissistic traits that would need further attention, perhaps through therapy elsewhere.

Now I never talk like this in therapy. For one thing, I avoid technical terms. They only invite intellectualization. And narcissism is one of those all-purpose insults, like immaturity, that conveys little beyond rejection. As for trying to introduce a new theme in the last days of therapy—whatever did I have in mind?

I did try to appear kindly; my purpose was not confrontation. I had simply given up, and I hoped that common conversation would do the young woman some good. In my own terms—in terms of my art—I was out of control. I did not feel I was sailing close to the wind, merely swamped and drowning. My referring to further therapy meant I had lost hope of a structured termination and was tacitly agreeing with my patient's impulse to avoid facing the emotional consequences of the end of our relationship.

But no disaster ensued.

Instead, the patient began to associate to the mythic origins of the word "narcissism." She had, she said, dreamt of looking at herself in a mirror. In this dream, the the top of her dress disappeared, and she found she had not her own breasts but those of a friend whom she secretly scorned for having a less striking figure. This image was accompanied by anxiety.

After recounting this dream, the patient was filled with emotion. She said she believed her troubles had begun years before, when her mother underwent a double mastectomy for breast cancer. The cancer and surgery had aroused strong ambivalent feelings in the young woman. I understood at last that in encouraging the patient's growth away from her mother I had inadequately addressed the guilt this new distance engendered, in light of the real and symbolic mutilation of the mother.

I now saw the patient's urgent emphasis on her own attractiveness not as nonspecific regression (and seductiveness) in the face of termination, but as an attempt hurriedly to work on an issue in the last weeks of therapy. Her insistent ignoring of my first mild comments represented another aspect of that work: a demand (expressed through making me feel inadequate) that I understand that her father, despite the strengths she had come to see in therapy, really had disappointed her in certain ways in childhood.

We discussed the unease she felt in her new closeness to father and

[216]

distance from mother. In her fantasy, to rejoin her husband without attacking him would represent a betrayal of her mother – and of her own childhood memories. At the last moment, termination was possible after all.

But where do we place the intervention which turned the tide, my irritated accusation of narcissism?

It is just the sort of thing I teach residents never to do: to intellectualize, to distract a patient from the anxiety of termination. If you asked me at the time what I was doing, I might have confessed I was trying clumsily to get outside therapy, to try to halt regression through an appeal to good sense. I had failed to puzzle out any of the complexity of the situation. I had missed the boat.

But my missing the boat turned out to be useful.[23] Losing control and accusing the patient of narcissism had very much the same effect as Max's calm refusal, in my own psychoanalysis years before, to accept my explanation of the identity of Penthesilea: the patient was able at last to come to terms her inner constructs of a threatening mother and passive father. The attempt to escape therapy put us at the core of therapy.

I suppose this would not be a bad definition of psychotherapy: the creation of a context between people in which mistakes are useful. So that – and is this true in art? – bumbling and mastery can be very much alike.

Therapy is the thing where, when you stop doing it, or fail to do it, or feel furthest from doing it – where you no longer intend to do it – you may be doing it all the more. It is the relationship where crossing the outer limit puts you back at the center of the enterprise. Or where transcending the tradition puts you squarely within the tradition.

So psychotherapy is an art. Except that it is often bumbling and mundane. And it is not always clear which participant is the artist. Well, perhaps some other arts are like that as well.

Because it is an art, psychotherapy eludes simple description. It is in large part defined by its traditions, which include both its history and its ordinary daily practice, but it is subject to change and continually transcends, challenges, or ignores tradition. Attention to theory, intent, and genre (or to such key elements as empathy, interpretation, and the feeling of engagement) can only ever partly characterize the art, because it encompasses acts and objects with overlapping resemblances but no universal common feature. Psychotherapy is difficult to examine because when defined in static terms it disappears entirely.

Like philosophy, psychotherapy's subject matter includes its own boundaries; testing the boundaries of the field is the constant occupation of patient and therapist alike – except that therapies which do not test boundaries also characterize and help define the field. Its essence is improvisation and immediacy, except that it relies every day on slogging and set pieces.

It is a mistake to say merely that art characterizes how one applies the tenets of psychotherapy or how one administers psychotherapy to patients; it is an art altogether – except that it is a medical discipline the practice of which relies on a working knowledge of science, a discipline whose only justification is the progress patients make and where aesthetics have a legitimate role only if they make a practical difference. To call psychotherapy an art is to say something metaphorical; it is an art, but only in a certain sense – only if we are also willing to concede that it is also not an art as we ordinarily understand the arts.

What psychotherapy is feels self-evident, and yet it resists definition. Its nature is, I think, best but always inadequately reached by metaphor, a limitation which is perhaps appropriate for a field whose work depends on metaphors, ones which are, however, always inexact and often good enough.

Refraction

Accounts of apprenticeship often begin with the author's decision to enter a profession. I would like to end with such a story, in the belief that it may serve as a lens through which to refocus the stories and arguments I have already told and made. I hope this unusual structure will prove appropriate to a consideration of a profession which often uses the technique of "peeling the onion," looking ever further into the past to understand the present.

I can, as it happens, remember the precise moment I found my calling. I was standing lost in the Negev Desert outside Be'ersheba, and I thought, if I make it back from here, I will become a psychiatrist. Like many epiphanies, and like many other events in the profession, this one was, even as it occurred, *à la fois posé et déçu*, at once stated and undermined, consequential and foolish.

I was en route from Jerusalem to Be'ersheba, where I was to meet up with friends to travel through the Negev. But my Hebrew was poor, nonexistent really, and whatever I said to the public bus driver led him to discharge me by the roadside far from the city.

He may have intended a conscious act of sabotage, because the path he set me on led not to a hostel but only ever further into the sand. It was near midday, and I realized after perhaps 40 minutes of walking that I had no sense of how to retrace my steps. Except for a change of clothes in my day pack and two bottles of orange pop, I was without supplies. The liquid might get me through the afternoon, and layers of clothes might suffice for the night, but even so, as I headed back in what I thought was the direction of the road, I began to think about dying lost in the desert.

What, I asked myself, would I regret not having done? Maybe you have to be the age I was then, just out of college, to ask this sort of question in these circumstances. It is, we can see with the distance of time, with any distance at all, a purely romantic question in a romantic setting, straight out of Chateaubriand. In answering myself, I began with mistakes or unkindnesses I might have rectified and went on to women and sensual experiences I might have pursued. But more and more, as I became certain I was well and truly lost, I understood that if I died in that spot I would regret not having gone on to become a doctor. And not just a doctor but a psychiatrist, which to me at that time meant a psychoanalyst.

The issue was one of seriousness, in the way that late adolescence is about seriousness. What in life is serious? What is serious enough in terms of a life's work?

I was in Israel "finding my roots" by visiting various relatives. This was on spring break of that first year in England (some months into my psychoanalysis with Max), where I was studying modern literature at University College, London. Something about Israel – not just the land but the presence and life story of a particular relative – made that work, of writing precious papers in the academic cloister, seem frivolous and decadent.

Chanan, an older cousin of my mother, was then in his late fifties, an owl-eyed scholar habitually dressed even on warm days in a worn and oversized black tweed sports-coat. He spoke little English and I less German and, as I have said, no Hebrew; and he was partly deaf from birth. To me, in that romantic and seeking state, these obstacles seemed to give weight to the words we spoke. I would in any event have understood that his words were always chosen carefully and worth struggling with.

He had been born to well-to-do parents in a small town in Germany. The parents owned the local department store, and as Hans was a scholarly boy it was expected, as in many Jewish families who could afford it, that the son would make the transition from *Kaufman* to *Lehrer*, businessman to professor. As a teenager in Germany, he had been drawn to literature, but he was drawn to the dream of Zion more, so over his family's objections Hans enrolled in an agricultural high school. With skills as a farmer and (borrowed from an understanding aunt) a thousand pounds sterling, the requirements for immigration set by the British Mandatory government, he entered Palestine.

He tried to convince his parents to join him, and they came for a visit. But the country was too harsh and foreign, and they returned to Germany, where they were killed.

For over 20 years Chanan (he had renamed himself after a character in a favorite short story) worked as a farmer, sometimes tilling land for ground crops, sometimes supervising citrus orchards, finally tending a flower garden. As each kibbutz became better established and more bourgeois, he would move to another more radically socialist group.

Meanwhile, he held to his love of learning. He translated Heine from German into Hebrew in the fields and wrote out the verses at night. On one kibbutz, he uncovered noteworthy artifacts while digging and helped establish a small museum. He became expert in the flora and fauna of the Middle East. But the focus of his learning was Biblical philology. He taught himself to read ancient Semitic languages, and in his middle fifties he produced a monograph on the Book of Isaiah so impressive that he was invited to join the Hebrew University.

He moved to a kibbutz near Jerusalem and at age 55 left communal life at last for his own apartment, one and a half rooms within cycling distance of the university. A former believer in free love, he was married for the first time at 57 to an Egyptologist, another quiet and exact scholar with another tale of survival and dedication and sacrifice.

When I met him, Chanan was working on a Hebrew dictionary based on historical usage, modeled on the *Oxford English Dictionary*. Each morning he would bike to a small room filled with file cards, one word to a card. I think I fell most in love with the image, from Borges more than from life (I read better than I saw), of a fragile, partly deaf man surrounded by words in dead tongues.

He seemed to know everything about Israel and Hebrew. On the walks we took, every stone or plant, every valley or streetcorner, had a story. As he talked, he stopped now and then to teach me about particular words, their precise usage and metaphoric overtones. But he had too much respect for words to publish widely. He assumed that any educated man would know what he knew. What he did write was brief and precise; most of his effort went into the dictionary.

He was a happy man. "*Bescheiden*" was his wife's word for him, modest, and sparing in his needs. Always on the kibbutzim he had been the last to accept housing, sleeping under trees or in a tent while young married couples moved indoors.

What impressed me most was his respect for the word. Praxis first— the land before the book. And then great care before pen is set to paper.

As a graduate student in English and philosophy, I was writing plenty without much thought. In college I had written more, almost become a journalist. This man's life seemed to speak to my dissatisfaction. No wonder I was ungrounded. Like Spinoza, the lens-grinder, like those medieval rabbis who studied practical trades before writing *responsa*, I needed a *handwerk*. Praxis first. Writing might come later, when what needed to be written would be so clear it would write itself.

It was these notions of seriousness and caring and service which rose up around me in the desert. I was not struck in epileptic fashion like Saul on the road to Damascus, but what with the hormones of late adolescence and my tiredness and the inadequacy of the treacly pop, my conversion took place in a hazy and affectively disordered state—I was incredibly happy—which a neuropsychiatric diagnostician might have considered quasi-ictal. Perhaps it was heat stroke.

I had never before considered becoming a doctor. My father is a pharmacist, so I had often been asked the question. Blood, I always answered, made me queasy, and anyway I understood doctors to be glorified plumbers. But now I asked myself what was so bad about blood or plumbing. The physical facts of life appealed to me, the grimier the better. The important thing was to have a useful role in society. By the time help arrived, the decision was made.

I was rescued by an angry Israeli soldier. He drove his jeep straight at me, jammed on the brakes and jumped out with rifle aimed. What was I doing here? Didn't I know I was on forbidden land, a military reservation? Once he saw I was harmless, he bawled me out with polyglot curses for wandering in the desert without supplies. Then, softening, he drove me to a city bus stop—I had been miles out of town—and sent me on my way.

And without looking back I applied to medical school, took the required premed courses in hasty fashion after having applied (it can be done—chemistry and half of biology one summer; physics nights in England while doing literature days; and organic chemistry with the other half of biology the summer before med school), and entered in the fall two months after completing my scholarship program.

Psychiatry would be my handcraft, grinding lenses for the mind's eye.

What an odd notion! A person does not choose psychiatry the way he might settle on (what?) scrimshaw, as a way of freeing the mind while the hands are at work. In literal terms psychiatry is the profession farthest from handcraft. So in what sense is psychiatry a *handwerk*?

Oh, it is, I would have answered at the time, under the spell of Max's scupulous technique.

But I wonder. Isn't it fairer to say I chose psychiatry because I loved Max (and Chanan, and my father) but found it easier to focus on craft than intimacy? I should have mentioned that my mother is an occupational therapist who later became a school psychologist. So that we might say I had to go to England and adopt Max and then to Israel with Chanan and finally to get off at the wrong bustop—the desert instead of the city—in order to allow myself to do what my family and I had wanted all along. I wonder whether most romantic journeys are not overdetermined in this way.

Also, working with Max had allowed me to come to terms with a certain part of myself, the part that favors routine and certainty over stimulation. I remember as a child spending occasional Saturdays at the drugstore where my father worked; I counted and packaged honey-and-horehound drops, or I restacked the toothpaste shelves. I loved these mundane tasks; though I was a very intellectual child, I loved busywork as much as anything. So that labeling psychiatry a craft involved a successful reconciliation with a denigrated part of myself.

And I know I saw in psychoanalysis a literary romance—the sort of thing the Penthesilea story typifies. So that standing nobly in the desert, I could tell myself I was settling for blood and dullness while secretly I hoped to retain the very same intellectual sensibility I was in theory abandoning for a handcraft. I was ready to throw myself into life, but of course I still had hopes of holding back.

* * * * *

The self-deception in this decision also had to to with the sort of craft psychiatry is. As do many college students for whom issues of dependency loom large, I had a stake in my treatment's being well-defined and theory-bound, because I wanted my cure to come from the method and not the person in authority. But I had other strong reasons for that preference which were entirely of that time, of that place.

I had come to London fresh from the anti-war struggles of American college life in the sixties. As an undergraduate, for months I had woken each morning full of guilt over not having done enough to change history. I could not imagine—had no inner permission to consider—a career which lacked, to use the dread expression, social relevance.

London was far from Vietnam. I enrolled first in the London School of Economics. But as I became acclimated, and as I asked myself what I was capable of caring about with sustained attention, I requested my scholarship committee to allow me to transfer to a program in literature, under the sponsorship of the critic and scholar Frank Kermode.

Even this decision, in favor of the soft over the hard, of intellect over relevance, was confused. As it turned out, literary criticism had become political and relevant. Kermode conducted an advanced seminar in structuralism which drew attendance from an array of international thinkers. There was a buzz of excitement over the deconstruction of novels and its meaning for the way we saw the world.

I found I had gone through my undergraduate days ignorant of the importance of ideology in contemporary intellectual life. In this respect and others, I was a Henry James American naïf abroad. Despite four years of anti-war turmoil, I was unprepared for the seriousness with which British students took subtle points of socialist and communist theory. I had studied political philosphy all right, but my political psyche was still awash in American pragmatism.

It was in under these influences—longing for the beauty and intricacy of literature, searching for a morally acceptable alternative to the imperative to political action, and newly moved by the intellectual force of ideology—that I came to my personal psychoanalysis.

I should also add something about the position of psychoanalysis in the small intellectual and academic community in which I lived. It was entirely mainstream.

Since my literary research involved different ways of describing objects in fiction, Kermode had introduced me to the philosopher Richard Wollheim, who early in his career had worked in aesthetics, defining the problems inherent in specifying the object of art. But by this point

Wollheim had written a biography of Freud and was now considering philosophical questions related to the nature of thought and emotion, the scientific basis of which he approached through the psychoanalysis of Melanie Klein.[1] Wollheim kindly permitted me to sit in on his graduate seminar, and though I had come looking for insights into literature, I found myself dealing, partly in psychoanalytic terms, with such questions as "Is thought constitutive of emotion?"

Putting aside the particulars of theory, the way psychoanalysis approached the world — looking for small symbols of historical significance and explicating their ramifications with great thoroughness — seemed to be the way good scholars approached any problem. Through Wollheim and Kermode, I came to attend Ernst Gombrich's now-famous lectures at the Warburg Institute on the role of decorative motifs, especially the acanthus, in the art of different civilizations. Kermode encouraged my reading in Panofsky and other iconographers who subscribed to Aby Warburg's dictum, "God dwells in detail." Warburg, Gombrich, and Kermode were hardly Freudians, but I took their work to imply that an understanding of what mattered in life came through attention to the particularity of images in the context of a system of belief.

I was familiar with arguments to the contrary. In Kermode's seminar we read the essays of the French "new novelists," not least Alain Robbe-Grillet who wished to rid the object of its role as a source of meaning. The object, Robbe-Grillet wrote, had become overburdened with significance, and he intended in his novels to disrupt this layering of intentionality so that readers might be liberated to see the world afresh, free of unexamined and ideology-bound meanings. But when I read his novels, I saw that they were filled with obsessionality and paranoia explained only though symbols; or else they "erased" that most object-ridden of literary forms, the murder mystery (in which the blood-stained statuette and the locked French window potentially contain all the meaning), only themselves to turn on the Oedipus myth. It was in Robbe-Grillet that I first read the phrase *à la fois posé et déçu*, but it seemed to me that his attempt to rid the world of signifiers was itself stated and undermined — he could do it only though immersion in ideology and symbolism.

Part of my own work involved an ambitious attempt to characterize the different ways objects contained significance in the literature of disparate periods. Having begun my stay in lodgings in Bloomsbury, I perused the novels of Virginia Woolf. I was struck by the ending of *Jacob's Room*, in which the young man's death is represented by a pair of old shoes. For some reason, the passage reminded me of the one in that "earliest novel," *Robinson Crusoe*, in which deaths in a shipwreck are represented by "two shoes that were not fellows." The thought would have passed but for another detail: when I went to read Woolf's diaries, I found she had been reviewing an edition of Defoe just as she was completing *Jacob's Room*.

I had stumbled onto (or discovered through empathy) the sort of nugget from which graduate school papers, not to say careers, are made. Not only that, but the reading to which Wollheim had referred me included Heidegger's essay on aesthetics which uses as its example Van Gogh's painting of the worn pair of peasant's shoes, so I was very much in danger of writing a far-reaching thesis on the ways in which the depiction of shoes creates significance in Western art, a contribution the academic world has so far had to do without. This effort both prepared me to leave academics in favor of more down-to-earth work and created the context in which I was to embrace psychoanalysis.

As did my social life. My girlfriend was a student of Wollheim's. Shortly after we met, she began a psychoanalysis with an eminent Kleinian. Together she and I rented a house with a friend from my scholarship program, a student of legal history who was also in psychoanalysis.

It was only a matter of time before we began demanding of one another the sort of honesty which is inevitably ruinous to close relationships. And we interpreted one another's foibles, wittily if we could. Expatriate and left-wing politically, for all intents and purposes we lived, 40 years too late, in the world of thirties intellectuals.

One of our less endearing qualities, I am sad to relate, was the way we took pride in the purity of our analyses. My girlfriend and I suffered repeated shocks of disbelief when our roommate reported on his treatment. For starters, his analyst, another prominent Kleinian, during sessions drank tea ostentatiously from an oversized porcelain cup (a copy of which was soon in said roommate's possession, a sign of weakness and genital competition, we felt). Moreover, this same self-aggrandizing analyst took the liberty of introducing our roommate to other patients, recommending reading, and suggesting career choices. My girlfriend and I flirted with envy over this privileged relationship but settled instead on contempt and even pity. Of an analyst who violated the rules of absti- nence, anonymity, and neutrality, nothing good could be expected. This extravagance made our own analysts' abstemious habits seem by contrast all the more saintly and allowed us to take pride in their orthodoxy.

Through the roommate's contacts, we came to know part of the London analytic scene. London boasted a vigorous young, cosmopolitan analytic community quite different from any psychiatric group I am aware of in the States today. Because the Tavistock Clinic, and I think also the Hampstead, allowed nonphysicians to train as child psychoana- lysts, people with accomplishments in diverse fields, usually the arts, leavened the group. And bright young doctors from Latin America, Africa, India, and the Continent came to study. People felt lucky to be in London. There was an intellectual excitement among the elect which seemed mostly free of defensiveness.

Mostly but not always. The group spoke the language of psychoanal- ysis, and free association out loud was encouraged. I remember attend- ing a party dominated by a vivacious, exhibitionistic young woman doctor from Chile. She had an explosive laugh which served to draw attention to her, something which given her decolletage was hardly necessary. Our hostess, a young analyst with an Eastern European ac- cent, dismissed her guest with the cryptic insult, "I'm sure her orgasms are just like her laugh." If this comment was intended to diminish my interest in the Chilean, it did not, but it did give me a sense of the sort of judgment the group was likely to render, one which took any surface occurrence as an indicator of inner sexual maturity or its absence.

I also remember analysts comparing their analysts' utterances, the way meditators illicitly compare mantras. One man tried to impress on me the significance of a couplet with which D. W. Winnicott had entrusted him. It began something like "Breathe me in, life's hope begins; breath me out . . . " or "Breathe life in . . . " I could not make head nor tail of it, but I understood it was meant to be a precious object because of the giver.

We enjoyed ourselves. I dwell on these memories in part because they are mostly sweet, in the were-we-ever-that-young sense. But what I took from this overemphasis on the person of analysts, and from the trivial use of analytic ideas, was an increased respect for the more rigid and dogmatic side of the calling. The job was important enough to be done scrupulously, and I was proud that my psychoanalyst did it that way.

*　　*　　*　　*　　*

Max's simplicity—his dowdiness—stood out handsomely against this background of aestheticism and frivolity. And his methods meshed well with my sense of intellectual enterprise and my requirement for high seriousness.

He sat silently behind me while I associated to the events of the day or certain ongoing concerns. His few comments were clarifications and interpretations of the most traditional sort. Of course, this posture on his part was facilitated by my own; I cooperated, I worked hard, I was willing to bear pain.

My girlfriend lied to her analyst, something I could not fathom. It would not be until the third or fifth time she told a story that it came out right, and she hated herself the whole while lies were on the table. She acted out, too, doing small dishonest or self-destructive acts that mirrored her shame. (But analysis transformed her. She taught me how different therapies are and must be. So did our roommate. In a sense I had three analyses; how could I help tolerating eclecticism?)

My acting out did not go beyond repeatedly losing umbrellas (my roommates and I considered buying umbrellas in bulk at a British Rail lost property auction; loss, I came to believe, symbolized prior loss, the losses of childhood), arriving a minute or two late for sessions, blocking in my work, and socializing with analysts. Free association and interpretation were for me the whole of psychoanalysis.

The goal was resolution of oedipal conflict, where oedipal conflict referred to the strong forces of love and death, not to vaguer yearnings for attachment and separation. (Therapy did not depend merely on the analytic *method*; Max held to the credo, set down by Ernest Jones in 1929, that the Oedipus complex is the finding by the truth of which psychoanalysis stands or falls.) What one learns from such a self-examination is the passion, the viciousness, the hunger behind simple feelings. Today, our patients are reluctant to believe, and we rarely have

[228]

the conviction to persuade them, that the short arrow of affection is really the infinite vector of infantile lust projected on a skewed and distant screen. I lived for months under Max's care in easy contact with a turbulent unconscious whose main elements were the fiery rage and desire of the id.

Today, I remember little of that perfect analysis. The resistances and interpretations have faded from memory. Most of what I do recall is at odds with the classical theory of cure through insight which I imagined Max championed.

I remember, to give a small example, a time when I was in despair over my method of studying physics. Scraps of paper covered my desk, I had lost all ability to organize, my mind wandered. I knew Max would interpret to me my resistance, against experiencing the fears dredged up by my becoming a doctor, a competitive act directed at my parents and him alike.

Instead he said only, "Perhaps that's just how you do study."

And, of course, it is just how I study, a truth I was glad to remember when I flailed about in medical school and after.

One has to have experienced the spartan quality of Max's analysis to see this comment as atypical, even seductive. It would have been much more usual for him to let me focus on the disorganizing anxiety aroused by the task at hand. That I remember this simple statement of fact as a gift is, I suppose, not different in quality from another man's remembering Winnicott's verse.

Another time, when I was about to receive a visit from a group of relatives, I wondered out loud what I might tell them I had gotten out of analysis. "I can say it's improved my tennis game," I ventured.

"Oh yes, tennis," Max said. He said this with just enough dryness for me to understand that he approved of my vigorous sexual behavior of the preceding weeks. And this permission to enjoy sex was, I suppose, as important as any interpretation of my superego's prohibitions against pleasure.

I have any number of such memories—jokes Max let slip, and adages, and comments and advice, and minor acts of reframing or relabeling— each of which was tangential to our main purpose or in violation of our mutual rules. If I were to try to reconstruct our work together, it is with these that I would have to begin.

That and the memory of Max himself. I see him as a warm and self-sacrificing man. He seemed utterly without egoism; it was impossible to insult him or puff him up with praise. He concentrated unblinkingly on the patient and the cure, which for him meant the unconscious. He was not elated by progress nor downcast by failures. Sly challenges did not get a rise out of him. He betrayed no curiosity, but he was willing to hear whatever I had to say. We sometimes mock this sort of neutral distance today as unnatural, even demeaning or discourteous to the patient, but it suited me perfectly. I understood I did not have to court nor please my analyst. We did not engage in small talk. I said whatever came to mind. I understood that the aimless action in my life was my own.

But for me to say this much is also to undermine the contention that the therapy rested on interpretation. If what counted for me was Max's calm center, then the cure was in part a transference cure. I do not think Max aimed for identification as a critical element in the analysis, but it was.

He was enormously kind and generous, something I knew without being able to say how I knew it (students of his later remarked on these qualities to me), so that much of the warmth I attributed to the therapy did not come from the positive transference alone but from real qualities within him.

I admire his steadfast abstinence even more with the distance of time and in light of my own later experience in trying to approach it as a therapist. What he did was so difficult, and he did it so well, that the analysis was bound to contain the seeds of destruction of its own theories. If therapy works through identification, re-education, permission, and the like, why must we place the interpreted unconscious at the center? My regard for Max made me a good patient but a poor disciple.

Although I wonder sometimes what it would mean to follow in Max's footsteps. He was a dedicated psychoanalyst and an instructor at the more conservative of the London institutes, but his technique was perhaps not so rigidly directed as I have so far portrayed it to be.

There were a number of hints throughout our time together that it was I, as much as he, who cared about adherence to rules. I remember a time when the consulting room was invaded by noise from construction elsewhere in the building. I went on associating, oblivious to the racket. I doubt I heard anything, so hypnotized was I by the routine. Max pointed out to me what I was ignoring. If I heard what was around me, would I experience anger? Would I worry Max was distracted? Was my obedience a form of avoidance and resistance? To associate in the midst of that noise was preposterous, and analysis is not a farce.

I remember also our last session together. It was scheduled for a few hours before I was to leave for the airport to return to the States, and I free-associated vigorously right to the end, hoping through adherence to technique to squeeze the last drop of goodness from the therapy.

Max interpreted my overcompliance as he said good-bye. He invited me to stay in touch and to visit him if I passed through London. "I can imagine you ringing up," he said, "and saying, 'You know—the American in the blue jeans who was here on scholarship at University College,' as if I wouldn't remember you without a reminder." And he was right. I had come toward the end to believe in and act on a parody of a human relationship. And the analysis surely was a human relationship first, not the pairing of an utterly impersonal therapist with a perfectly goalless free-associating patient. I had used obedience as a defense against acknowledging intimate sentiment.

I was losing him, him in particular, and he was losing me, and we were both sad over it, and I knew it.

And I came to wonder whether the Max I had experienced was the same one every patient knew. I knew in some respects he was, but I also began to ask myself whether some of his extreme abstinence—the minimalism of the therapy—had not been in response to me, because it was what I wanted and needed (because of the time and the place, and my reaction to authority, and the stacking of toothpaste boxes, and all the other reasons), and even whether it had not in part been created by me, through my fantasy of therapy.

It was not that Max's withholding, ideological, enquiring, symbol-laden variant of psychoanalysis just happened to mesh with certain social and developmental needs of mine; we had together created the therapy to meet those needs. It was our sonnet.

I did come back and visit. This was in the first year of medical school. (The time when I flew in to find Max had died was three years later, just before internship.) I had begun to see psychiatric patients of my own, and after the first encounter, where I frightened a patient into cure by interpreting wildly, I had tried to imitate Max's method of leading me into therapy. And when I did, I remembered that the way our therapy had begun did not comport entirely with our later standards. It had a subtly seductive quality.

When I began the analysis with Max, I was romantically involved with a young woman whom I saw as caring and even saintly. I tormented myself over the shortcomings of the affair. Somehow Max helped me realize—surely not by saying so directly, but through grunts and quiet questions—that in the relationship with me this girlfriend was in fact demanding, aggressive, and castrating. As I began through further corroborating memories to illuminate this less attractive aspect of her behavior, he then put her back in a more appealing, and more human, light by analyzing her and helping me understand her motivation.

In other words, Max led me into therapy by relieving my anxiety about my own behavior and placing blame on someone else; to a degree he gratified my narcissism. Certainly he empowered me socially. I was able to see the girlfriend's hidden demands, and also the struggles which produced those demands, and to deal with her according to her needs, not just her angelic façade.

Of course, we were left with many useful questions. Why had I chosen such a lover, and how had I managed to mistake her character? What about me encouraged her to act as she did? What was there for me in the idealization of women? Where was my own hostility? And so forth. To the extent that I accepted his analysis of the girlfriend's motivation, we had a model at hand for posing answers to these questions about my own. So I was thrown into my analysis by a sort of trick or technique of engagement. Max first helped me by analyzing a woman who had power over me, and once I accepted that help I could not deny the legitimacy of the same methods when applied to my case. This beginning provided a basis for the later examination of the Penthesilea dream.

So when I returned to London early in medical school, I asked Max about engagement and seduction.

We talked face-to-face, and for some reason tears streamed down my cheeks for most of the interview. I loved Max but already felt some distance from psychoanalysis.

In medical school, when I had begun a therapy by interpreting to a patient about someone else in her life—the kind of interpretation that is easy to take—a supervisor had cautioned me about seductiveness. How serious a failing, I wondered, was this leaning toward seduction?

Oh, Max said, that's why we use people as therapists and not computers. He spoke dismissively, as if I had happened into the middle of an argument he conducted regularly with colleagues, a matter long since settled in his mind. Indeed, I understood him to be welcoming me into the fold as a colleague and, in his quiet way, inviting me to take a broad view of the requirements for psychotherapy.

* * * * *

Some years into my practice, I had the opportunity to return to Israel. I almost passed it up. I was not eager, I found, to reacquaint myself with the urges of adolescence nor to see the past with new eyes. I was satisfied with the myth.

But in the end I went. Chanan and I walked again in Jerusalem. Less, though. He had aged; not so much as I had feared, but enough to make a difference. He wondered whether at times he had small delusions; we talked of senility. But on our walks his mind remained sharp.

The greater change was in the stories. On my trip 15 years ago I had gotten eveything wrong. He had in fact finished *Gymnasium* in his home town and had been denied access to higher education because he was a Jew. His turn to farming was more out of necessity than desire; an apprenticeship with peasants was demanded by the Zionist group sponsoring his *Aliyah*, and he had acquiesced. In Israel, too, he had wanted to attend college, to study Semitic languages, but the kibbutz required labor, and he was loyal.

He had changed kibbutzim for political reasons only once, and then to join a less radical group. (How could I have understood the reverse?) And of course the split was as much a function of group process—petty squabbles, jealousy and stubornness—as politics. The second kibbutz had no library, and by the time he was able, financially, to leave, he was ready. It was in fact as a student that he applied to the university, in his forties. Only later did he join the dictionary project.

After 15 years, they were still on Aleph. And this was in part because of turmoil among the researchers. The head of the project apparently had various faults as a manager—the usual ones, the ones we find in academicians here. My relative had published an annotated version of an ancient fragment of Isaiah, but now he had left the university to be able to write on his own, without having to allow superiors' names to appear on his papers. It was all familiar, no different from the American academic scene.

[233]

The story took on specificity, became less mythic. Some acts that had seemed to bespeak dedication were done out of need, and not always with perfect good will. Some self-sacrifice seemed to call for explanation of the sort we as psychiatrists like to supply: family dynamics, teenage rebellion, the vagaries of identity formation. The politics were less clear-cut, the struggle to clarify the origins of Hebrew more tainted by human foibles.

I did not regret having gone. I loved the present man as much as the past. It is good at a certain age to revise the stories of one's youth.

In fact, it is just these new hard-boiled stories, of mundane reality behind what was once romance, which suit me today. No doubt the new reality is as much tainted by fantasy as was the old myth.

Chanan's life still was and is one of dedication, perhaps more than he now remembers or cares to recount. His story was useful to me in the past and is now. (Just as the notion of a selfless, rule-bound, technically simple psychoanalysis served me well both as an ideal and as a myth requiring re-examination.) The way I first constructed Chanan's history helped me to change careers; the way I constructed it the second time allows me some freedom from the demand for a degree of self-abnegation I am unlikely to achieve. We have two listeners, two tellers, and two tales. All our professional instincts tell us not to work too hard to arrive at one true account; settling for ambiguity is our forte.

* * * * *

It is funny how transparent we look with time. Not just standing in the Negev with two bottles of orange pop, but every piece of the story, seems overdetermined: the way Max's room resembled my immigrant grandmother's apartment; the ideology and the reflections of the analytic method in British academics; the analyzed girlfriend and our roommate and his psychoanalyst friends; the two visits back to see Max; my struggles on the inpatient ward; the stubborn, contentious, and rebellious patients whose pride and anger mirrored my own; and the many silent and deaf patients with their echoes of Max's silence and Chanan's deafness and my childhood perceptions of relatives whose language I did not speak or understand. Overdetermined, every bit; overdetermined in every aspect.

Posé and *déçu* or not, my epiphany in the desert served me well. I found a craft. But having found it, I discovered that I had mistaken the nature of craft—or that the nature of craft had changed.

It is as if I had apprenticed as a sculptor, imagining sculpture to be something like stonemasonry, only to find that in this era what was called for was the creation of monumental mobiles activated by computer-driven engines, and that the relevant skills were metallurgy, physics, and electronics. Or perhaps it is not so much a matter of change in the field as of my own naïveté, as if I had entered architecture ignorant that the art required a mastery of structural engineering. Or else the confusion may be of another sort, as if it took me some time to understand the difference between learning rules and applying them, as if I did not understand the amalgam of technical knowledge, aesthetic sensibility, confidence, experience, spontaneity, passivity, immediacy, impotence, energy, idiosyncrasy, mastery of routine, and acceptance of compromise which underlies every art. Most likely, it was a combination of all three sorts of error.

Certainly I had something wrong about craft from the start. One does not perform a craft to save oneself for other work. Done well, craft is the use of self, and of every skill the self can bring to bear, in a difficult endeavor; when the result looks simple, it is only because the plethora of theories and techniques have been well hidden, by further craft. One does not grind lenses in the morning and perform rabbinical functions in the evening; craft and spirit are intertwined.

Psychiatry does serve me as a *handwerk*, because that is the aspect of the profession on which I choose to concentrate. I know it is not only for others that I grind lenses but also for myself, for the pleasure of making them and of trying them on, to see things afresh if I can, and without any real belief that vision without distortion or scotoma is possible.

Notes

PREFACE

[1]The quote is from the author's introduction to *The Stories of John Cheever* (New York: Knopf, 1978).

Elsewhere in the introduction, Cheever writes of publicly presenting his early stories: "A writer can be seen clumsily learning to walk, to tie his necktie, to make love, and to eat his peas off a fork. He appears much alone and determined to instruct himself. Naïve, provincial in my case, . . . sometimes obtuse, almost always clumsy, even a selected display of one's early work will be a naked history of one's struggle to receive an education in economics and love." A psychiatrist gets more help along the way than most writers do, but otherwise I would say the feelings on presenting one's early cases are much the same.

MYTH

[1]Avery, C. B., ed., *The New Century Classical Handbook*. (New York: Appleton-Century-Crofts, 1962). It is from this volume that the quotes which follow are taken.

[2]For purposes of brevity and to avoid stylistic awkwardness, I often throughout these essays use the masculine pronouns to apply to both sexes. I understand and am sympathetic with the arguments for abandoning this tradition but do not know of a good alternative.

SILENCE

[1]Originally anthologized in Twain's *The 30,000 Bequest and Other Stories* (New York: Harper & Bros. The copyrights run from 1872 to 1906).

INTRUSIONS

[1]Having written this sentence, I went to the library to glance at Will and Ariel Durant's *A Dual Autobiography* (New York: Simon & Schuster, 1977), just to be certain

that the Durants really were stable and happy. They were, but the autobiography contains a few surprises, particularly regarding the beginning of their love affair, which are worth thinking about.

[2]For instance, David Greenfeld's fine book, *The Psychotic Patient: Medication and Psychotherapy*. (New York: The Free Press, 1985).

[3]This dichotomy extends to much of our work: not only in medicating but also in providing interpretations we represent both nurturance and intrusiveness, a dialectic which I sometimes think is no less pervasive than the oedipal one between protection and arbitrary power.

[4]More than one early reader of the manuscript for this chapter asked me what happened to the young woman. I consider this reaction to be empathic to the experience I have tried to depict: we are often ignorant of what is wrong with a patient, what will help, and what the future portends, and with certain patients we remain in this state for a long time. We wish we knew, but we do not.

Although she developed a close psychotherapeutic relationship with me, the young woman complied poorly with medications as an outpatient. Her condition waxed and waned, and in a period of terror she demanded to be hositalized. On the local inpatient ward she was diagnosed as having a psychosis on the basis of a subtle seizure disorder, and for a time she seemed to improve slightly on an anticonvulsant regimen.

The family moved to another city where the young woman deteriorated and was rehospitalized; the second hospital diagnosed schizophrenia but discharged her to a psychiatrist who considered the problem to be developmental and treated her with psychotherapy for a personality disorder. The last I heard, new sophisticated EEG results were moving new doctors to consider anticonvulsants. Athough I now know her well on a personal level, if the young woman were to return to me today as a patient, I wonder whether I would be able to face her with immediacy as a psychotherapist. At this late stage, legitimate diagnostic considerations would still stand between us.

THE MIND-MIND-BODY-PROBLEM PROBLEM

[1]Garetz, F. K., Raths, O. N., Morse, R. H., "The Disturbed and Disturbing Psychiatric Resident," *Archives of General Psychiatry* 33: 446–450, 1973. The researchers studied a 100 percent sample of 25 years of trainees, comprising 200 residents.

The best outcomes were among "maverick residents": those who were disturbing because they acted overly independent and resisted faculty interventions. Many of these had come to residency with more than the usual level of experience. Four of five mavericks went on to outstanding careers, as compared to 14 percent of "undisturbed and undisturbing" residents. I try to remember these results when dealing with my feelings towards rebellious residents.

[2]In retrospect, I think this conflict reflected widespread ill feeling over true splits in psychiatry of the time. The psychoanalytic community carried on in functional ignorance of what was going on elsewhere—not that individuals were unaware of the existence of descriptive psychiatry, but psychoanalysts as a group had not been forced to take diagnosis seriously. There was as yet no need for integration, and a host of strong

psychiatries, ranging from mainstream Freudianism to object relations based psychoanalysis to absurdist family therapy to pure neuropsychiatry, coexisted within miles of one another.

Boston, New Haven, and Philadelphia—not to mention St. Louis—each represented a different approach to the patient and a different theory of mind, and in each it was possible to teach and practice without inner conflict. The parochial quality of the ward on which I floundered can be understood as arising from a feudal separation of localities, each having its own truth.

We might call the American psychiatry of 15 or 20 years ago a personality disordered member of the medical community, overly proud of its independence, self-assured, contemptuous—and isolated. Like the young patient in this vignette, like me on the ward, when forced to swallow a large dose of biology, it gave up its oppositional traits with relief—almost too readily, one might say, forsaking the good with the bad. Consequently, psychiatry departments today are better integrated with other medical departments, more scientific and academic, more uniform nationally, and perhaps less individually interesting and less skilled at teaching what is unique to the field.

[3]"The Beginning of Wisdom Is Never Calling a Patient Borderline," Brown University/Butler Hospital Psychiatry Grand Rounds, Providence, Rhode Island, May 28, 1987.

[4]In college I had the privilege of attending Lionel Trilling's Charles Eliot Norton Lectures at Harvard, later published as *Sincerity and Authenticity*. Trilling saw the advent of the self-questioning hero as the historical entry point of Western culture into modernity. But beyond and after the self-aware man, Trilling brought to our attention characters who took responsibility for their unconscious selves—the new heroes of the contemporary world. If we abandon the concept of the unconscious, how will we understand authenticity? What will we admire, and what will we see as expressing our own condition? Our concept of our identity will have to change to meet a new scientific paradigm.

Or, to give a concrete example of a slightly different phenomenon: when Primo Levi, the concentration camp survivor who was also a renowned chemist, essayist, and novelist, committed suicide, the initial reports noted that, already stressed by his mother's suffering a stroke, he had been exhausted by prostate surgery and been placed on antidepressants; the suicide was said to have been an impulsive act possibly related to a change in dosage of the antidepressants. (An expert on Italian Jewery, Alexander Stille, wrote an essay in *The New York Times Book Review* in part challenging this reductionist view.)

I know nothing further about the suicide—but what extraordinary times we live in, when the first thought about a Holocaust survivor's suicide concerns its likely organic basis. I understand that this reaction is in part a defense against addressing the possibility of defeat, with time, of a brave man. But it also straightforwardly represents a necessary way of viewing events. If you were Levi's doctor, would you not be remiss if, on discovering him depressed, you failed to inquire into a post-anesthesia syndrome? Or a frontal stroke during surgery? Or brain tumor? When antidepressants were added, was another medication withdrawn? And so forth.

Do we factor in the Holocaust years as having "kindled" an organic depression?

Regarding his reaction to his mother's illness, what do we make today of bereavement or post-traumatic stress syndrome?

How much clearing away of brush we must undertake before we are allowed to take into account the mind, the depressed man's thoughts—even in this case, in which the most thoughtful of men has been confronted with the most painful of circumstances!

Likewise: in *Maus: A Survivor's Tale* (New York: Pantheon Books, 1986), a brilliant retelling in cartoon form by Art Spiegelman of encounters with his parents' experiences in Auschwitz and after, Spiegelman shows us a cartoon-within-the-cartoon, "Prisoner on Hell Planet," recalling his reaction to his mother's suicide some years after the war. In one frame we see him in despair on his bed, with his tortured and contradictory thoughts printed across the frame: "menopausal depression" and "Hitler did it." This duality of thought is today inescapable even in the face of extreme events whose single cause would in other eras have seemed self-evident.

[5]I once directed a general hospital psychiatric outpatient clinic staffed mainly by nonpsychiatrists. The best scientific evidence at the time was—still is—that psychotherapy works equally as well as antidepressants in the treatment of ambulatory nonpsychotic depression; the combination of medicine and psychotherapy works better than either alone, but for the ordinary case therapy does well enough.

I noticed that certain social workers were worse than I was. No matter if a patient had cardiac conduction defects, orthostatic hypotension, hepatitis, and all the stigmata of an anaclitic depression, they wanted a psychiatrist to prescribe medication. Seduced by the lure of the physical, they were overcome by an urge to betray their profession's central tenet, that social and psychological forces determine men's well-being.

The story is told of B. F. Skinner that he went to the Pentagon, or perhaps it was the Congress, early in World War II with a plan to train pigeons to guide missiles. The pigeons would sit in the nose cones and peck to the left or right depending on how the bomb was off course. No one would take a risk on birds (imagine being an officer trying to argue for this course of action); the military opted for electronic guidance systems, a choice which stimulated the modern electronics field generally. But, so the story goes, by the end of the war electronic systems could not do as well as Skinner's pigeons did at the start of the war.

The issue is not efficacy nor evidence. Hard technology drives out soft.

[6]The history of views of autism was recently summarized in Volkmar, F. R., and Cohen, D. J., "Neurobiologic Aspects of Autism" (editorial), *New England Journal of Medicine* 318: 1390-1391, 1988.

[7]Collaboration is not without its virtues. The "therapist-administrator split" was once widely used on inpatient units to prevent struggles over ward rules from becoming focal points in the psychotherapy of patients who used contentiousness in self-destructive ways; the T/A split can be useful for outpatients who might otherwise struggle unproductively over medication for transferential reasons. But this division of labor is based on a clear rationale related to the patient's habitual behavior; it has nothing to do with the therapist's inner struggle over how to understand and act in response to symptoms whose origin and proper treatment are ambiguous.

[8]I am thinking here of what Paul R. McHugh and Philip R. Slavney, in their *The*

Perspectives of Psychiatry (Baltimore: The Johns Hopkins University Press, 1983), pp. 130–133, call "life-story reasoning": "Although life stories embody the analysis of function both for particular clinical problems and for the general theories that can arise from this method, it is difficult to define the source of the story's authority. . . . The story is composed in the relationship between patient and physician. . . . It mediates a common vision for the patient and the physician, and by altering the patient's understandings, intentions, and other relationships, it suggests ways of confronting the future."

[9]If my notion of this odd illness is difficult to understand, I should say I have in mind something like the "kindling" paradigm for affective disorder.

In many biological systems, habituation determines responses. The more a stimulus is applied, the less response it evokes.

In contrast, epilepsy is a kindled illness, one in which repetition of the stimulus evokes a heightened response. If you stimulate a monkey brain in a particular spot with an electrode, it takes less and less current to evoke a seizure. Eventually the animal will seize spontaneously from that focus, and repeated stimuli will decrease the periodicity of the seizures.

Some scientists, and Robert Post of the National Institute of Mental Health is a leading proponent of this view, believe that many affective disorders are kindled. That is, it takes progressively less psychic (or other) stress to set off a depression, and eventually the episodes become spontaneous.

I use this mixed biological-psychic model to illustrate the possibility of a paradigm in which dynamic conflict might contribute to an illness whose periodic manifestations might nevertheless not all be meaningful.

PIÈCE DE RÉSISTANCE

[1]This truth puts analytic teachers in a difficult position. If you believe something ought to be taught slowly, you are at a disadvantage if everything else in the curriculum can be learned fast — and if what can be learned fast is also effective.

By the way, I do not want to imply that good human qualities are not important in strategic therapists. But it does seem that the virtues admired in master strategists differ from those valued in senior analysts. Strategic therapists are prized less for their sanctity than for their incisiveness. The local virtues are cleverness, power, humor, radical imaginative freedom, and ruthlessness.

Like psychoanalysis, strategic therapy is dangerous in the hands of a therapist who has his own ax to grind. But the extirpation of character flaws seems less integral to the teaching of strategic therapy than to the teaching of analysis. This less virtue-centered approach has the advantage of dropping the pretense that only saints make good therapists; but it has its attendant dangers, too.

LIMITS OF INTERPRETATION

[1]I believe there are patients, and those with chronic pain syndromes are often in this group, for whom therapy must be either highly intrusive and shocking or highly

supportive and based on exquisite empathy. The ordinary strategy which lies between these two extremes provides neither enough protection for what Heinz Kohut called transmuting internalization nor enough threat and ordeal to chase the patient into health.

[2]Later published as Mann, J., *Time-Limited Psychotherapy* (Cambridge: Harvard University Press, 1973).

[3]Looking back on the Penthesilea episode, in the chapter "Myth," we can say I may myself have been one of those patients for whom interpretation provided as much support as insight. Perhaps my intellectual loyalty, in medical school and early in residency, to an over-strict view of the role of interpretation, even in the face of my comfort in practice with support, stemmed from a wish not to rethink my own psychoanalysis; I preferred to continue to experience it as based on emotional and intellectual revelation rather than as a reparenting experience enjoyed and required by a late adolescent.

[4]"In Memory of Sigmund Freud (d. Sept. 1939)," in Auden, W. H., *Collected Shorter Poems 1927–1957* (London: Faber, 1966), pp. 166–170.

[5]Peterson, M. J., "The Victorian Governess: Status Incongruence in Family and Society," in Vivinus, M., ed., *Suffer and Be Still: Women in the Victorian Age* (Bloomington: Indiana University Press, 1972). Dr. Edward Brown, the psychiatrist and historian of science, brought this article and its relevancy to the Lucy case to my attention. Peterson's study of the English governess shows how few occupations consistent with a "lady's status" were available to the gentlewoman who found herself in need of employment. For the governess with a ruined reputation, there was nowhere to fall. Methods of denying the sexuality of governesses were all but openly discussed in books of social advice for the well-run household. Understanding the conflicts inherent in the governess role, those of the well-bred woman unable to participate in the social intercourse of the class in which she had been raised, makes Freud's deduction in the Miss Lucy case seem less idiosyncratically brilliant but all the more shocking.

The vulnerable position of the governess is also made strikingly clear in certain Sherlock Holmes adventures.

[6]"Miss Lucy R, age 30" in Breuer, J., Freud, S., *Studies on Hysteria* (1893–1895), in *The Standard Edition of the Complete Psychological Works of Sigmund Freud*, Strachey, J., tr., (New York: W. W. Norton, 1955), Vol. II, pp. 106–134. The quote is from p. 117.

[7]I have in mind, for instance, Martin Amis's novel *Money: A Suicide Note* (Penguin, 1984); for a slightly more complete discussion see my column "Climate of Opinion," *Psychiatric Times*, May 1988.

[8]*The Standard Edition of the Complete Psychological Works of Sigmund Freud*, Strachey, J., tr., (New York: W. W. Norton, 1959), Vol. XX, pp. 77–174.

[9]This is a metaphor frequently used in self psychology. I associate it with the work of Drs. Paul and Anna Ornstein.

[10]Consider, for example, the following quite representative passage from Kohut about the psychoanalysis of neurosis, a condition which he characterizes in terms of underpinnings similar to those attributed by both object relations theorists and self

psychologists to personality disorders: "The differences between the traditional and the self psychologically informed therapeutic approaches to the classical transference neuroses relate to their different conceptions of the basic pathogenesis. The classical position maintains that we have arrived at the deepest level when we have reached the patient's experience of his impulses, wishes, and drives, that is, when the patient has become aware of his archaic sexual lust and hostility. The self psychologically informed analyst, however, will be open to the fact that the pathogenic Oedipus complex is embedded in an oedipal self-selfobject disturbance, that beneath lust and hostility there is a layer of depression and diffuse narcissistic rage." Kohut, H., *How Does Analysis Cure?* Goldberg, A., ed., (Chicago: University of Chicago Press, 1984), p. 5.

11The role of actual interventions in the patient's life is rarely discussed, but we all are aware of respectable psychiatrists who do this sort of thing. Milton Erickson is well known to have intervened actively in patients' social lives. A eminent psychoanalyst and object relations theorist I knew of in England is said to have virtually used his consulting room as a salon, introducing patients to one another when he believed it appropriate. One disturbed older woman I treated—she responded to MAO inhibitors after years of suffering—said her life was saved in her suicidal teenage years when her therapist took her into her (the therapist's) home to live.

12Gould, S. J., *The Panda's Thumb: More Reflections in Natural History* (New York: W. W. Norton, 1982).

13The laughter links this interaction in my mind to one in which my behavior on the surface appeared quite different—a case in which I declined to interpret the obvious.

I was working with a highly intelligent woman who had lost her (idealized) father young and later been sexually abused by a stepfather. She nonetheless went on to lead a successful life, except in the area of relations with men.

Some time into our work together, she began an outrageous, sexually masochistic menage-à-trois with a doctor and his wife. This behavior was well beyond her usual range, and I guessed that she knew as well as I did that the relationship was a form of acting out. It had the element of implying doctors were abusive like bad fathers and also loving like good fathers. She used the material in provocative ways in the therapy, telling me how at last she was sexually fulfilled, and I had better not say anything critical about this wonderful solution to her problems, and the like.

I said nothing. I knew there were some risks in the situation, but so did she. At last she came in angry and said, "I don't know what he sees in that woman," meaning what the doctor saw in the his wife. This comment was so clearly related to her own oedipal complaints about her mother that I must have raised an eyebrow.

The patient broke into peals of laughter—the feeling was one of self-recognition, embarrassment, and relief—and went on to say as much as I ever could have about the meaning of her behavior. She never saw the couple again.

The two therapies could not appear more different in terms of my behavior in the sessions, but I see this sequence as similar in its underpinnings to the one in which I interpreted so vigorously about the young man's eyeglasses—except that here it was the absence of any interpretation that served as a series of messages, about responsibility, locus of control, the type of rescue the patient could expect from me, my faith in her ability to manage her own affairs, and even the Oedipus complex. Certainly the volume of interpretations says little about what is going on in a therapy.

JUST GOOD FRIENDS

[1]Lest this transformation seem too miraculous, I should say that in later years this patient suffered setbacks. Even then, her many early months of success under my gaze served as a helpful backdrop for a more troubled and technically demanding therapeutic relationship.

[2]The Sachs quote, as well as some of the characterization of the nonspecific hypothesis in the first sentence of the following paragraph, comes from an article by Hans H. Strupp, "The Nonspecific Hypothesis of Therapeutic Effectiveness: A Current Assessment," in the *American Journal of Orthopsychiatry*, 56:513–520, 1986. Strupp writes: "The therapist's personal and technical skills are inextricably woven into every aspect of the structure and process of his or her relationship to the patient." I want to go further and say that there are some skills which are neither specific nor nonspecific, in the narrow sense of these terms, but professional and specifiable without being obviously theory-bound.

[3]As in many of these examples we can ask whether this rent-a-friend treatment was really supportive. Wasn't it more a dynamic interpretive treatment, one in which the early exploration came all from the patient? Or, alternatively, given how the patient saw the situation, wasn't this really structural family therapy with only one family member in the room? The therapist's "doing nothing" may have a variety of active meanings for the patient. This is part of what I mean when I say that support and exploration are difficult to distinguish.

[4]In *Making Contact* (Cambridge: Harvard University Press, 1986), pp. 188–189, Leston Havens quotes Carl Rogers writing about the patient's perception of the therapy as impersonal: "In this sense it is impersonal . . . the whole relationship is composed of the self of the client, the counselor being depersonalized for the purposes of therapy into being 'the client's other self.'" In other words, the therapist is rented precisely as an object onto whom to project.

Havens once speculated to me in passing that much of the efficacy of psychoanalysis is due to the therapist's taking a silent stance with just those patients whose parents have been too present in their childhood lives.

Much of Havens' genius, it seems to me, is in his ability to gauge the proper distance between patient and therapist, and then to maintain that distance.

[5]Alexander, F., *Fundamentals of Psychoanalysis* (New York: W. W. Norton, 1948).

[6]Laurens Van Der Post recounts a treatment of C. G. Jung's which I would put in the rent-a-friend category, one which also contains a surprising element of touching. Jung was referred a "simple girl of the hills" who appeared to be going insane. He understood her problem to be her discomfort in a modernizing Swiss community intolerant of traditional beliefs.

Jung got the girl to talk to him about the things she had enjoyed from childhood

(Isn't there a cure like this in *The Sound of Music*?), and he joined her in singing and dancing "and at times took her on his knee and rocked her in his arms."

The girl was cured, and when the amazed referring doctor asked how it was done, he could not believe Jung's reply: "'I listened to her fairy tales, danced with her a little, sang with her a little, took her on my knee a little, and the job was done.'" *Jung and the Story of Our Time* (New York: Pantheon, 1975), pp. 57–58.

Despite the liberties I have described Jung and Whitaker taking, I am suspicious of therapies that involve the therapist touching or holding a patient; I have never had occasion to undertake one myself. These stories are helpful mainly in defining the extent or limits of our freedom. An example of my own variety of "rising to action" is presented in the last section of this chapter.

[7]Leston Havens makes note of the opposite phenomenon in openly depressed patients: "Often if the therapist of a depressed person feels depressed himself, the patient improves." *Making Contact*, p.18. I have had this happen in my work, and it can be a striking occurence. Here, the same action in a different context results in a different form of support (ego over superego and id).

IS EMPATHY NECESSARY?

[1]"And empathy, especially where it is surrounded by an attitude of wanting to cure directly through the giving of loving and understanding, may indeed become basically overbearing and annoying; i.e., it may rest on the therapist's unresolved omnipotence fantasies." Kohut, H., *The Analysis of the Self* (New York: International Universities Press, 1971), p. 307.

[2]Gill emphasized this point in his lecture "Psychoanalysis and Psychoanalytically Oriented Psychotherapy: A Revised View of Their Relationship," at the 1984 Annual Meeting of the American Psychiatric Association in Dallas, Texas. See also Gill, M. M., "Psychoanalysis and Psychotherapy: A Revision," *International Review of Psychoanalysis* 11:161–180, 1984.

[3]Kohut, H., *The Analysis of the Self*, p. 302. I will return to this issue later.

[4]Book, H. E., "Empathy: Misconceptions and Misuses in Psychotherapy," *American Journal of Psychiatry* 145:420–424, 1988. I presented a brief discussion of this article in a letter to the Editor, *American Journal of Psychiatry, 146*(3), March 1987.

[5]Kohut, *op. cit.*, p. 300.

[6]Havens, L., *Making Contact: Uses of Language in Psychotherapy* (Cambridge: Harvard University Press, 1986), pp. 18–20.

[7]Symposium, "Empathy in Psychotherapy," at the 1983 Annual Meeting of the American Psychiatric Association in New York City.

[8]I have in mind here and elsewhere Minuchin, S., *Families and Family Therapy* (Cambridge: Harvard University Press, 1974), and Haley, J., *Uncommon Therapy: The Psychiatric Techniques of Milton Erickson* (New York: W. W. Norton, 1973).

[9]"In what language?" is a question I like to ask when residents speak to me about "communication." "Improving communication" often means foisting one spouse's (in American couples, generally the wife's) verbal fluency, and also demands for greater

intimacy and for a greater role for responsibility, guilt, and so forth, on a spouse (generally the husband) whose language is one of action and clear individual autonomy.

Often couples communicate all too well – we can say that Wendy communicated her neediness all too well – and with such couples the proper goal of treatment is not communication but something else, like a change in the balance of power or even an increased ability on the part of one member to disguise or withhold data.

[10]When at a lecture I expressed this scruple, a listener said to me, you say you felt no empathy for your patient, but to worry (over his response to discovering you felt nothing for him) was highly empathic. This listener's remark is clever; it illustrates the many uses of the word under discussion. Is worrying over how someone will take a hurtful remark empathic? We might say it is, but then it is also the sort of thing one might feel for someone in whom one had only a very slight emotional investment. In hearing someone else tell of an anempathic therapy, we might worry about the patient involved, even if the therapist reporting the case had failed to describe the patient well. To express such a worry may indicate the speaker is generally an "empathic person" (this is yet another use of the word, with its own similar problems), but it says nothing about the worrier's relationship to any particular patient.

[11]Novey, S., The Second Look: the Reconstruction of Personal History in Psychiatry and Psychoanalysis (Baltimore: Johns Hopkins University Press, 1968).

[12]"From the History of an Infantile Neurosis" (1918) The Standard Edition of the Complete Psychological Works of Sigmund Freud Strachey, J., tr. (New York: W. W. Norton, 1955), Vol. XVII, pp. 3–122.

[13]We might even say that in some contexts showing caring is just a sort of apt speech – a way of reaching someone on his own terms. The many patients who need to experience that their therapist values them speak the language of intimacy and dependency. To show care for them is to speak their language, to enter appropriately (courteously) into their world. There are other patients who want the therapist to be competent and distant, or at least they are more easily engaged when the therapist takes this posture, and we can say that they require a different language.

[14]It is tempting to make a similar error with regard to the sensation one of my medical school mentors called "sailing close to the wind." "Sailing close to the wind" (or "close reaching") bears a relationship to empathy but is perhaps not identical. It refers to a certain way that therapy can be for the therapist: dominated by a sense of movement, of oneness with the vessel and wind and water, suffused with strain, danger, and exhiliration. (Empathy often lacks this sense of progress; and this feeling can arise at times in therapy when we are not yet quite in empathy but, for instance, on the trail of emotion. Or the excitement may be in the patient, whom we understand to be on the verge of discovering something quite new and unknown to either of us.)

I wonder whether it is possible to consider oneself a psychotherapist without having had this experience: a patient begins to tell a story, perhaps in a perfunctory way. We begin to grasp what it is about, and the telling deepens. Feelings and episodes rush by, as if we were passengers on a high speed train careering through a distinctive landscape.

We say nothing, and the tale continues, now more filled with emotion. Or else we venture a word or two, summarizing something, perhaps not what the patient has reason to expect at all, something from our own trance state. And as a result of this comment, the train takes a hairpin turn, revealing the other side of the ambivalence, an icy landscape where moments before there was jungle. The ride continues. The session ends, and we say a word more, or not. And though we have done nothing, nothing visible or audible of any note, and though the telling may seem to have contained much pain for the teller, the patient rises and thanks us, made newly shy by the depth of his gratitude. "Thank you, thank you for listening. I have meant to tell you how much this means to me."

The temptation is to say that *this* is therapy. I think we are tempted in this way, if we are, because the experience is so precious to us.

But in our practice many therapies pass — and ought to pass, because they work quite well on a different basis — without such a moment occurring. If we hold this quasi-spiritual inner definition of psychotherapy, we may feel uneasy about our uninspired therapies, as if we have cheated someone, however satisfied they may be. In the course of therapy we may blame the patient for not letting us get close, or blame ourselves for our obtuseness or distraction.

Feeling this way about our own work, we may apply a similar standard to the work of others. We may believe we know on the basis of this sensation what is not therapy (as if we had an *Rx Gefühl* to match our *Praecox Gefühl*), disdaining treatments which lack movement and risk. But the quasi-spiritual definition is wrong and misleading. It is like trying to base a definition of poetry on the English romantics and leaving no room for Pope or Dryden. Xanadu and Kubla Khan are wonderful, but not all poetry needs to be wonderful in that way. If we succumb to this temptation, we will end in blaming ourselves needlessly over perfectly good courses of treatment which lack the particular magic we favor.

WHEN IT WORKS

[1]What I mean is, our therapeutics arises out of our opinions about human development, cultural norms, ethical relativism, and the like. It is through these filters that we see the patient, his life history, and the problem to which we will apply our technical remedies. In this sense all therapies are strategic and problem-solving. To choose psychoanalysis today is to select a certain strategy.

Putting it differently, Michael Basch has called psychotherapy "applied developmental psychology." (He made this remark during the informal discussion portion of symposium on "Recent Contributions to Psychoanalytic Psychotherapy" at the May 1988 Annual Meeting of the American Psychiatric Association in Montreal, Quebec.) This is true, and it is also true that developmental psychology is an exciting, confusing, rapidly changing field, so that psychotherapy must have a volatile, unsettled quality.

[2]There are, of course, many types of uncodified beliefs, some having to do with the natural history of illness or symptoms, some with behavioral norms, some with more or less subtle aspects of technique; certain ones of these may be subject to scientific testing, but the mass of beliefs is so great and the number of salient factors in each clinical situation so many that the field would have to change in character for it to become

testably scientific as regards the many individual choices during courses of treatment.

³An account of this case, much of which I draw on in this retelling, appeared in Kramer, P. D., "Integrated Psychiatric Treatment of a Dying Patient," *General Hospital Psychiatry* 5:291–299, 1983. In each instance I have varied certain identifying details.

⁴I will reluctantly mention an issue which always arises in these cases: whether we expect the psychotherapy will help the patient to live longer. There is a popular literature to this effect – therapists who claim in mass-market books never to have lost a patient to cancer, and the like. I do not believe anyone has this ability. Although for the sake of our patients we might hope for it, I am not sure for my own sake that I would want such a messianic power; how would we feel about the cases we lost?

Because she wanted it, I very much wanted Julie to live. But I had no belief or hope that I would influence the course of her illness. Lack of such a belief or hope allowed me to focus in a practical way on the series of mundane problems at hand.

It may be worth touching on an aspect of psychotherapy with dying patients which is special and which arises from the refusal to entertain false hopes. Once we acknowledge the reality of the patient's impending death, certain of our professional conventions begin to lose their rationale. It is evident, for example, that while I tried to go out of my way to restore Julie's autonomy, at the same time I was not overly wary about inducing psychic dependency. A patient who can hardly stand cannot avoid a degree of dependency, and I as a therapist had no need to fear the sort of draining demand for support we sometimes anticipate when treatment is potentially endless. Each of our rules needs to be reexamined in light of the truth that the patient is about to die. This examination can result in quite freewheeling therapies.

⁵I recommend his account of his work and of the psychiatric epidemiology of Martha's Vineyard: *People and Predicaments* (Cambridge: Harvard University Press, 1976).

⁶I have seen good therapists move directly to suggesting concrete courses of action in the psychodynamic treatment of obsessional patients. The patient may perseverate in ruminating about whether a certain sort of job is available, and the therapist will whip out the classified section of the newspaper and hand over a telephone. Leon Salzman does not go quite this far in his wonderful practical guide, *Treatment of the Obsessive Personality* (New York: Jason Aronson, 1980), but, while stressing the need for sensitivity to the obsessive's tender emotions, he makes it clear that one must introduce forceful, guiding interpretations and insist on them as a way of clarifying to the patient what are resistances and what are realistic obstacles.

⁷C. G. Jung wrote, "The knowledge of human nature that I have accumulated in the course of 60 years of practical experience has taught me to consider each case as a new one in which, first of all, I have had to seek the individual approach. Sometimes I have not hesitated to plunge into a careful study of infantile events and fantasies; at other times I have begun at the top, even if this has meant soaring straight into the most remote metaphysical speculations It all depends on learning the language of the individual patient . . ." Cited in Havens, L., *Approaches to the Mind: Movement of the Psychiatric Schools from Sects toward Science*. (Cambridge: Harvard University Press, 1973), p. 313.

⁸See my review of Norcross, J., ed., *The Handbook of Eclectic Psychotherapy* (New

York: Brunner/Mazel, 1986) in "Patchwork," *The Psychiatric Times*, May 1987, p. 3ff.

[9]I sometimes wonder whether all school therapies are not technically eclectic. I happen to have at hand Aaron Beck and Gary Emery's *Anxiety Disorders and Phobias: A Cognitive Perspective* (New York: Basic Books, 1985). In his section on technique, Emery allows the occasional use of paradoxical prescriptions, similar to those used in strategic therapy, and also recommends desensitization *in vivo*, drawn directly from strict behavioral therapy. Both interventions presumably act independent of cognition.

[10]Kaiser, H., "Emergency: Seven Dialogues Reflecting the Essence of Psychotherapy in an Extreme Adventure," *Psychiatry* 25:97-118, 1962. I would like to thank Dr. Edward Brown of Brown University for bringing this work to my attention.

[11]*Statesman* 294a-299. I want to thank Professor Julia Annas of the Philosophy Department of the University of Arizona for acquainting me with the diverse references to physicians in Plato's dialogues.

WHAT IS PSYCHOTHERAPY?

[1]Wolberg, L. R., *The Technique of Psychotherapy* 3rd ed. (New York: Grune & Stratton, 1977).

[2]And I fear they are ill-represented here. The researcher is Dr. Leslie Gise, of Mount Sinai Medical School. Her research has inherent interest, and I do not mean to slight it; I hope it is clear by this point—and becomes yet more evident as this section progresses—that my intention is to use a sketchy account of a certain sort of interaction with patients as a taking off point for a "thought experiment" about intention and psychotherapy.

[3]Smith, M. L., Glass, G. V., and Miller, T. I., *The Benefits of Psychotherapy* (Baltimore: Johns Hopkins University Press, 1980). Placebos included group discussions and informational meetings, as well as relaxation training and the like (pp. 73-74). The effect size of placebo therapies was substantial, especially for "measures of emotional-somatic disorders."

[4]And will any professional relationship do? Is it enough, say, that the professional relationship be that of a doctor? Or does the particular profession have to be psychotherapy? But if so, haven't we just pushed the need for a definition back one level?

[5]Schafer, R., *The Analytic Attitude* (New York: Basic Books, 1983).

[6]Symposium on "Recent Contributions to Psychoanalytic Psychotherapy" at the May 1988 Annual Meeting of the American Psychiatric Association in Montreal, Quebec. The vignette appears in Basch's *Understanding Psychotherapy: The Science Behind the Art* (New York: Basic Books, 1988).

[7]Wittgenstein, L., *Philosophical Investigations: The English Text of the Third Edition* Anscombe, G. E. M., tr. (New York: Macmillan, 1958), pp. 31-32.

Rereading this passage I recalled what my 2¹/₂-year-old son said when he first saw a volleyball game at the beach: "It's just like my dinosaur quiz game." This is a child's game involving cards with pictures of dinosaurs. "How is that?" "They both have points."

[8]Wolberg, *op. cit.* The definitions are respectively from Melzoff, J., and Kornreich, M., *Research in Psychotherapy* (New York: Atherton, 1970); Fisher, V. E., *The Meaning*

and Practice of Psychotherapy (New York: Macmillan, 1950); and Frank, J. D., "Psychotherapy," *Encyclopedia Britannica*, 18:804, 1972.

[9]I quote Paul Chodoff to this effect in the column "Actual Evidence" in *The Psychiatric Times* of June 1988. In that column and a prior one, "MacGuffin Down the Backstretch" (April 1987), I discuss in more detail some of my technical objections to the methods of comparison outcome trials.

[10]Müller, C., "Psychotherapy in Schizophrenia: The End of the Pioneers' Period," *Schizophrenia Bulletin* 10:618–619, 1984.

[11]I say "if it succeeds" because at least one study has shown that, even under the auspices of a manual, therapists treat different patients quite differently—doing exploration with healthier patients and supporting the more impaired. (Jones, E. E., Cumming, J. D., and Horowitz, M. J., "Another Look at the Nonspecific Hypothesis of Therapeutic Effectiveness," *Journal of Consulting and Clinical Psychology* 56:48–55, 1988.) This inhomogeneity of similarly diagnosed patients, along with lack of homogeneity in similarly-labeled treatments, may go a long way toward explaining why comparison trials rarely show differences between supposedly distinct treatment conditions.

[12]Given the strength of my objections, I want to be clear in saying I do not find any researcher dishonest in the reporting of his experimental results. I only mean that as a field we are disingenuous if we try to define our boundaries by means of this sort of research, or even if we say that these results demonstrate the superiority of any treatment for any indication. Like much other research troubled by design weaknesses, the horseraces have, and perhaps even ought to have, a suggestive power to influence our overview of our work. And there is reason to be hopeful about the helpfulness of process studies which will emerge from the horserace data; though perhaps even these would have been stronger if done using real therapies in natural settings.

[13]Gardner, J., *The Art of Fiction: Notes on Craft for Young Writers* (New York: Vintage, 1985).

[14]For me, "the really interesting question," to appropriate a phrase of Lytton Strachey's, is precisely whether psychotherapy is an art. Assuming research design issues could be resolved, it would be interesting to test the hypothesis that artful therapies are more effective than mechanical ones.

I have often wondered whether one could design a psychotherapy study pitting a manual-driven intervention against a condition in which experienced therapists act as they ordinarily do, deciding whether there is an indication for them to take on individual patients and treating the patients as the therapists see fit—in other words pitting draw-by-numbers against ordinary craft. If craft failed, we might have to rethink our premises.

There is, by the way, a disturbing hint in a psychotherapy outcome study involving treatment of drug addiction conducted by researchers at University of Pennsylvania. (Luborsky, L., McLellan, T., Woody, G.E., et al., "Therapist Success and Its Determinants," *Archives of General Psychiatry* 42:602–611, 1985). In that research using manual-circumscribed treatment, when it came to supportive-expressive therapies ("SE," a supportive treatment derived from psychoanalysis), *those practitioners who stuck to the manual* (had a high "purity" rating) *had better results than those who did not* (low purity). Cognitive-behavioral (CBT) therapists had, on average, lower purity than did the SE group; but the range of their ratings was such that correlating purity with outcomes was impossible.

What does all this mean? Well, it may mean that when using SE with drug addicts one had better go by the book. The Penn studies are among the best extant.

But this material is subject to a number of questions. Can one really measure purity? And are purities comparable between treatments?

For starters, there is a problem parallel to one cited earlier in the main text (in a theoretical example regarding therapist confidence). Since CBT is a didactic therapy, it seems likely that therapists can stray a good deal and then say, now let's get back to work. But in a transference-based psychotherapy, even a small deviation may throw the treatment off course for weeks. Low purity will almost certainly have different meanings in different therapies.

Even within a therapy, how do we compare impurities? In SE therapy, if all one's interpretations are psychodynamic but one makes them with a complicit smile or seductive leer, is one more or less pure than a therapist whose mask remains neutral while he admixes cognitive interpretations with his dynamic ones?

We might also want to know more about the patients. Did therapists stray mainly in those difficult cases in which they felt the restricted therapy was failing? In that case failure determines purity, and not vice-versa. Or did less talented therapists flail about while the more skilled found less need to? Then purity is just a marker for ability; the pure therapists might do better yet if given more room to maneuver. A fair test of eclecticism (or the value of purity or conformity) would not focus on aberrations from a protocol but would from the start include a "natural" condition as a cell of the outcome research; the difficulties with validity and pseudo-parametric measurements would, of course, persist.

[15]I do not in this essay attempt to distinguish art from craft. (How much do we differentiate the art of fiction from the craft of fiction, or the art of medicine from the craft of medicine? Consider the title of Gardner's book.) Any such distinction is difficult, especially since art can serve quite practical aims, such as political persuasion. If enterprises are ranged on a spectrum from the purely aesthetic to the largely practical, with art at one extreme and craft at the other, then of course psychotherapy is a craft. I want first to say that it certainly is at least a craft. Among crafts, I would place it toward the art portion of the continuum. It is a craft which is, as I try to show by the comparison with Gardner's conception of fiction, learned and practiced as certain arts are, although as an art it seems odd in ways I specify in the last section of this chapter. I do not want to deny that psychotherapy also partakes of the scientific; it is grounded in developmental and abnormal psychology, neurology, and other biological sciences. But I wonder whether it does not look as odd among the sciences as among the arts and crafts. To frame it entirely as a science is, I think, to lose sight of its nature altogther.

[16]Of course, Gardner is referring to the writer as writer, not as a human being after hours. The same is true of the therapist, whose persona Roy Schafer calls a "second self." Schafer (*The Analytic Attitude*), p. 44 puts it this way: "I wish to emphasize that this second self presented by the analyst is analogous to the second self (or 'implied author') presented by creative writers."

[17]But then all art is subject to questions of this sort. See the Richard Wollheim's wonderful short book, *Art and Its Objects* (Harper & Row, 1968).

[18]"From the History of an Infantile Neurosis" (1918) *The Standard Edition of the Complete Psychological Works of Sigmund Freud* Strachey, J., tr. (New York: W. W. Norton, 1955), Vol. XVII, pp. 3-122.

[19]"Nuns fret not at their convent's narrow room," Wordsworth wrote, explaining why he continued to favor sonnet form in an era which permitted innovation. But the writing of sonnets and the observance of holy vows, both admirable occupations, have different meanings in an age of free verse and unbelief than they did when the alternatives were less evident. Even orthodox psychoanalysis today is colored by therapists' and patients' awareness of alternatives (I mean this in the sense that I take Borges to mean that Menard's *Quixote* differs from the original because it is written in a different century).

[20]Lazare, A., Eisenthal, S., and Wasserman, L., "The Customer Approach to Patienthood: Attending to Patient Requests in a Walk-In Clinic," *Archives of General Psychiatry* 32:553-558, 1975.

[21]*The Analytic Attitude*, p. 49. The meaning of this passage is perhaps slightly different in context; Schafer's essays, indeed his books, have such a fine organic quality that it is difficult not to quote out of context.

[22]See Bowen, M., *Family Therapy in Clinical Practice* (New York: Jason Aronson, 1978), particularly the later chapters on differentiation of self.

[23]I think it happened this way: the patient set out to make me feel her anxiety, in part as punishment for being, in the transference, an underinvolved father or an insufficiently attentive lover. She correctly saw my change in approach as a response, and she then was able to entrust me with the further work she had done on areas inadequately explored in therapy.

REFRACTION

[1]I have referred earlier to his lovely small book, *Art and its Objects* (New York: Harper & Row, 1968). The Freud biography, also short and excellent, appeared in the Modern Masters series edited by Frank Kermode (London: Fontana, 1971). The work on affect in the seminars I attended in London later formed a small part of Wollheim's 1982 William James Lectures, published by Harvard University Press in 1984 as *The Thread of Life*.

Index

FOR THE BEST IN PAPERBACKS, LOOK FOR THE 🐧

In every corner of the world, on every subject under the sun, Penguin represents quality and variety—the very best in publishing today.

For complete information about books available from Penguin—including Pelicans, Puffins, Peregrines, and Penguin Classics—and how to order them, write to us at the appropriate address below. Please note that for copyright reasons the selection of books varies from country to country.

In the United Kingdom: For a complete list of books available from Penguin in the U.K., please write to *Dept E.P., Penguin Books Ltd, Harmondsworth, Middlesex, UB7 0DA.*

In the United States: For a complete list of books available from Penguin in the U.S., please write to *Consumer Sales, Penguin USA, P.O. Box 999— Dept. 17109, Bergenfield, New Jersey 07621-0120.* Visa and MasterCard holders call 1-800-253-6476 to order all Penguin titles.

In Canada: For a complete list of books available from Penguin in Canada, please write to *Penguin Books Canada Ltd, 10 Alcorn Avenue, Suite 300, Toronto, Ontario, Canada M4V 3B2.*

In Australia: For a complete list of books available from Penguin in Australia, please write to the *Marketing Department, Penguin Books Ltd, P.O. Box 257, Ringwood, Victoria 3134.*

In New Zealand: For a complete list of books available from Penguin in New Zealand, please write to the *Marketing Department, Penguin Books (NZ) Ltd, Private Bag, Takapuna, Auckland 9.*

In India: For a complete list of books available from Penguin, please write to *Penguin Overseas Ltd, 706 Eros Apartments, 56 Nehru Place, New Delhi, 110019.*

In Holland: For a complete list of books available from Penguin in Holland, please write to *Penguin Books Nederland B.V., Postbus 195, NL-1380AD Weesp, Netherlands.*

In Germany: For a complete list of books available from Penguin, please write to *Penguin Books Ltd, Friedrichstrasse 10-12, D-6000 Frankfurt Main 1, Federal Republic of Germany.*

In Spain: For a complete list of books available from Penguin in Spain, please write to *Longman, Penguin España, Calle San Nicolas 15, E-28013 Madrid, Spain.*

In Japan: For a complete list of books available from Penguin in Japan, please write to *Longman Penguin Japan Co Ltd, Yamaguchi Building, 2-12-9 Kanda Jimbocho, Chiyoda-Ku, Tokyo 101, Japan.*